**Arthur Waley** was a poet and major authority on Chinese and Japanese literature. He introduced this work to a wider public through his well-known and accessible translations. He taught himself the languages while he was working in the Print Room of the British Museum and his first book, *A Hundred and Seventy Chinese Poems*, was an immediate critical success. He claimed it was popular because it appealed to those who do not normally read poetry. Written with clarity and intelligence, his translations are usually unrhymed. Arthur Waley also published many articles and books on Oriental art, history and culture but, despite many invitations, he never visited the Far East. He lived most of his life in London and was friends with many of the Bloomsbury Group.

# ARTHUR WALEY

# The Secret History of the Mongols

## and Other Pieces

HOUSE OF
STRATUS

This edition published in 2008 by House of Stratus, an imprint of
Stratus Books Ltd., 21 Beeching Park, Kelly Bray,
Cornwall, PL17 8QS, UK.

www.houseofstratus.com

Typeset, printed and bound by House of Stratus.

A catalogue record for this book is available from the British Library
and the Library of Congress.

ISBN 07551-160-4-6

# CONTENTS

# CONTENTS (CONTD)

# PREFACE

his book consists in the main of articles, broadcasts and so on, later than 1952, when my last miscellany *The Real Tripitaka* was published, together with some earlier pieces going back as far as 1921, but not previously reprinted. I have also included one or two pieces which have never been published before, of which by far the longest is *The Secret History of the Mongols*, which gives its name to the book.

Of the *Secret History*, I have translated only the parts founded on story-tellers' tales. These are some of the most vivid primitive literature that exists anywhere in the world. I have used the Chinese version, but with constant reference to the Mongol text. *The Secret History* (so called merely because it was meant for the Mongols and not for the Chinese, who might have got from it the impression that the Mongols were barbarians) has been chiefly studied from a learned point of view, by scholars addressing themselves only to other scholars, and its quality as literature and hence its value to ordinary readers have been to a great extent overlooked. I hope that my extracts will introduce it for the first time to many who do not have access to learned publications. It is a work which it would be possible to furnish with endless annotation. I have preferred to dispense with footnotes and give only a few indispensable explanations in brackets. A full translation by Professor Cleaves of Harvard, intended for scholars, with

i

abundant annotation, exists and will, one hopes, soon be published.

I have not explained place names because hardly any of them can be identified with certainty, with the exception of the principal river names, such as the Onan, the Selenge, the Orkhon, which still exist almost unchanged and will easily be found on modern maps. That the Erdis is the Irtysch of modern maps is perhaps not so obvious. Almost the only mountain name that can be identified is that of the Altai range. Contrary to some scholars I regard the historical value of the *Secret History* as almost nil and it is as legendary story-telling not as history that I offer it here. The parts I have selected may date from about the middle of the thirteenth century. There is one passage, not translated here, which I have shown to be considerably later than 1258.

Despite the fact that in this book I translate from Chinese, Japanese, Ainu, Mongol and syriac, I do not want to give the impression that I am a master of many languages. Chinese and Japanese I do know fairly well; but though I know a good deal of Ainu I have often helped myself out by use of the Japanese versions of the texts. Mongol I have been studying for some thirty years, but I am far from being a Mongolist. To translate the *Hymn of the Soul* I learnt a certain amount of Syriac (already knowing some Hebrew, which was a help), but I leaned heavily on existing translations, such as that of W Wright in *The Apocryphal Acts of the Apostles*, 1871. But none of these translations, least of all that of Montague James (1924), which is the best known, give or even try to give the reader the feeling that he is reading poetry, which is what I hope I have succeeded in doing. Several people have said to me that till they read my version they had not realized that the *Hymn* is poetry and poetry of a high order.

At the end of my book will be found a few original stories and poems, and a review. Like most elderly men of letters I have in the course of my career written enough book-reviews to fill a whole volume and it seems that in a retrospective collection of this kind so considerable a writing activity ought to be represented. But most of these reviews were of specialized books and would not interest the general reader, for whom the present collection is chiefly intended. I have therefore included only one short review which seemed to me on re-reading it to be both amusing and suitably non-technical.

For permission to reprint I am grateful to *History Today, The Listener, Oriental Art, The Atlantic Monthly, The News Statesman, Encounter* and *The Cornhill*. Also to *Folklore*, the Royal Asiatic Society and the School of Oriental and African Studies.

# ANQUETIL-DUPERRON
## AND SIR WILLIAM JONES

W hen it had barely run half its course the eighteenth century grew tired of itself. Turning away from its classical and Biblical heritage it fled in its dreams to the Druids, the Middle Ages, Egypt, India, China. It looked for new mythologies, new arts and above all for new legislators, such being the term it applied to the supposed founders of ancient civilizations. Among the legislators of antiquity none held a higher reputation than Zoroaster. Eudoxus, a pupil of Plato, regarded his teachings as the 'most enlightened and useful' form of philosophy, and the library of Alexandria treasured his complete works, in two million verses! Of this immense literary output not a line was available in the eighteenth century. True, Dr Hyde (1636–1703) had collected what Moslem writers asserted about Zoroaster and his teachings. But such sources were late and for obvious reasons unreliable. It was known that there were still small bodies of Zoroastrians in Persia, but Persia was at that date difficult of access. The best hope seemed to lie in India where Zoroastrians (commonly known as Parsees) had fled from Arab persecution. In 1723 the Bodleian at Oxford had acquired a text in an unknown script. It was said to be a book by Zoroaster; but not even the great Dr Hunt could make out a word of it. Some years later a merchant called Fraser made an attempt to learn ancient Persian from the Parsee priests at Surat, on the north-west coast of India; but they proved unwilling to help him.

In 1754 a young man of 23, who held an appointment in the Bibliothèque du Roi at Paris, was shown as a curiosity a copy of the opening passage of the mysterious Oxford manuscript. He at once determined to go to India and learn how to read it. This young man was Abraham-Hyacinthe Anquetil-Duperron. He was the son of a Paris tradesman – a grocer whose shop was in the rue de la Verrerie. He had studied theology at the Sorbonne and (in 1751–52) at Old Catholic (Jansenist) seminaries near Utrecht. The Dutch Jansenists at this period specialized in Oriental studies, both for missionary purposes and for those of Biblical exegesis. Anquetil (as I shall henceforth call him) does not seem to have been influenced by Jansenist ideas. But he did not forget these early schismatic associations nor expect others to forget them. Many years later (in 1791) he sent a rather crazy letter to the Pope, subscribing to the sanctity of the monarchic principle and declaring his own 'inviolable attachment to the Holy See'. When no reply came he attributed the Pope's silence to disapproval of his early association with schismatics.

He was the fourth of seven children. His father had very modest means and could not possibly afford to pay for a passage to India. Anquetil accordingly enlisted in a regiment that was going to Pondicherry, the French settlement south of Madras. This was a brilliant move. His friends, admiring his determination, took steps on his behalf; the King granted him an allowance, he was discharged from his regiment and given a free passage, with the right to dine at the Captain's table. Of his journey and his doings in India I shall give only a brief account. They have been admirably dealt with by M.

Raymond Schwab in his *Anquetil-Duperron, sa Vie* (1934). My chief concern will be with his eventful stay in England on his way home in 1762. Eighteenth-century sea voyages are all much alike – a long sequence of tempests, pestilences and semi-starvation. Suffice it to say that he arrived at Pondicherry in the summer of 1754 and there set to work to learn modern Persian, then a general *lingua franca* in India. After some excursions in the interior he set sail for Chandernagore, a French settlement north of Calcutta. Here he hoped to find Zoroastrian texts; but they were not forthcoming. His interest, however, was not confined to Zoroaster. The Brahmins had, in romantic European circles, an almost equal reputation for wisdom, and he determined to make for Benares, where they were believed to be in very strong force. Later he would strike westward again and crossing the whole breadth of India arrive at Surat, where recent information assured him that the Parsee priests were prepared to oblige him in every way they could. But the French and English were at war. Early in 1757 Chandernagore fell to the English and Anquetil, who had not yet started for Benares, was obliged to quit Chandernagore precipitately and put himself under the protection of the French army at Cossimbazar. The commander was the famous Law of Lauriston, great-nephew of an Edinburgh banker who had thrown in his lot with the French. It was a characteristic of Anquetil that he always knew how to do everything better than anybody else, and being a very obliging man he invariably told people of their own or their subordinates' mistakes. The French army was apparently wandering about without a map. Anquetil had a map and became indispensable. In his *Mémoires* Law of Lauriston notes, 'We had with us at this time a certain M. Anquetil, a clever young man, very observant, but over-critical. My Staff happened accidentally to become aware of some criticisms of them that he had made and complained to me about him;

THE SECRET HISTORY OF THE MONGOLS

whereupon he decided to leave us.' It appears from Anquetil's own account that the officers got hold of a notebook in which he had listed their defects, intending no doubt to assist Law by acquainting him with the shortcomings of those who served him.

English armies blocked the way to Benares. He determined to make for Pondicherry, where the French were strongest. To go by sea would have been to court capture; he set out by land, on foot. After innumerable hardships, sicknesses and narrow escapes he reached Pondicherry and as these waters were less frequented by the English navy he was able to take ship to Mahé, a French possession on the south-western coast. Not far away lay Cochin and Malabar, with their mysterious Indian Jews and Indian Christians. Anquetil, laying aside for the moment his Zoroastrian project, turned south, interviewed Rabbis, obtained copies of the charters accorded to them at various dates and of other documents bearing on their history, and disentangled the Black Jews from the White.

The Christians of St Thomas proved to be a much more difficult problem. They claimed to be descended from converts made by the Apostle St Thomas, whose mission in India is described in that enchanting and too little-known book, the apocryphal *Acts of St Thomas*. Their church is now generally believed to have been founded by Nestorian missionaries from Syria in about the fifth century. This theory was known to Anquetil and he searched for evidences of heresy among them, for example the use of the apocryphal *Infancy of Jesus*. He found none, and this was natural enough, for the Portuguese had forced orthodoxy upon them a hundred years before. Apart from the Thomas Christians there were many other Christian sects, whose beliefs he disentangled with the aid of a Polish bishop. His most picturesque find was a peculiar sect of low-caste Catholic fishermen.

4

Turning north again he spent some time at Goa and then set out (in March 1758) on his second formidable tramp, over the Ghats and parallel with the west coast of India, to Surat. He passed through Ellora and made a complete iconographic survey of the rock-carvings there. For the arts as such he cared nothing, and Ellora interested him simply as a repository of Hindu mythology.

He arrived at Surat on May 1, 1758. Here his brother Anquetil-Briancourt was sous-chef of the Surat branch of 'Campagnie des Indes', the French equivalent to our East India Company. The temperaments and aims of the two brothers could not have been more different. Briancourt was a cautious, conciliatory public servant, bent upon keeping the French upon tolerable terms with the various interests (English, Dutch and Moslem) which prevailed in Surat. Anquetil, on the other hand, was bent on getting hold of the Parsee scriptures and soon found that he could only do so by exploiting the quasi-political factions that divided the Parsee Church. There was a pro-French party and a pro-Dutch party. Both were determined, in return for teaching Anquetil ancient Persian and letting him copy their books, to get out of him every penny they could. The existence of these two factions enabled him, by siding first with one and then with the other, to demonstrate to them that neither had a monopoly. When after months of intrigue he had learnt old Persian and procured the texts he wanted to copy, he was obliged to guard them with fire-arms – the famous *deux pistolets* that always lay ready loaded on his work-table. In March 1759 Surat was captured by the English. The French Company existed on sufferance and the utmost tact was needed to safeguard even a remnant of French commercial interests. Anquetil, intent upon his texts, was conscious of political events only in so far as they helped or interfered with his studies. The brothers got upon one another's nerves and towards the end of Anquetil's stay in Surat, Briancourt wrote to a friend: 'I would a thousand times rather be married to an ugly, ill-tempered wife than have a person of this kind permanently on my hands. But he is my brother, and I make a virtue of necessity.'

In September 1759 Anquetil was attacked in the street by the irate husband of a young lady to whom he had been giving French lessons. In defending himself he received severe wounds but was unfortunate enough to kill his assailant. As soon as he was able to move he left his brother's house and put himself under the protection of the British flag. He believed (whether rightly I do not know) that under French law his position was perilous and preferred to be tried by a Moslem court under British supervision. He was acquitted; but it was not till a year later that he ventured to return to the French Settlement.

We know extremely little about his relations with women. At Goa it seems that he commissioned a friend to transmit a statuette of Cupid to a lady. Apart from this and the ill-starred French lessons we know only of unsuccessful advances made by admiring ladies – the tall tender-eyed 'Fakiresse' who offered to cook for him near Puri and the Moslem ladies at Surat who sent their duenna to him with the message 'Come tonight!' He never married and seems in later life to have had no female friends.

But I am concerned here rather with the actual circumstances of his Zoroastrian discovery than with his personal relations or the politics of British-occupied Surat. His medium of communication with his Parsee teachers was modern Persian which, as I have said, was a common *lingua franca* in eighteenth-century India. The native language of the Parsees in Surat was Gujarati. How fluently they spoke Persian it is quite impossible to discover, but we may at least suppose that they were better at Gujarati. How well Anquetil spoke Persian is also quite unknown. Travellers (and he is no exception) are apt to be cagey about the exact extent of their linguistic acquirements. About ten days after their arrival in a strange country comes the stereotyped announcement, 'I was now able to converse freely with the natives'. One wonders sometimes whether there is not in this an element of Epic convention, similar to the poetic device that enables Greeks to chatter to Trojans. It is clear that he knew some Bengali, some Malayalam, some Hindustani. How far his Persian went and how far he had found opportunity during his travels to practise it we simply do not know. One thing however is clear. If he had from the start gone for Gujarati and learnt it thoroughly he would have given himself a much better chance of benefiting from his Zoroastrian lessons.

He left Surat in March 1761, with the copies he had made of Zoroastrian scriptures and a mass of other Indian manuscripts. During the latter part of his stay at Surat he was in close relations with the English, and he now obtained the permission of the English authorities (though France was still at war with England) to leave in an English ship. On November 17th he landed at Portsmouth, and at this point the reader of his memoirs experiences considerable relief, for he was one of those travellers who while in exotic surroundings interlard their accounts with native words which convey nothing to the mind of the average reader. For example, page 63: 'Je fus arrêté à une demi cosse de Nerengar par un Tchoki qui voulut voir la Tchape de mon Dastok.'

His first impressions of England were not favourable. Just outside the harbour a number of HM seamen put off secretly in a jolly-boat in order to land somewhere up the coast and so escape the press-gang which though they had been away for ten years would have promptly carried them off to a man-of-war. When the passengers came ashore they were surrounded by hordes of Portsmouth prostitutes. 'It was amusing,' says Anquetil, 'to see on the one hand the Customs officers with their pirate faces rummaging through our clothes and turning out the contents of our pockets, and on the other, a crowd of pretty girls, trying out their few words of broken French, particularly such phrases as belonged to their profession, clutching at us, kissing our little native servants, swearing they would not charge a penny to poor prisoners such as we, who had come from so far away. The Fusileers had to drive them back; but they followed us to the inn to which we were taken and early next morning they were still at the door, and nothing would content them but that they should come with us to the Customs Office.' No instructions about Anquetil had reached the authorities at the port. He had arrived along with a number of French military prisoners, and he now found himself despatched with them to the neighbouring village of Wickham, where he was held on parole. Here he was soon visited by the local squire, a cultivated country gentleman called George Garnier, who henceforth took him under his protection. He was of French origin, had travelled widely, was a good classical scholar and possessed an excellent library. He loved France, but 'so passionate was his adoration of the English Parliament that he felt bitterly towards our Government'. Some years later he became Sheriff of Hampshire.

Meanwhile Anquetil's luggage with his books and manuscripts, was still at the Portsmouth Customs in a water-logged store-room. Through Mr Garnier's good offices he got permission to go for two days to Portsmouth. Though it had rained every day throughout December, the flood had not yet reached his luggage. He was not allowed to remove the trunk, but only a few MSS. at which he was actually working. Orders now came that the French prisoners at Wickham were to be repatriated. It seemed as though Anquetil would inevitably be forced to go with them, but he was determined not to leave England till he had been to Oxford and seen for himself whether there were (as had often been stated) Zoroastrian

MSS. there in ancient Persian. In the nick of time a letter from the French King's librarian, appealing for Anquetil's release and the restoration of his effects, reached Mr Stanley at the Admiralty. What civilized days those were! It was in the middle of a war; but Anquetil was at once released, told he could go to Oxford if he pleased and could have his luggage restored to him. Mr Garnier furnished him with introductions to the Oxford dons and 'malgré les *turn-pikes* (barrières qui vous arrêtent presqu'à chaque double mille)' he arrived at Oxford on January 17, 1762, and at once presented himself to Dr John Swinton to whom he had a letter of introduction. Swinton (1703–71), famous for his knowledge of abstruse subjects, such as Etruscan inscriptions and Parthian coins, and also for his bizarre absent-mindedness, concerning which Dr Johnson heard an anecdote[1] when he visited Oxford in 1754, gave him a reception which 'it would be an exaggeration to describe as *assez gracieuse*'. Grace was not in Dr Swinton's line. 'He is,' writes Anquetil, 'a little shrivelled fellow. His eyes which look like holes bored with a drill are framed with red and half-hidden under thick, grey-white eyebrows.' Elsewhere he describes him ironically as the Apollo among the 'opulent Doctors' of the University. In the Bodleian he was at once shown the *Vendidad*, Oxford's great Oriental treasure, so precious indeed that it was kept on a chain 'dans un endroit particulier'. This was the Zoroastrian MS., an extract from which had fired his imagination in 1754 and started him off on his eight years' pilgrimage. The Bodleian was unheated and the weather bitterly cold. Anquetil calmly proposed carrying off the *Vendidad* to his inn. To his surprise and indignation Dr Browne, Vice-Chancellor of the University and Keeper of the

---

1 The gist of which was that preaching to convicts who were to be hanged next day he referred to what he would be telling them a week hence; forgetting for a moment that he was not preaching to dons in the University Church.

Bodleian, rejected his request. Next day, in intense cold, he spent an hour at the Bodleian examining the MS. Helpful as ever, he pointed out to the librarians that they had labelled their treasure wrongly, displaying indeed such ignorance that *Vendidad*, the name of the book,[1] was given as though it were the name of the author. He was invited to dine (i.e. take his midday meal) at the house of the Rev. Philip Barton, DD, Canon of Christchurch Cathedral, Fellow of the Society of Antiquaries from 1752 till his death in 1765. Anquetil was pained to observe the obsequious manner in which Dr Swinton behaved towards Dr Barton. He could find no cause for this except the fact that though Dr Swinton was rich, Dr Barton, owing to the many benefices which he enjoyed, was richer still. He seems indeed to have been irritated, as many other outsiders have been, by the cosy opulence of donnish life. At three o'clock they set out for the house of Dr Thomas Hunt (1696–1774), also a Canon of Christchurch, Laudian Professor of Arabic and, later, Regius Professor of Hebrew. Here he was to be shown further Zoroastrian MSS. that Hunt was putting in order for the Radcliffe Library. 'As we crossed the court of Christchurch,' Anquetil writes, 'I could not help laughing to myself at the figure cut by my two guides. Dr Swinton, all huddled-up in his gown, his head poked forward and crowned with a filthy old three-cornered cap, looked the complete Academic stooge. Dr Barton, tall and well-built, walked several paces ahead of him, solemnly fluttering a noble gown with satin-lined facings which were well matched by a velvet cap, the front peak worn well down over his forehead, an arrangement which seemed to enhance his air of pride. Add to that a continual turning of the head, now this way, now that

1 Now read 'Vidēvdat'.

10

as though better to admire his own stately progress, and you have the faithful portrait of an opulent English Canon.'

Helpful once again, he informed Dr Hunt that what the Doctor imagined to be ancient Persian was in fact simply modern Persian written in ancient characters. Anquetil had brought with him some of his own manuscripts and, to show that he was duly impressed, Dr Hunt embarked upon a rather heavy pleasantry. 'I am a Justice of the Peace,' he said, 'and I have a good mind to arrest you for this affair of yours that made you put yourself under the protection of the British flag, and confiscate your manuscripts.' Anquetil (how dangerous it is to make jokes to foreigners!) took this playful threat quite seriously and replied heatedly that Hunt would in that case find himself answerable both to 'le Ministre anglais, M. Pitt et au Roi de France', both of whom had been informed of Anquetil's discoveries. He had, we must remember, all the over-sensitivity of a newly released internee; moreover, this was his first experience of that very singular product, British Academic humour. Afterwards he realized that he had taken Hunt 'trop à la lettre'.

At Dr Swinton's that night a grave *contretemps* occurred. The Doctor produced a Persian royal medallion with a very effaced inscription which Anquetil was expected to read. 'In vain I declared to him that the characters, where not wholly effaced, were different from Zend: in his eyes my failure to decipher the inscription ranked as a defeat.' He was back at Wickham on January 21st. On his journey he found the country people he met friendly to a Frenchman and heartily sick of the war. Prices were soaring; at Winchester a cup of coffee cost him three shillings (3 livres). It was in the heyday of the beef-steak. Wherever he alighted he was told that he could have anything he fancied; but what was eventually served was invariably beef-steak. He had to go to Portsmouth to clear his luggage at the Customs and arrange for it to be sent to London. At Portsmouth Church he heard the congregation, though 'sustained' by an organ and professional choir, sing horribly out of tune.

He arrived in London on January 31st. The inn which had been recommended to him by his landlord at Portsmouth turned out to be little better than a tavern. Here he was treated with hostility; whereas if he had been at one of the '*bagnos* where people of quality put up' he would (he was certain) have been received with open arms. His general remarks about London are of a familiar kind. He was struck above all, like so many other visitors, by the deplorable state of the streets. Only in a small area round Pall Mall were they paved; elsewhere they were mere oceans of mud. His remarks on the position of learning and letters in England are more interesting, and to some extent still hold good. In France, he says, learning is concentrated in Paris. But Paris is a cosmopolitan centre and this fact saves French scholars from the awkwardness and heaviness that result from studies too long pursued in the arid and sombre atmosphere of the library. In England, on the contrary, learning is confined to Oxford and Cambridge, places quite cut off from continental comings and goings, but so impregnated with study that the air for a mile round stinks of Greek, Latin and Hebrew. Outside the two university towns learning, unless directly useful to commerce, has no prestige at all.

He found that the British Museum was 'one up' on the Bodleian: 'En hiver il y a du feu.' Apparently visitors had to make an appointment beforehand, and only twelve were admitted at a time. He found the exhibits, both in the Antiquities and the Natural History sections, 'very ordinary'. In the latter he saw 'common stones and quite ordinary insects' classified as rarities. Mr Morton, one of the curators, imagined that he possessed the Zend alphabet, i.e. that in which the early Zoroastrian MSS. are written. 'Je le tirai de cette erreur,' remarks Anquetil characteristically.

He tells us that at the theatre of the great Mr Garrick he saw ' "Le Couronnement", pièce de Shakespeare'. It was followed by a turn in which a pack of fifty sailors bawled out imprecations against the enemies of England. A young gentleman sitting next to him (so Anquetil tells us) deplored the fact that Garrick, to propitiate the mob, found it necessary to stage such puerilities. Garrick, it will be remembered, was of French descent; moreover, in 1755 when he brought over Noverre and his ballet company a patriotic crowd smashed the theatre and even attacked Garrick's London house.

But I think what the young gentleman actually told him was that *even* Garrick found it necessary at *his* theatre to placate the mob by sometimes staging vulgar turns. For there is not the slightest doubt that Anquetil, making a mistake that is still sometimes made, went to Covent Garden thinking that it was Drury Lane. On February 10th, for one night only, 'King Henry IV, with the Coronation' (that is to say, a potted version of Parts I and II) was played at Covent Garden. Nothing of the kind was given at Drury Lane during Anquetil's stay in London. Hoping to see the great Garrick (whom he might have seen at Drury Lane on February 8th in *Cymbeline*) he went to the wrong theatre and saw, as Henry IV, an obscure actor called Gibson. The world is not composed of Anquetils, and no one took the trouble to 'le tirer de son erreur'. The episode was indeed another demonstration that Fate did not intend him to see us at our best. He arrived on a Sunday. He was in England from November to February, certainly not the pleasantest season. He was here when we were at war with France and war-fever was at its height. He was interned; he was subjected to donnish humour; he saw a scrappy, unsuccessful show by an inferior company, when he might have seen Garrick at his best. He confesses that in a fortnight one cannot get very far in one's study of a vast nation. If he had been longer in London he would, he says, have liked to study further the various classes and categories of Englishman; for example, the clergy whose daughters, upon the death of their father, often 'remplissent les lieux publics de Londres', a rather odd statement, if it means (as it appears to) that clergymen's daughters frequently become prostitutes. The only class for which he reserves unstinted praise are the serious, demure English girls, quite as pretty as 'nos petites maîtresses', but wholly lacking in the 'folies et le papillotage' that make French girls so intolerable.

He embarked at Gravesend on February 14th and travelling via Ostend arrived at Paris on March 14th. Here he continued to work at his *Zend-Avesta*, which appeared in three enormous volumes in 1771. The first of these contained, in 500 crowded quarto pages, a complete account of his journey, including the derogatory remarks about Oxford dons which I have quoted above. A few months later a London printer put out an anonymous French pamphlet of some fifty pages, in which the author declares the MSS. which Anquetil had translated to be modern forgeries, and trounces him for his remarks about England in general and the Oxford Orientalists in particular. It did indeed soon become known that the author of the pamphlet was called Jones. But from anonymity to 'Jones' is no great step in advance. 'You, Sir,' writes Jones, 'put yourself under the protection of the English, they duly protected you against your own nation. You returned to Europe in an English ship, you landed in England in time of war, the most distinguished men in that country hastened to your assistance; you went to Oxford and were there received with equal courtesy. How came it then that you looked with so jaundiced an eye upon a nation that the whole of Europe respects and will continue to respect?' Another aspect of the book to which Jones takes strong exception is Anquetil's repeated references, both direct and indirect, to his own good looks – his 'teint de rose et lys'. The passages in question do indeed figure oddly in the preface to a learned work. But they have at least the merit of telling us all we know about his personal appearance; for so far as I can discover no portrait of him exists.

Jones, it turned out, was a young Orientalist who had arrived at Oxford two years after Anquetil's visit. He was to become Sir William Jones, author of the famous Persian Grammar, translator of Indian drama, authority upon Indian law, founder of the Royal Asiatic Society of Bengal and indisputably the foremost European pioneer of Asiatic studies. Undoubtedly his main object in writing the pamphlet was to come chivalrously to the rescue of the Dons whom Anquetil had derided. It does not seem, however, that they saw it before it was printed; for Dr Hunt, in a letter written soon after its appearance, begs Jones, if he prints an English version (which he never did) to delete the rash statement that the whole of early Persian literature had irretrievably perished. But there were other motives. To publish a pamphlet or open letter deriding some new play or book was at this period a recognized way for a young writer to bring himself before the public. To excite curiosity such pamphlets were usually anonymous; but steps were soon taken to let the authorship be known. Boswell and Erskine's *Critical Strictures* (1763) was a work of this kind. Jones' pamphlet, it is fair to surmise, was written with the object of displaying his own powers of invective and mastery of the French language rather than of damaging Anquetil's reputation. He expressly denies that he is accusing him of deliberately deceiving the public. It is Anquetil himself whom the Parsees have deceived. However, on the next page Jones declares that Anquetil does not really know old Persian and has only translated what the Parsees dictated to him in modern Persian. As Anquetil tells his readers that he did know old Persian, Jones is in fact accusing him of bad faith. As proof that Anquetil did not know old Persian he points to a glossary appended by Anquetil to his book, in which occur a number of words that Jones declares to be Arabic and consequently post-Mohammedan. Here he was being too clever. The kind of Persian under discussion does contain words (such as 'Malke', king) which look like Arabic; but they belong in fact to another Semitic language, Aramaic. And they really do occur as loan-words in ancient Persian. Here he had at least raised a serious and debatable point. His main and more general argument is that Zoroaster, hailed by antiquity as the most enlightened of philosophers, could not possibly have written such dreary stuff as was contained in Anquetil's book. This was an objection that Anquetil had himself anticipated. 'I am afraid,' he writes in his *Discours Préliminaire*, 'that the works that I have here translated may not correspond to preconceived ideas about this Legislator (i.e. Zoroaster). But should this fear prevent me from submitting my translation to the learned world? On the contrary, I think it will be felt that a few hours of boredom are a small price to pay for the satisfaction of knowing the truth about this matter.' Anquetil was in fact, at any rate at this period of his life, a scientist in attitude. No one thinks the less of a botanist's discovery because his new flower is not particularly beautiful or has not much scent. The fact that it was unknown and has now been made known is enough. And that was Anquetil's attitude towards the texts he had discovered. It is perfectly true that early Zoroastrian writings, interesting though they are to the historian of religion, the anthropologist or the linguist and inspiring though they may be to living Zoroastrians, are not calculated to make a universal appeal. The *Vendidad*, for example, which occupies so large a space in Anquetil's first volume, consists chiefly of minute directions about ceremonies of ritual purification and the art of combating demonic influences. Much of it is wearisome even in the more fluent modern translations, and in Anquetil's crabbed version it is almost unreadable.

Jones, on the other hand, was an artist. It was not his aim simply to fill gaps in knowledge. He loved to communicate not to scholars only but to the world in general whatever he found particularly beautiful or interesting in his Oriental reading. It was perhaps this temperamental antagonism, as much as any other motive, that was responsible for the savageness of his attack. In any case, in light-heartedly and irresponsibly accusing a fellow-scholar of fraud and condemning his productions as worthless he committed a very grave fault, of a kind particularly surprising when we consider that the beauty of his moral character is a theme that reverberates through the memoirs and correspondences of the late eighteenth century. Modest, 'harmonious', sincere, generous, affectionate – the epithets pile up. But 'Les défauts des gens parfaits sont terribles', as Anquetil himself wrote in an unpublished note-book quoted by M. Schwab. Was he thinking, one wonders, of what he had suffered at the hands of that paragon of all the virtues, Sir William Jones?

Meanwhile, the harm was done. It may be said, speaking in a general way, that the pamphlet wrecked Anquetil's reputation, both here and abroad. Typical is a letter of the great Baron Grimm (January 1, 1772) who quotes 'un Anglais, M. Jones', agreeing with him that Anquetil is to be 'strongly suspected' of having only the haziest and most superficial knowledge of old Persian. Most continental scholars followed suit. Not till de Sacy, in 1793, successfully used Anquetil's glossary in the decipherment of the Sassanian royal inscriptions did the tide begin definitely to turn. The nearest that Jones ever got to an apology was a passage in his Sixth Discourse (1789): 'M. Anquetil had the merit of undertaking a voyage to India in his earliest youth with no other view than to recover the writings of Zeratusht, and would have acquired a brilliant reputation in France, if he had not sullied it by his immoderate vanity and virulence of temper, which alienated the goodwill even of his own countrymen.' Here there is no longer any suggestion either of ignorance or fraud; but the reparation was of a very negative kind.

Anquetil, on his side, never replied; so far as I know he only refers twice to Jones. In 1787 he praises him for his good work in founding the Asiatic Society of Bengal; later (writing *c.* 1796) he describes him with justice as 'eruditus et leviter de omnibus disserens', learned, but too ready to hold forth on every possible subject. No one now doubts that Anquetil's translation was an honest attempt to convey the sense of the original or that he had a great knowledge if not of early Persian grammar, at any rate of vocabulary. Above all, he never tried to improve upon his originals by clothing them in the language of Christian piety. The same cannot be said of the translators from Chinese trustfully quoted by Sir William Jones in his *Discourse on China*, where Confucius is made to talk about 'the Lord of Heaven who governs the Universe' and the Sage who 'conforms to his knowledge of God'.

In the latter part of his life Anquetil did a lot of theological and political pamphleteering, with which I am not here concerned. Much of his energy went into trying to persuade the French Government to recapture India by an overland campaign through Turkey or Russia. His hatred of England and his perfectly orthodox though slightly orientalized Catholic mysticism grew continually more intense. After passing unscathed (though a violent Monarchist) through the revolution, he died at the age of 73 in 1805. Only one of his later works was of any importance – his translation of fifty-one Upanishads. It is instructive to reflect that this work, which had so profound an influence on European thought, ought not, according to the current laws of scholarship, ever to have been undertaken. The Upanishads are Sanskrit philosophical texts; Anquetil retranslated them from a modern Persian translation. Today we frown upon retranslations, and a scholar who presented such work as a thesis at any of our universities would quickly be sent about his business. But it turned out that his Upanishads, despite the indirect way in which he had access to them, were to mark a new epoch in the relation between European and Indian thought. In 1813 they fell into the hands of Schopenhauer and soon permeated his philosophy. Moreover, when in 1897 Paul Deussen published in German a second great collection of Upanishads, he was obliged in some cases to fall back upon Anquetil's translations; for the Sanskrit originals had still not come to light.

The history of his Upanishad translations is a curious one. The manuscripts reached him in 1775. In a morbid excess of fidelity he translated them into French word for word, in the Persian word-order, which is quite different from that of French. This took him twelve years. He then realized that what he had written was too far removed from idiomatic French to be publishable, and began to make it less 'pidgin'. But qualms of conscience seized him again, and he set to work to make a translation into Latin, on the ground that this language 'admet les inversions comme le Persan'. The work was finished in 1796 but not printed till the beginning of the nineteenth century. The commentary (also in Latin) ranges very widely, and even contains a eulogy of the British Sunday School system, a topic which figures oddly in an exposition of the Upanishads.

Thirty years ago when I first became interested in the Jones–Anquetil story, though knowing only the bare outlines of it, my sympathies were entirely on Anquetil's side. Now, after further study of the whole affair, I feel differently. In the particular case at issue one cannot of course help being on his side. But when one has lived with him, as I have done recently, for some weeks on end, one cannot help agreeing with Sir

William that his 'virulence of temper' ends by 'alienating' one. There was also a touch of sordidness about the asceticism of his later days which I find distasteful. He claims, for example, that he lives (apparently not by necessity but by deliberate choice; for at almost the same period he offers the Government a contribution of fifty louis a year if they will start an all-out war against England) on four *sous* a day. 'Nulla corporis lintei lotio, mutatio'; a Tacitean way of saying that his underclothes are never washed or changed. But certainly he had courage, as is shown by his formal declaration, when asked to swear loyalty to Napoleon in 1804: 'Je ne jure ni jurerai fidélité à l'Empereur, comme on n'a pas droit d'exiger d'un Français, simple particulier, sans places ni fonctions.'

(*History Today*, January 1952.)

# A Chinese Poet in Central Asia

W hat, you may well ask on reading the title of this paper, induced the Chinese (whose own country is, Heaven knows, large enough) to push out into remote regions, from which they were separated by immense tracts of desert? The main reason was an economic one. And here we are not, as so often with regard to economic motives in ancient times, simply left guessing. We are specifically told that the attack on Turfan in AD 639, a hundred years before the time of our poet, was made because the Turfanese were preventing caravans from the West from reaching China. This did not interfere with China's basic economy; as regards food and clothing China was self-sufficient. The trade in question was one in luxury articles such as perfumes, jewels and drugs. On these the Chinese levied heavy import duties which were an important source of public revenue. There were, however, for the seventh-century conquest of Turkestan, political as well as commercial reasons. The T'ang dynasty, which had just come into power, followed upon a number of short-lived dynasties, most of which only ruled over part of China. There were still people alive who had lived under four or five successive dynasties and few people can have seen any reason to suppose that the new dynasty would last any longer than its

21

predecessors. It was necessary to get people to think of the T'ang dynasty as a régime that had 'come to stay', to equate it in their minds with, for example, the Han dynasty which had ruled for over four hundred years (*c.* 200 BC–AD 220). The best way to make clear the parallel was to re-enact the Central Asian conquests of the Han dynasty; loyal documents of the period constantly congratulate the T'ang Emperor on having done so. Similarly, one of the motives for the recent Chinese occupation of Tibet (nominally undertaken in order to free the Tibetans from Americo–Imperialist oppression) was no doubt in reality to assert equality with the last great dynasty, the Ch'ing, who conquered Tibet in the eighteenth century.

What made occupation of Turkestan possible in the seventh century was the break-up of the great Turkish confederation (the Western Turks) which had till recently controlled the whole area from Mongolia to the Caspian and beyond. Similarly, the break-up of an earlier nomad power, the Hun confederacy, had enabled Chinese armies to march into Turkestan in Han times.

It must not be supposed that the attack in 639 met with universal approval. We know, in fact, that a number of officials drew up a joint protest, declaring that a campaign carried on so many thousand miles away could not succeed, and that even if Turfan were eventually taken it could not be held. They proved to be quite wrong. The expedition won an easy victory and, as we shall see, over a hundred years later the Chinese were still in Turfan.

So much by way of historical introduction. Now let us turn to our poet, through whose verses we shall learn something of what it felt like to be keeping open vital trade communications, for the benefit of the exchequer, three thousand miles away from home. The poet Ts'ên Shên was born in AD 715, into a family that had produced three Ministers of State in the last hundred years. At the age of 19 he presented to the

Examination authorities, as a recognized alternative to sitting for the Literary Examinations, some of his essays and poems; but they were not accepted. In the years that followed he married, travelled in various parts of northern China and worked at the prescribed examination subjects. In the winter of 743, just before going in for the Literary Examinations, he addressed to some person of influence a prose-and-verse composition (*fu*) describing the past splendours of the Ts'ên family and in a veiled way asking his patron to put in a word for him with the examiners. For candidates to solicit support of this kind was a general practice. Ts'ên Shên had a particular reason for doing so. His grandfather and great-uncle had both rendered conspicuous services to the dynasty. The great-uncle had indeed died a martyr to his loyalty; for he resisted the attempts of the Empress Wu Hou to set up a new dynasty and was executed during the period of her usurpation, along with his five sons: 'She shattered our house,' he says; 'she destroyed our clan.' But after the restoration of the legitimate régime (the T'ang) an uncle of Ts'ên Shên's was accused in 713 of intriguing against the accession to the Throne of the reigning Emperor, Ming Huang. One object of Ts'ên Shên's composition was to remove the prejudice against him that the régime might feel in consequence of his uncle's offence. 'It was as the result of concerted slander and false denunciation,' he writes, 'that my uncle the Duke of Ju-nan was punished by the Son of Heaven.' The appeal seems to have worked, for in the spring (744) he duly passed the examination. He was given a small clerical appointment in the administration of the Crown Prince's Bodyguard. For five years he seems to have got no promotion. Some desperate step was necessary if he were ever going to make his way in the world, and he accepted a secretarial post on the Staff of General Kao Hsien-chih who in 749 was back in Ch'ang-an (the Capital) after his famous campaign in the Pamirs. I say 'desperate step' because service even a few hundred miles from the Capital was regarded as exile, and General Kao had been appointed Governor-General of An-hsi region, with its centre at Kucha many thousand miles away to the west, in what is now Turkestan. In 751 General Kao went back to Ch'ang-an to report and was moved to a post at Liang-chou in Kansu, considerably nearer home. His Staff (including Ts'ên Shên) went to Liang-chou expecting the General to join them there. But in the early summer there was a rumour that the natives of Turkestan had appealed to the Arabs to come and liberate them from Chinese rule. General Kao raised an army of 30,000 men and marched against the Arabs, who were advancing from Samarkand. While Kao was besieging Talas, some 200 miles east of Samarkand, the Karluk Turks (who were nominally on the side of the Chinese) revolted and came to raise the siege of Talas. General Kao decided to retreat under cover of night. In the darkness his troops got out of touch with their officers and the retreat became disorderly. It is probable that the Arabs captured a considerable number of stragglers. We know at any rate that Tu Huan, afterwards the author of a famous geographical work, fell into the hands of the Arabs, ultimately made his way to the 'Western Ocean' (presumably the Persian Gulf) and got back to Canton by sea. Kao Hsien-chih himself seems to have abandoned his troops and to have fled precipitately to the east. The scattered contingents were rallied by his second-in-command, Li Ssu-yeh, who led them back to their headquarters at Kucha.

We are told by Al-Thaalibi (AD 961–1038) that the Chinese prisoners taken by Ziyad taught the inhabitants of Samarkand, who had hitherto written on papyrus and parchment, how to make paper, an art of crucial importance to the Arabs, who were on the eve of becoming a great literary nation.

The Arabs did not follow up their victory. Their own internal situation was chaotic. Only a year before the battle of

Talas the Abbassids had set up a new dynasty with its capital at Baghdad. The generals who put the Abbassids into power were in 751 already quarrelling among themselves. In 752–3 Abu Muslim, the general chiefly responsible for the rise of the Abbassids, was suspected of separatist tendencies, and Ziyad (the victor at Talas) was ordered to revolt against him. The revolt failed, and Ziyad was beheaded. Abu Muslim was lured by the Abbassids to a conference in Baghdad in 755, and treacherously assassinated. Chinese and Moslems did not, so far as I can recollect, meet in battle again for many centuries.

Whether Ts'ên Shên was present at the siege of Talas we do not know. The fact that he does not allude to it proves nothing, as the subject was one which it would have been indiscreet to mention. He may, of course, have been left behind at Kucha or somewhere else on Kao Hsien-chih's lines of communication. His only allusion to the episode is contained in a poem addressed to a certain Censor Hsüeh who was apparently also a member of the disgraced General's Staff:

Now that the General has fallen into disgrace
What is to become of those that were clients at his gate?

Ts'ên Shên returned to China and passed the years 752 and 753 in Ch'ang-an, so far as we know, without a job. It was at this time, however, that he got to know the famous poet Tu Fu, whose friendship was later so advantageous to him. In the autumn of 752 Ts'ên Shên, Tu Fu, Ch'u Kuang-hsi and Kao Shih, together with another less famous poet, climbed the pagoda of the Monastery of Maternal Love, where a hundred years before the pilgrim Hsüan-tsang (Tripitaka) had worked, and each wrote a poem to commemorate the visit. Here is Ts'ên Shên's poem:

Like a jet of water this tower springs from earth,
Lonely and high, brushing the palaces of Heaven.
As we climb the steps we leave the World of Men;
The stone stairway winds in an open void.
Its looming presence daunts our holy land;
Its storeyed heights seem made by demon skill.
Its four corners block the light of the sun;
Its seven storeys brush the vault of the sky.
I look down, to point at the highest bird;
I raise my head to listen to the startling wind.
Mountain chains, like wave on wave of the sea,
Hurry forward, bearing their tribute to the West.
Green sophoras flank the Imperial Road;
Faultless in beauty stand the mansions of the great...

And the poet ends with the resolution, so common in poems of this kind, to give up official life and devote himself to Buddhism. The poem that Tu Pu wrote on the same occasion is much less plain-sailing. It is full of mythological allusions which are themselves apparently veiled allusions to current events; but as regards the real meaning of the poem commentators are hopelessly at variance.

In 754 Ts'ên Shên decided to try his fortunes once more in the west and managed to attach himself to the Staff of General Feng Chang-ch'ing who had just been given a command at Pei-t'ing, north of Turfan, near the modern town of Guchen, in north-eastern Turkestan. Among Ts'ên Shên's other functions was now that of Inspecting Censor (8th Rank, 2nd Class) and (later on) Assistant Commissioner of Expenses in Pei-t'ing and Kucha. Next year (755) he was chiefly at Pei-t'ing and Lun-t'ai near Urumchi, the modern capital of Turkestan. Some of the places that he now visited and about which he wrote poems he had probably already seen in 750 and 751. But for convenience I will deal with them here. We will begin with the Mo-ho-yen desert, on the way between the Kansu frontier and Hami, a wilderness of gravel and crumbling rock, with a width of over 200 miles.[1] This was the desert that the pilgrim Hsüan-tsang crossed in 630, all alone, plagued by phantom hosts and demon voices, without water for four nights and five days. 'An endless prospect of fearfully barren desert,' writes the Swedish traveller Sven Hedin, 1,300 years after Ts'ên Shên's time, 'not a blade of grass and not a trace of any wild animal; only a deathly silence.'[2] It was here that Ts'ên Shên wrote the famous quatrain:

Over the desert I saw the sun rise,
Under the desert I saw the sun sink.
And to get here I travelled ten thousand leagues!
What thing is fame that we buy it with journeys such as this?

Much of his time in Central Asia was spent at Turfan,[3] an oasis which though it is at a considerably more northern latitude than Peking, has a tropical climate, with temperatures of over 130° Fahrenheit; for it lies, in part at any rate, more than 300 feet below sea-level. The German traveller von Le Coq speaks of the 'bare red hills, strangely rent and torn' which surround this depression. They are the Fiery Mountains (*Huo Shan*) of our poet.

I came at evening to the city of Chiao-ho;
The Fiery Mountains loomed jagged and red.
It was late autumn, but still my sweat flowed;
A flaming wind swept the sandy dust.

1 Aurel Stein, *Ruins of Desert Cathay*, Vol. 2, p. 339.
2 Sven Hedin, *The Sino–Swedish Expedition*, Vol. 3, p. 234.
3 Now Yarkhoto, west of the present town of Turfan.

> How comes it that Maker of Wet and Dry
> To this one place sends no rain or snow?

Or again, when crossing these mountains:

> Their red flames burn the Tartar clouds,
> Their blazing fumes scorch the desert's void.

Turfan at that time had a population of about 50,000, of whom only a small proportion were Chinese. Christian, Manicheans and Buddhists lived side by side. Its products were carpets, myrrh, grape-wine and punch. In photographs[1] the great streets seem at first glance to be intact. Then, as one looks, like a mummy exposed to sudden light, the town dissolves and one sees a picture of endless ruins, projecting no more than a few feet above the ground.

Much of his time was spent at Lun-t'ai ('Wheel Terrace'), about 100 miles north-west of Turfan:

> At Lun-t'ai everything is strange,
> For in ancient times this was the land of the Huns.
> In the third month there is no green grass,
> At every homestead white elms grow.
> The native books use a strange script,
> The people of the place have a language of their own.
> Looking westward, to the north of the Flowing Sands,
> I gaze sadly at a jutting corner of the lake.

The language of Lun-t'ai was almost certainly Tocharian, an independent Indo-European language, having affinities with Latin, Greek, Celtic and Germanic, thus having the air of a

---

1 For example, Aurel Stein, *Serindia*, plate 273 (p. 1166).

sort of natural Esperanto. An ox is *okso*; the word for 'new' is *ñu*. The script (Brahmi) came from India. The mention, in this and other poems, of a lake near Lun-t'ai might help to identify its site; but lakes in Turkestan have a way of appearing and disappearing in the course of the centuries.

Ts'ên Shên writes again:

> In a strange land, beyond the Yin-shan,
> In a lonely town by the side of a snowy lake,
> Where autumn brings only the wild geese,
> Where all summer the cricket never sings –
> A brush of rain and the carpeted walls drip,
> A puff of wind, and the felt awnings stink –
> At Lun-t'ai, ten thousand leagues from home.
> How little has happened in all these three years!

At Lun-t'ai too was written the 'Snowy Song made when seeing off Assessor Wu on his return to the Capital':

> The north winds coil the earth, the pale grasses break;
> The Tartar sky in the eighth month is made of flying snow.
> Suddenly (as when in one night the spring wind comes –
> On a thousand trees, ten thousand trees the pear blossom
> opens)
> It finds its way through the bed-curtains and wets the gauze
> hangings,
> The fox-fur quilt gives no warmth, the padded coat feels thin,
> The Army-leader cannot draw his horn-spliced bow,
> The Governor-General's iron cuirass is too cold to wear.
> From the fencing along the desert lake the ice hangs yard
> on yard,
> Ten thousand leagues of dreary cloud are packed stark and
> still.

Here in the camp we set wine and drink to the departing
        guests;
The pipa sounds, the violin and the Tibetan flute.
Thick, thick the evening snow falls on the camp gate,
The wind tears at the red banners, frozen too stiff to flap.
To the eastern gate of Lun-t'ai we come to see you off
And as you go snow fills the road to the T'ien Shan.
A turn of the hill, a bend of the road and you are lost to sight;
All that is left is the track on the snow where your horse's
        hoofs trod.

Writing of the defile just to the west of Kharashahr Sir Aurel
Stein says that at the narrowest point 'a wooden gate across
the road, with troglodyte quarters for a guard, marks a watch-
station still in being.'[1] This was what the Chinese in ancient
days called the Iron Gate Pass. In a poem called 'Inscribed
upon the tower of the Iron Gate Pass' Ts'ên Shên, evoking a
strangely similar image, describes the same spot:

The Iron Gate, at the limit of the Western World!
Scarcely a traveller, far as the eye can see.
At the pass gate a solitary watchman stands
All day, facing the rock wall.
The bridge bestrides a chasm of a thousand feet,
The road winds pressed between tall cliffs.
I go up to the western tower and look;
A look is enough to make one's hair turn grey.

In 'At the rest-house to the west of the Silver Mountain
Desert', also near Kharashahr, he writes:

---

1 *Serindia*, p. 1228.

At the mouth of the Silver Mountain Desert the wind is
    sharp as an arrow:
To the west of the Iron Gate Pass the moon shines white as
    floss.
Two by two my sorrowing tears wet my horse's mane;
With hiss on hiss the Tartar sands slash the rider's face.
But a hale man, still in his thirties, cannot be content
Without wealth, without rank, to pore over inkslab and brush.

These are all private poems, not meant for the eye of his
superior officers or of authorities at the capital, but addressed
to equals and friends. In them he is free to express the feelings
of loneliness and horror that the deserts and vast snow-ranges
inspired, feelings akin to those of early European travellers
when they crossed the Alps. He makes no attempt to hide the
fact that he is here merely to mend his fortunes and would far
rather be leading an unadventurous life at home. Quite
different (and wholly without interest as literature, though
they fill in some gaps in our historical knowledge) are the
conventional poems of flattery that he addresses to superiors
such as the Generals Kao Hsien-chih and Fêng Chang-ch'ing.
These speak only of victories, of glory, of extending the might
of the dynasty, of whole nomad tribes surrendering with their
tents and flocks and camels, of feats surpassing those of
legendary conquerors in early days.

But to return to his private life in the oases, all was not
sadness. In many poems there are allusions to the feasting,
music and dancing that went on at these isolated Chinese
camps and Government-houses. In a poem written at Lun-t'ai
(which, as we have seen, was near the modern Urumchi) he
says 'Here in the camp we have set wine. It is night; we beat
the drums. Brocaded mats, red candles, the moon not yet full
risen. The Uighur General is good at native songs; the foreign

31

prince from Shê River (north-west of Lun-t'ai) can talk to us in Chinese.'

The natives of Central Asia were and are great dancers and musicians. They were numerous in the towns of western Kansu, and their music dominated that part of China. 'One out of every two natives is a *pipa* player,' writes Ts'ên Shên, speaking of Liang-chou. At Kan-chou, farther west, he saw Governor T'ien's girls dance the Whirling Dance called 'Like the Lotus Flower'. Turkestan is still famous for many forms of whirling dance. In this variety the girls whirled round long poles which they planted now to the right, now to the left, accompanied by the music of pipa and flute. Ts'ên Shên found the music incomparable. It made 'Gathering the Lotus' and 'Falling Plum-blossom' (two famous Chinese tunes) 'seem (as he says) mere senseless din.' But above all the dancing amazed him: 'the dancing that is commonly taught,' he says, 'is dancing and nothing more. It does not aspire to postures such as these.' To this we might of course object that dancing ought to be 'dancing and nothing more' and that Ts'ên Shên showed bad taste in preferring acrobatics.

The documents brought back from Tun-huang, the starting-point for caravans taking the southern route across the desert, by Aurel Stein, Pelliot and others tell us a great deal about the administrative and religious life of Chinese officials there, but very little about their social life. Ts'ên Shên has a poem about a party given by a Governor of Tun-huang:

When the moon came out over the town wall and stars
    filled the sky
Wine was set in his inner room, brocade mats were spread.
His singing girls, freshly rouged, all looking their best,
Droop sideways their tall coiffures, to stick in the golden pins.

While he sits drunk they hide his belt-clasp in front of the
    red candle:
'I can't imagine what has become of that belt-clasp of mine.'

This may possibly refer to the New Year game of guessing
which guest is holding a belt-clasp in his closed fist. Another
Governor, this time at Su-chou, a little further east, enlivens
his dinner-party by dancing the sword-dance. But soon the
Tartar pipers burst in with their shrill tune, reminding the
guests of how far they were from their homes and, as so often
happens at the end of Chinese poems, 'their tears fell like
rain'. We find him on another occasion feasting with a
General Kai in 'a warm room with embroidered curtains and
a glowing ground-stove: the walls covered with woven stuffs,
the floor with patterned rugs'. Young ladies are straining the
wine into jade cups and scattering here, there and everywhere
a profusion of bronze bowls full of wild-camel cream. They
wear purple sashes and have gold slashings on their coats. The
poet asks who they are and is told they are merely the
General's 'ordinary household slaves'.

In the winter of 755 the An Lu-shan revolution broke out:
Lo-yang, the eastern capital, fell after a few weeks' fighting,
and the T'ang dynasty seemed to be on the point of collapsing.
Ts'ên Shên must have heard the news early in 756, but in the
summer of that year we find him unconcernedly cultivating
his garden. 'In the year *ching-shên* of the T'ien-pao period', he
writes, 'when I was… Assistant Commissioner for Expenses at
Hami, Turfan and Pei-t'ing, my business left me a great deal
of leisure and in the garden of the Government House I
planted trees, grew medicinal herbs, made hillocks, dug ponds
and found it an agreeable distraction enough to potter about
among them.' In a rare wild flower brought to him by a
colleague from 'south of the T'ien Shan' Ts'ên Shên saw a

symbol of his own unhappy destiny. Just as the flower, unknown in China, had wasted its fragrance and beauty in a sequestered fold of the hills, so Ts'ên Shên was wasting his best years in obscure employment at a remote frontier town. He describes the flower at some length, but I have not succeeded in identifying it.[1] In the late summer, however, events at home took an even more serious turn. The rebels captured the capital, Ch'ang-an, and at the end of the year we find Ts'ên Shên on his way back to China.

My main object in this essay has been to give some account of his life in Central Asia and of the poems written there. But you will perhaps be glad to have a brief account of his subsequent career.

Ming Huang had abdicated in the autumn of 736. In 757 his son Su Tsung was at Fêng-hsiang, about a 100 miles west of Ch'ang-an, collecting forces for a counter-attack against the rebels. Many Chinese officials had been captured or were cut off from access to Fêng-hsiang. It was necessary to set up some sort of skeleton administration. The usual Civil Service examinations could not, of course, be held and posts were given in a haphazard way to such members of the governing class as happened to be on the spot. It was an opportunity not to be missed, and in the late spring or early summer of 757 Ts'ên Shên presented himself at the new Emperor's headquarters. Here he met his old friend the poet Tu Fu who had escaped from occupied Ch'ang-an and had at last (he had never succeeded in passing the examinations) under these exceptional circumstances managed to secure a tolerably good post. In the sixth month Tu Fu and some other friends recommended Ts'ên Shên as one who had 'early established a

---

1 I wish to thank Sir Edward Salisbury, Director of Kew Gardens, for his kindness in trying to get this plant identified for me. The description sounds like the Bella Dona lily.

reputation for clear judgment and sound principles and was highly respected by his contemporaries'. In consequence of this recommendation he was made *pu-chüeh* ('pointer-out of defects') in the Grand Secretariate. He was now Seventh Rank, Second Class; none too good a position for a man of 43.

It was the custom, on the ninth day of the ninth month, for those who were away from home to climb the nearest hill, drink together and look towards their native land. On this day, in 757, Ts'ên Shên wrote what is perhaps his best-known poem. The sense is:

> I should dearly love to climb to some high place,
> Had I only a friend to bid me drink wine.
> Piteous to remember that in far Ch'ang-an
> My chrysanthemums are flowering beside a battlefield.

It is not poetry in English; but one could only give it rhyme and lyric form at the cost of misrepresenting the meaning.

In the winter of 757 Ch'ang-an was retaken from the rebels and the Court moved back. After two years Ts'ên Shên was given a post in the Sixth Rank, and shortly afterwards he became Senior Officer (*chang-shih*) at Kuo-chou, near the modern Ling-pao, in Honan. This too was nominally a move-up, as the post belonged to the Fifth Rank. But it was one that at this period was generally given to administrators who had got into trouble of some kind, and this was clearly Ts'ên Shên's case, for he speaks of himself as 'awaiting punishment' at Kuo-chou. On the wall of the Kuo-chou commandery he wrote:

> Throughout my life all my plans have failed:
> I have tripped and tumbled till now my hair is grey.
> I have plotted and schemed, but all to no effect;
> My wife and children must share in my disgrace.
> But though our Enlightened Ruler has cast me aside

A loyal heart still beats in my breast.
When sadness comes, having nowhere else to go,
I climb to the upper storey of the Western Tower.

Whether his wife had remained in occupied Ch'ang-an or had escaped to the south we do not know. The above poem perhaps indicates that she was with him at Kuo-chou. He had a son called Tso-kung of whom, however, nothing is known.

He was at Kuo-chou till the spring of 762. He then returned to Ch'ang-an and held, in rapid succession, a great number of small posts including one in the Crown Prince's Household and one in the Household of the Emperor. In 764 he became Secretary of the Department of Forestry. It was typical of China's highly literary and idealistic civilization that an office of this kind, dealing solely with material affairs, should have been considered as of little importance. The Secretary was the head of the department, but he belonged only to the Fifth Rank, Second Class. We might justifiably be surprised that such a post should be given to someone who presumably lacked all technical knowledge or previous experience of forestry, were it not that our own attitude towards the filling of such posts is almost as frivolous as that of the ancient Chinese.

In 765 he was transferred to a slightly higher position (Secretary to the Arsenal). Then, at the end of the year, he got his first Governorship. His district was Chia-chou, near Mount Omi, in Szechwan. Governors of important districts were in the Third Rank, but Chia-chou was only a Middling District and its Governor belonged to the Fourth Rank. For the moment the appointment turned out to be purely nominal. A fresh insurrection was going on in Szechwan and after reaching Han-chung in southern Shensi he was obliged to return to Ch'ang-an. In 766 the great statesman and soldier Tu Hung-chien (709–769) was entrusted with the task of quelling the Szechwan rebellion. He took Ts'ên Shên on to his civilian Staff and they reached Ch'êng-tu, the capital of Szechwan, in the autumn. Tu Hung-chien's campaign was successful and in the summer of 767 Ts'ên Shên was at last able to take up his Governorship at Chiachou. Tu Fu, who was lying ill at Yün-an, in eastern Szechwan, sent him a present of carp. They had corresponded, but had not met for nearly ten years. So far as we know they never met again. In 768 Ts'ên Shên was recalled to the capital, but at Jung-chou on the Yangtze he was held up by a fresh insurrection. In a poem called 'Held up by bandit forces between Lü-chou and Jung-chou', after describing the reign of terror set up along the Yangtze River by these fugitives from the battle areas in the north, he warns them that Government troops are at hand and he calls upon them to repent while there is still time. 'It is with sadness that I think of you', he says 'for I know that you are doomed men.' The poem is extremely like several written by Tu Fu at this period, and it may be that besides sending fish to Ts'ên Shên he had also sent some of his recent verse.

Giving up the attempt to get to Ch'ang-an Ts'ên Shên went north, to Ch'êng-tu, where he fell ill and died in the early days of 770. Tu Fu died in the autumn of early winter of the same year. Ts'ên Shên's Central Asian poems have, of course, a considerable value from an ethnological, historical and topographical point of view. I have indeed confined myself mainly to his frontier poems not because of their documentary interest, but because the Western Regions with their strange alternation of featureless desert, luxuriant oases and gigantic snow-peaks, moved him profoundly and wrang from him poems of a vividness and intensity rare in the poetry of his day. Another feature of these poems which at any rate makes it relatively easy to convey some impression of them in English is their freedom from literary allusion. A poet writing in Central China was at every turn reminded of local celebrities and their legends, of historical events and of previous poems written in the same locality. The poetic impact of his surroundings lost its freshness and became veiled by a cloud of historical references and literary allusions. The Turfan region had no such associations. 'From ancient times till now few poets have been on the frontier', Ts'ên Shên himself writes, and apart from a few poems written near Lake Barkul by a well-known poet called Lo Ping-wang, some eighty years earlier, so far as I know no Chinese poet had written about Turkestan. A poem such as the one about the Iron Gate Pass near Kharashahr, recording a vivid, momentary and completely personal impression, would have been impossible to write in China where, at such a geographical key-point, a medley of historical and literary reminiscences would inevitably have intervened between the poet and his subject.

I must not close this essay without paying a tribute to Wên I-to, the great scholar who was assassinated in 1946 by Kuo Min Tang extremists. It is upon his researches into the chronology of Ts'ên Shên that this essay is largely based.[1]

(*History Today*, November 1951.)

---

1 See Vol. 3 of the Collected Works published after Wên I-to's death (*History Today*, November 1951).

# Lo-yang and its Fall

I n AD 311, Lo-yang, the capital of China and the greatest city of the whole eastern world, was captured and sacked by the Huns. For several centuries northern China was under foreign rule, and when at the end of the sixth century the north passed once more into Chinese hands the culture of the great native dynasties that ruled a powerful and united China (such, for example, as that of the T'ang) was in many ways a synthesis of nomad Turkic and traditional Chinese elements. The year 311, then (like the year 410, when the Goths sacked Rome) marks a turning-point in history. Gibbon, before describing the sack of Rome, pauses to give a general account of the city and the people who live in it. We may well follow his example. What, then, materially and spiritually, was Lo-yang at the beginning of the fourth century? The name is familiar to modern readers, for it figured fairly constantly in war-news at the time of the Japanese invasion. It lies in the north-west corner of the province of Honan, some 20 miles south of the Yellow River. The population at the beginning of the fourth century was about 600,000. That of Rome may have been somewhat larger; otherwise there was probably no city in the world of that size. It measured about 2 miles from north to south and was about 1¹/₂ miles wide. The main streets were divided into three parts. In the middle, the Imperial Road ran between walls about 3¹/₂ feet high. Only the Emperor and his family and the highest officials (Presidents of Boards, and the like) could use this central road. Ordinary people used the tracks that ran on each side of it, and these tracks were 'One Way'; traffic going from one of the city gates to the centre used the left-hand track; traffic going in the reverse direction used the track on the right. These main roads were flanked by avenues of elm and sophora.

The public buildings were of the utmost magnificence. The Indian monk Jīvaka who came to Lo-yang about 305 declared that the great cluster of palace buildings corresponded exactly with the thirty-three palaces of the paramount god Indra, as seen by the religious in ecstatic vision, 'allowing (he added) for the fact that they are human work, not divine.' The blinds of these palace buildings were of mother-of-pearl, and at sunset flashed with a blinding radiance. The great boulevard that led up to the palace buildings was called Bronze Camel Street, after the huge bronze figure of a camel that stood at its head, in the square outside the Palace gates. The Government offices were in the Palace precincts; the city offices of the provincial administrations lay near the eastern city gates. There were three markets: the Metal Market in the centre of the town, the Horse Market in the east and a general market outside the southern walls. It would be possible to give a much more detailed picture of Lo-yang at other periods, both earlier and later. For Lo-yang *c.* 311 our sources are limited; but perhaps the few facts that I have brought together will suffice to give some idea of the city.

When we turn from the city to the people that lived in it we naturally find ourselves provided with ample information about the educated, governing class, but are left completely in the dark about the lives and thoughts of the ordinary people who formed the bulk of the population. This is inevitable; for all the records come from members of the ruling class (which was at this period almost completely hereditary) and this class was interested in the common people mainly in regard to their corporate utility as soldiers and tax-payers, though always with an eye to the menace that they constituted as possible insurgents.

The prevailing faction in this ruling class was strongly Taoist. They justified conservative *laissez-faire* of a familiar kind by the argument that Being must have sprung from Non-being. Thus Everything is the product of Nothing, and this Nothing (which had the power to produce a whole universe) must be a prodigious force. They identified this force with Tao, the Absolute of the early Taoists, and believed that by conforming to it one can share in its magic; that one has only to do nothing, and everything gets done. This led to (or was the excuse for) a contempt for administrative duties and social obligations. The basis of this as of most philosophies was an irrelevant analogy. Traditional Chinese thinking was concerned with the family, viewed as a tree. The founder of the family was the stock (*pên*) of the tree and its 'ramifications' were of course the branches. Transferring this metaphor from the origin of families to the origin of Everything, the Taoists naturally regarded the manifold forms of Being as branches that had sprung from a single ancestral 'stock', anterior to Being. This 'stock' could only be Non-being, that is to say 'Nothing'. 'Nothing' thus becomes an Ancestor, a 'stock', and it was a maxim of traditional religion that 'every man must reverence the stock from which he springs'. This same word 'reverence', *ch'ung*, which means also 'exalt', 'worship', was applied by the Taoists to their cult of Nothing. They were not merely people who had reached a speculative conclusion about the priority of non-Being. They had transferred traditional ideas about the Ancestor to what M. Sartre calls *le néant*, and believed that by behaving in a way conformable to the character of their new Ancestor they could share in his *tê*, his magic power. In doing so they overlooked the fact that they had turned Nothing into Something – albeit Something very insubstantial and mysterious; which, if I remember rightly, is just what Professor Ayer once accused Heidegger and Sartre of doing.

As representative of these aristocratic Nihilists let us take Wang Yen (AD 266–311), Prime Minister at the time of the fall of Lo-yang. He belonged to one of the most distinguished families in China, the Wangs of Lang-yeh and was descended from a long line of high officials. He was famous for his great beauty and in particular for the jade-like whiteness of his hands. He subscribed to the theory that though exceptional people can acquire transcendent powers through the cult of *le néant* (to use M. Sartre's convenient term), inferior people (among whom he modestly ranked himself) must be content if through their cult of the *néant* they manage (in a dangerous world) to save their own skins. He did his best to take a negative line towards everything, merely to drift with the tide of events; and as he belonged to the privileged class, had great ability and, despite his principles, a considerable capacity for decided action, he 'drifted' into high post after high post, until (as we have seen) he became Prime Minister, though still protesting that he had 'never had any such ambition' and had only reached his present eminence 'by a series of routine promotions'.

The favourite distraction of Wang Yen and his friends was 'pure conversation', that is to say talk for talk's sake, as opposed to talking with a view to action. 'Mysteries' (*hsüan*), such as how the universe came into existence, were discussed, and problems about the relation of words to facts. For example, is a white horse a horse? And interwoven with these high themes were endless discussions about the characters of absent friends. The conversation, in fact, was very like that of clever undergraduates at our own universities. Of the endless anecdotes about Wang Yen the one that I like best has also the convenience of introducing us to P'ei Wei, Wang Yen's chief philosophical opponent. At the height of his reputation as an expounder of Taoism Wang Yen was besieged by students who came to ask difficult questions. Once when he had been talking continuously for two days he said wearily to a young enquirer, 'I am not feeling well today. P'ei Wei lives close by; you had better go and ask him'. It was as though Dr McTaggart, the great Idealist, had said to an importunate visitor, 'You had better go and ask Bertrand Russell.' For P'ei Wei's attitude was this: An absolute Negation could not possibly produce anything. 'Being' must have produced itself. Only what 'is', what 'exists', can affect what exists. To talk of a society being ruled by Inactivity (*wu-wei*) is absurd. How can the Void, the Non-existent, do any good to us human creatures who, unlike it, *do* exist?

P'ei Wei's doctrine was called 'exalting Being', as opposed to 'exalting Nothing'. According to him the ancestor whom we should reverence is not Nothing, but that mysterious thing 'Being', which performed the prodigious feat of producing itself out of nothing.

Essentially, then, what P'ei Wei preached was ordinary common sense; but such a view was far from being common at Lo-yang, where the cult of Nothing was being continually reinforced by the arrival from India and Central Asia of eminent Buddhists whose doctrine of the Void (*śunya*) was interpreted by the Chinese as an exotic version of their own Nihilism.

Such were the representations of the two opposing schools of thought at Lo-yang.

Now let us turn to the Huns. They were remote cousins of the Western Huns who invaded Europe in the fifth century.

Hard-pressed by another Turkic people, the Hsien-pi, they had been given permission by the Chinese at various times in the third century to settle in north-eastern China, where they were intended to act as a buffer against attacks by other nomads. Shih Lo, whom I am taking as the representative of the Hun side, was born in 274. His father was leader of one of the Hun tribes that had been settled by the Chinese on the north-east frontier. About AD 302 the Governor of this part of China who, like most provincial governors at that period, was a member of the Chinese Imperial family, found himself short of funds for military expenses and raised the necessary amount by kidnapping a number of Huns and selling them as slaves. Among those that were marched off 'chained in pairs' was Shih Lo. He was purchased by a man who lived at P'ing-yüan, in north-western Shantung, close to the Imperial horse-breeding pastures. Here he got into touch with one of the grooms, and with money obtained by petty brigandage bribed him to join a band of adventurers whom Shih Lo had collected, and mount them on horses from the Imperial paddocks. They were joined by a number of Chinese malcontents, and under the leadership of the groom, who had now become their General with Shih Lo as his second-in-command, they began to plunder north-eastern China. In 307 they sacked the great city of Yeh, about 115 miles north-east of Lo-yang, and slaughtered its commander who was, in fact, the Governor who had sold Shih Lo into slavery. Shortly after this the groom General was heavily defeated by Government troops and Shih Lo, retiring to the north, put himself at the disposition of the main Hun ruler. He had by that time made himself a reputation as a soldier and at once became one of the most important Hun generals. The Huns had now determined to get even with the Chinese, who for so long had treated them as chattels. In 308 they reached the gates of Lo-yang, but were driven off under the energetic leadership of our Nihilist philosopher Wang Yen, who apparently had only a limited faith in the magic of Inactivity. There were more Hun reverses in 309. These were thought by the Huns to be due to the fact that the spirit of Mount Sung, the guardian mountain of Lo-yang, had not been properly placated. After sacrifice to the spirit the Hun leaders were anxious to continue the attack; but their astrologer discovered that 311 not 309 would be the propitious year, and the Hun armies withdrew. In 310 the Hun chief died and there was a brief war of succession, which gave Lo-yang a breathing-space. In the winter of that year however the attack was renewed. Much of the country round Lo-yang was occupied by the Huns; food supplies in the city ran out and a terrible famine began. In the early summer of 311 the main Chinese armies, under the command of Wang Yen, were completely routed at K'u-hsien, about 150 miles to the east of Lo-yang. K'u-hsien, strangely enough, was the place where Lao Tzu, the legendary founder of Taoism, was supposed to have been born and where sacrifices were made to his spirit. Did Wang Yen, one wonders, pause at his shrine?

A number of high-ranking prisoners were brought to Shih Lo's tent and questioned about the state of affairs in Lo-yang. Among the prisoners was Wang Yen himself. He gave 'a full account of the reasons for the defeat'. What he considered these to be we are not told. He mentioned, presumably, the chaos produced by a long period of dissension between the various royal princes, and the refusal of the provinces to come to the aid of the capital. Shih Lo was much interested and sent for him again next day. In the course of the conversation Wang Yen spoke of his own career and once more protested, as he had done when he was made Prime Minister, that he was not interested in politics. It was Wang Yen's maxim (as we have seen above) that whereas the full-fledged Taoist saint can perform miracles by his detachment from concrete realities, the most that the common man can do is to 'save his own skin', undeterred by conventional non-Taoist ideas of dignity and morality. True to this principle and hoping (or so we are told) to curry favour with Shih Lo, he suggested that the Hun should proclaim himself Emperor of China. 'You took office when you were quite young,' said Shih Lo, ignoring Wang Yen's suggestion, 'made a name for yourself everywhere within the Four Seas, and now hold the highest office. How can you say that you have never had political ambitions? If any one man is responsible for the ruin of the Empire it is you.' And he ordered him to be removed. Then turning to his lieutenant, K'ung Ch'ang he said, 'I have travelled about a good deal in my time, but nowhere have I met with such a man as this. Oughtn't we to make use of him?' 'He is one of the Three Grandees of the Chinese Empire,' said K'ung Ch'ang. 'He would never work whole-heartedly in the interest of the Huns. Moreover he has certainly done nothing on this occasion to make us respect him.' 'We can at least not put him to the sword,' said Shih Lo, and that night he sent men to push over the wall of the room in which Wang Yen was sleeping and suffocate him. Death by suffocation was more honourable than decapitation.

The Hun armies entered Lo-yang from the south and east. The destruction of the city began with the burning of the offices of the provincial administrations which lay, as we have seen, just inside the eastern gates. Fierce street-fighting ensued and it was not till a fortnight later that the palace, in the northern part of the city, was reached. It was ransacked by the Huns who carried off everything of value, including the ladies of the Emperor's harem. The Emperor himself had made a previous attempt to escape by river to the east; but the Huns burnt his boats before the expedition was ready to start. He now slipped out by a back gate and attempted to escape westwards, in the direction of Ch'ang-an; but he was overtaken and captured. After being held captive for a short time he was sent to the Hun capital in the north-east where, stripped of all his grandeurs, he was made to carry round the wine at Hun banquets. After sacking the palace the Huns pillaged and burned the Imperial tombs, the ancestral shrines and the various ministries. There had been at one moment a plan to spare Lo-yang and make it the Hun capital. But it was still almost surrounded by unsubdued Chinese territory and the leaders decided that it might prove difficult to hold, The whole city was therefore burnt to the ground and no considerable town stood there till the Wei Tartars made Lo-yang their capital in 493.

News of the fall of Lo-yang, which was the terminus of a great Asiatic trade route, must have spread far beyond China. The one non-Chinese comment upon it that has come down to us occurs in a fragmentary letter (written probably in the summer of 313) by the Sogdian merchant Nanai-vandak to his colleague Nanai-dvar in Samarkand. It was found in the ruins of a watch-tower to the west of Tun-huang, on the western frontiers of China. The letter which is in Sogdian, an eastern dialect of early Persian, expresses astonishment that 'those Huns who yesterday were the Emperor's vassals' should now have overthrown the empire. 'And, Sir,' Nanai-Vandak writes, 'the last Emperor – so they say – fled from Saragh (i.e. Lo-yang) because of the famine, and his palace and walled city were set on fire... So Saragh is no more, Ngap (i.e. Yeh) no more!'

But the cult of Non-being, 'pure conversation' and Taoist indifferentism did not perish with Lo-yang. A large proportion of the official classes fled before the city fell, and after an unsuccessful attempt to set up a régime at Ch'ang-an in the West, the Chinese yielded the whole north to the 'barbarians' and made a new capital at Nanking, which remained in Chinese hands till its conquest by the Mongols in the thirteenth century.

The above account is taken from the original Chinese sources, except in the case of the Sogdian merchant's letter, for which I have used the translation of that brilliant Iranist, Professor W B Henning.

(*History Today*, April 1951.)

# SOME CHINESE GHOSTS

*T*here seem to be more ghost-stories in China than in any other part of the world; which is not unnatural, for more people have lived and *died* in China during more centuries than anywhere else. Here are a few such stories, taken from an eighteenth-century collection:

A certain Mr Yeh had a friend called Wang, and on Wang's sixtieth birthday Yeh mounted his donkey and rode off to congratulate Wang. At dusk, when he was crossing the Fang Shan (south-west of Peking), he was caught up by a big fellow on horseback, who asked him where he was going. When Yeh told him, he said, 'How fortunate! Wang is my cousin and I too am going to visit him on his birthday. Let us keep each other company!' Yeh was delighted to have a companion, and readily assented. After a time he noticed that the big fellow continually lagged behind. He invited him to lead the way, and the other pretended to accept the suggestion. But in a few minutes he had fallen behind again. Yeh began to suspect that the man was a bandit and kept on glancing at him over his shoulder. It was soon pitch dark, and he could no longer see his companion. But presently a storm began, there was a flash of lightning and by its light Yeh saw that the fellow was now hanging from his saddle head downwards, his feet moving in space, as though he were walking; and at every step he took there was a peal of thunder, each thunder-clap being also accompanied by a black vapour which issued from the fellow's mouth. Yeh saw that he had an immensely long tongue, red as cinnabar. He was of course much startled and alarmed; but there seemed to be nothing for it but to ride on as fast as he could to Mr Wang's house. Wang was delighted to see them both and at once asked them to have a drink. Taking Wang aside, Yeh asked him if it was a fact that he was related to the person he had met on the road. 'Oh yes,' said Mr Wang. 'That's quite right. It's my cousin Mr Chang. He lives in Rope-makers Lane at Peking and is a silversmith by profession.' This reassured Yeh, and he began to think that what he had seen during the night was simply an hallucination. However, when the time came for going to bed, he did not much like the idea of sharing a room with the fellow. But the other insisted upon it and Yeh was obliged reluctantly to concur, only taking the precaution of getting an old servant of Mr Wang's to sleep in the same room. Yeh could not manage to get to sleep. At the third watch though the candle had gone out, the whole room was suddenly filled with light, and Yeh saw the man sitting up in bed; the light came from his huge protruding tongue. He then came over and sniffed at Yeh's bed-curtains, saliva dripping from his jaws. But seeming to realize that Yeh was awake, he changed his mind and seizing the old servant, devoured him almost to the last bone. It so happened that Yeh was a devotee of Kuan Yü, the God of War, and he now hastened to call out: 'Great Sovereign, subduer of demons, where are you?' At once there was a resounding boom as though a gong had been struck, and Kuan Yü appeared from between the rafters, with a huge sword in his hand. He struck at the monster, who at once turned into a butterfly as big as a cart-wheel and spread its wings to parry the blow. After the combatants had pranced round one another for a moment or two, there was a loud crash, and both the butterfly and the god vanished.

Yeh fell fainting to the floor and was still lying there when at noon Mr Wang came to see what had happened to him. He had now recovered sufficiently to tell Wang the whole story, and Wang indeed saw for himself that there was fresh blood on the servant's bed. But both Mr Chang and the servant had disappeared, though Chang's horse was still in the stable. They at once sent a messenger to Peking, who on reaching Chang's workshop found him at his stove melting silver. He had been in Peking all the time and had never gone to Mr Wang's to congratulate him on his sixtieth birthday.

Here is another story:

In the year *Hsin-mao* of the Ch'ien Lung period (1771) my brother Yuan Shu went to the capital in company with his examination-mate Shao. They reached Luan-ch'eng on the 21st of the fourth month. All the inns at the Eastern barrier were crammed with travellers and their equipages. But presently they found an inn where there seemed to be no guests at all, and decided to stay here for the night. Shao took the outer room and my brother the inner room. When it was beginning to get late they went to bed each in his own room, but kept the lamps burning, and continued for a time to talk to each other through the partition wall. Suddenly my brother saw a man about 10 feet high, with a green face and green whiskers, dressed and shod all in green, come in at the door. He was so tall that his hat made a rustling sound as it brushed against the paper of the toplight in the ceiling. Soon a dwarf not so much as 3 feet high also appeared at my brother's bedside. He had a very large head, and he too had a green face, and was dressed all in green. He moved his sleeves up and down, and postured like a dancer. My brother tried to call out, but found he could not open his mouth. Shao was still talking to him from the next room but he was unable to say anything in reply. To add to his bewilderment another man now appeared, sitting on the low stool beside his bed. He had a pock-marked face and a long beard; on his head was a gauze cap, and he was wearing a very wide belt. He pointed at the giant and said to my brother, 'He's not a ghost'. Then he pointed to the dwarf with a big head, and said, 'But that one is'. Then he waved his hand towards the giant and the dwarf, saying something that my brother could not catch. They both nodded and began to salute my brother with their hands folded in their sleeves. At each salute they retreated one step. The last salute brought them to the door, and they disappeared through it. The man with the gauze cap then saluted in the same way, and also disappeared. My brother leapt up and was just on the point of leaving the room when Shao, screaming wildly, came rushing in, saying that he had been visited by apparitions. 'Was it two green men, one big and one little?', asked my brother. 'Nothing of the kind,' said Shao. 'When I lay down I at once felt a draught that seemed to come from a small closet close to my bed. It was so ice-cold that my hair stood on end, I was too uncomfortable to sleep, and that was why I went on so long talking to you, though after a time you did not answer. Presently I saw that in the closet there were about twenty men, some large, some small, with faces round as bowls, moving restlessly about. I made sure it was only my fancy, and took no notice. But suddenly their faces, big and little, appeared at the doorway, in rows, one above the other, till the whole opening was blocked up with faces, the topmost place of all being taken by a huge face as big as a grinding-pan. When all these faces began grinning at me, it was more than I could bear, and throwing aside my pillow I jumped up and came here. But of your "green men" I saw nothing at all.' My brother then told him of what he had seen, and they agreed to leave the place at once, without even getting fodder for their horses. At dawn they heard one groom whisper to another, 'That place we stayed at last night is said to be a ghost-inn. A lot of people who have stayed there have afterwards gone mad, or even died. The officials of the district got tired of having to enquire into all these cases, and more than ten years ago they ordered that the place was to be closed down. If these two gentlemen stayed the night there without coming to any harm, it must either mean that the haunting has ceased, or that the gentlemen are destined by fate to rise high in the world.'

The following story is headed: 'It is not always the most reputable people who turn into gods'.

A student called Li was going up to Peking for the examinations. At Soochow he hired a launch and had got as far as Huai-an, when there suddenly appeared at the cabin door a certain Mr Wang, who had formerly been Li's neighbour. He asked if he might join him. Li consented, and they travelled together for the rest of the day. At nightfall, when they anchored, Wang asked him if he easily took fright. The question surprised Li. He reflected for a moment and then said, 'I don't think so'. 'I should be sorry to scare you,' said Wang. 'But as you assure me that you are not easily scared, I had better tell you the truth at once. I am a ghost, not a live man. It is six years since you and I last met. Last year the crops failed, prices soared, and driven by hunger and cold I rifled a tomb, in order to get something valuable to sell for food and firing. But I was arrested, found guilty and executed. And now I am a ghost, hungry and cold as before. I boarded your boat and asked you to take me with you to Peking, because I have a debit to collect there.' 'Who is it that owes you money?'

asked Li. 'A certain Mr Piao,' said he. 'He is employed by the Board of Punishments, and he promised that when my papers passed through his hands he would erase the death sentence and substitute something milder, in consideration for which I was to give him 500 ounces of silver. I managed to collect the sum, but once it was in his hands he ignored his side of the bargain, and the sentence was duly carried out. So now I am going to haunt him.' This Mr Piao happened to be a relative of Li's. He was very much upset that a member of his family should have behaved in this way. 'The sentence pronounced upon you was of course perfectly in order,' he said. 'But my kinsman had no right to rob you in this way. How would it be if I were to take you with me to his house and point out to him how badly he behaved? He would then probably give you your money back and you would no longer feel so bitterly against him. But by the way, as you are dead, I don't quite see what use the money would be to you.' 'It is true that I have not now any use for it,' said Wang, 'but my wife and children are still living quite close to your home, and if we recover the money, I shall ask you to give it to them for me.' Mr Li promised to do this. Several days later, when they were approaching the capital, Wang asked leave to go on ahead, saying, 'I'm going off to your relative's house to haunt him. If he has already realized that he is in my power, he is more likely to listen to what you say when you put my case to him. If you were to go there straight away he would certainly take no notice; for he is a man of extremely avaricious disposition.' So saying, Wang disappeared. Li went on into Peking, found himself a lodging, and a few days later went to his kinsman's house. On arriving, he was told that Mr Piao was suffering from a 'possession'. Shamans, soothsayers, everything had been tried, but all to no purpose. As soon as Li reached the door, the 'possession' speaking through the sick man's mouth, shouted out, 'Now's your chance, people! Your star of deliverance has arrived.' The people of the house all rushed out to meet Li, asking him what the madman's words meant. Li told them the whole story, and Piao's wife at first suggested burning a considerable quantity of paper money in payment of the debt. At this the sick man roared with laughter. 'Pay back real money with make-believe money!' he said. 'Nothing in this world can be disposed of quite so conveniently as that! Count out 500 ounces of silver at once, and hand them over to our friend here. I shan't let go of you till you do.' The Piaos produced the money, and Mr Piao at once recovered his senses.

Some days later the ghost turned up at Li's lodging and urged him to set out for the South at once. 'But I have not sat for my examination yet,' said Li. 'You are not going to pass,' said the ghost, 'so there is no point in sitting.' Li, however, insisted on remaining at Peking. After he had sat for the examination, the ghost again urged him to start for home. 'Do let me just wait till the results are out,' said Li. 'You haven't passed,' said the ghost, 'so what is the point of waiting for the results?' When the results were published, Li's name was not on the list. 'Now perhaps you'll consent to start,' said the ghost, laughing. Ashamed of having kept him waiting for nothing, Li agreed to start immediately. On the boat he noticed that Wang sniffed at things to eat and drink, but never swallowed them, and that if he sniffed at anything hot, it at once became icy-cold. When they got to Sutsien, the ghost said, 'They are giving a play in that village over there. Let's go and look on.' When they had watched several episodes, the ghost suddenly disappeared. But Li heard somewhere nearby a sound of sand flying and pebbles rolling. He thought he had better go to the boat and wait till the ghost came back. It was getting dark when the ghost at last reappeared, dressed up very grandly. 'Goodbye,' he said, 'I'm staying here. I've got the job of being the God of War.' 'How have you managed that?' asked Li, very much surprised. 'All the so-called Goddesses of

Mercy and Gods of War down here in this world are merely ghosts passing themselves off as divinities. The play we saw was given in pursuance of a vow to the God of War. But the local "God of War" is in fact the ghost of a scamp who did far worse things than I ever did. I suddenly made up my mind I would oust him from his job, so I went and had a scuffle with him and drove him away. I daresay you heard the noise of sand flying and pebbles rolling.' With these words, the ghost bowed his thanks and vanished. Li went on down the canal, and eventually handed over the 500 ounces of silver to the ghost's family.

A story about the ghost of Chiang T'ing-hsi, a famous painter (1669–1732), well illustrates the 'clash of generations'. The men of the early eighteenth century were on the whole stern and puritanical, those of the mid-century pleasure-loving and tolerant, those of its closing years and the early nineteenth century, once more straitlaced and censorious. Chiang T'ing-hsi was a typical scholar of the old, severe school. He warned his sons and grandsons against ever having anything to do with actors, and as long as he was alive no actor or entertainer ever came near the house. When he had been dead for ten years (i.e. in 1742) his son Chiang P'u began occasionally to get actors from outside to give performances. But he still did not venture to keep a private troupe in the house. An old family servant called Ku Sheng, when chatting one day with Chiang P'u, got on to the subject of theatricals. 'A company of actors from outside,' he pleaded, 'is never so good as a troupe trained in the house, or so handy. A lot of the servants here have children. Why don't you get hold of a teacher, make him select the likeliest and have them trained as a company?' Chiang P'u was much attracted by the idea; but before he could answer he suddenly saw that Ku Sheng's face was transfigured by a look of abject terror. He held his two hands in front of him as though to receive handcuffs, and fell prostrate on the ground. Then he inserted his head between the legs of the table and worked his way from one table-leg to another till the table completely covered him, like the lid of a box. Chiang called to him, but he did not answer. He then sent urgent messages to shamans and doctors; but nothing they could do was of any avail. However, at midnight he began to revive and was able at last to say, 'What a fright I have had, what a fright! Just after my last remark to you, a huge figure appeared and dragged me off to a ball in which my old master was sitting. Looking at me reproachfully my master said in a stem voice, "I am surprised that you, who have been in the service of my family from generation to generation, should ignore my last wishes and persuade Wu-lang (Chiang P'u's intimate name) to keep actors." He then had me bound; I was given forty strokes with the rod and shut up alive in a coffin. I was completely stupefied, and did not know what to do. At last I heard voices calling to me and, still lying in my coffin, I tried to answer, but could not. After a time, however, I began to feel less confused; but I still did not know how to get out.' They looked at his back and saw there actually were blue-black weals on it.

The Chinese, as is well known, used to refer to Europeans as *kuei*, that is, 'ghosts' or 'demons'. Attempts have sometimes been made to show that this was not so rude as it sounds – that *kuei* is a harmless classificatory term, merely implying that foreigners were creatures that belonged to a different order of things. But it was certainly not a term of admiration. To call people *kuei* necessarily, I think, implies that they are both hideous and alarming. Many Chinese books of ghost-stories contain stories about *kuei* who were not spooks or spirits of the departed, but merely foreigners. Here is a story about the land of the Russian *kuei*:

General Umitai, a Mongol officer serving in the Chinese army, used to relate that when, as a young man, he was attached to a mission sent to Russia, he heard that to the north Russia was bounded by a great ocean and wanted to go and look at it. The Russians were opposed to this; but he begged so hard to be allowed to, that in the end they gave him an escort of foreigners, who carried compasses and implements for striking a light. For Umitai they provided a carrying-chair with a double lining of felt; his escort rode on camels. After going north for six or seven days they saw a mountain of ice, like a great bastion; so high that its summit was lost in the sky, and shining with so blinding a light that it was not possible to look straight at it. In the base of this mountain was a cave. He crawled into it, guided by his escort, who striking lights and consulting the compass wriggled their way through tortuous passages. After three days they came to the end of the cave and out into a region where the sky was brown, like tortoiseshell. Every now and then a black cloud blew their way, stinging them as though grit had been flung in their faces. The foreigners said it was what was called black hail. They could not bear it for long on end, and every few miles, when they could find a cavern in the rocks, they sheltered there, and started a fire, which they made with saltpetre; for nowhere in that region are there any bushes or trees; nor is there any coal or charcoal. After resting a little they would go on again, and after five or six days they came to two huge bronze figures, facing one another. They were some 30 feet high. One figure rode on a tortoise and the other grasped a serpent in his hand. In front of them was a bronze column with some characters on it in a script that Urmitai could not read. The foreigners said that the statues had been erected by the Emperor Yao. They had always heard that what was written on the pillar meant 'Gate into the Cold'. At this point the men of his escort refused to go any farther. 'Ahead of us,' they said, 'is a sea; but it is still 300 leagues away. When one gets there, neither the sun nor the stars are visible. The cold is so intense that it cuts one's skin, and if one catches it (i.e. gets frost-bite) one dies. The waters of the sea are black as lead. From time to time these waters part, and out of the rift come ogres and strange beasts, which seize people and carry them away. Even where we are now, water does not flow or fire burn'. To test this last statement Umitai held a lighted torch against his fur-coat, and found that, as stated, it did not burn. After a long rest, they started home again. On reaching the town, a roll-call was held, and it was found that out of fifty men, twenty-one had died of frost-bite. Umitai's face was black as pitch and he did not recover his normal complexion for six months. Some of those who went with him had blackened faces for the rest of their days.

Yao, it should be explained, was an ancient Chinese Emperor who thousands of years ago ruled over 'everything under Heaven'. So from a Chinese point of view it was not surprising to find that he had erected a monument in Siberia. The Chinese mission to which Umitai was attached was apparently the one that reached St Petersburg in 1732, and the story seems to be a more or less legendary account of an attempt to explore the White Sea.

What makes Chinese ghost-stories so different from ours is, I think, the fact that our belief in such things is an isolated survival from a whole pattern of thought that we have long ago cast aside; whereas Chinese ideas about ghosts were part of a vast structure of commonly accepted belief about that other universe, the World of the Dead, far apart from our world, yet so continually brushing against us with its cold touch that the fringes of these two worlds seem to overlap and entwine.

(*Listener*, March 1956.)

# SOME FAR-EASTERN DREAMS

here have been moments in modern Europe when people have begun to attach importance to their dreams. Some inkling that dreams are symbolic and have a secret (and not always very reputable) meaning leaked through from the works of Freud early in this century and a few earnest people began to take a rather awe-struck interest in their dreams. Later came Dunne's *Experiment with Time*, and the same people began writing down their dreams to see if they would come true – a possibility that does not seem to have interested Dr Freud. But on the whole we have regarded dreams as negligible aberrations of the spirit. In India and the Far East a very different attitude has been taken. True, one of the basic theories about dreams, found alike in India, China and Japan, is that they are due to small physical disorders or discomforts; for example, if one wears one's belt too tight one will dream of snakes, and one Buddhist school put forward the theory that dreams were due to arbitrary combinations of things familiar in waking life. 'When one is awake,' says the *Mahavibhasha Sastra*, 'in one place one sees a man and in another one sees horns. In dreams one combines the two things and sees a horned man.' But such ultrarational theories ignored the common folk-belief that dreams were sent by deities or were caused by the spells and drugs of magicians, and most Eastern theories about dreams, while attributing them to various causes, were concerned chiefly with those sent as warnings or encouragements by the gods. These concessions to popular belief were rather like Jung's revision of Freud's dream theory which to the layman appears rather drab and narrow, in its assumption that the dream is solely a product of the individual subconsciousness; whereas Jung's theory that dreams drew also upon a universal store of consciousness opened the door (as his theories have generally done) to traditional beliefs and mythologies.

In China at any rate it was not only men who received warning dreams from kindly spirits. Chang Hua, the famous poet and statesman, who died in AD 300, had a white parrot to which he was extremely devoted. One day when he was standing in the garden he called to it to come out of the house and perch on his hand. 'I had a bad dream last night,' said the parrot, 'warning me to stay at home.' Thinking that the parrot had merely overheard something said by a member of the household and was repeating the words without knowing what they meant, he went into the house, stroked its head and carried it out into the garden. It was at once attacked by a hawk. 'Peck its leg,' screamed Chang Hua; which the parrot did, and the hawk let go. But it was a very narrow escape.

Dreams, in these stories, not only give warning of what is about to happen in real life; they impinge on reality, sometimes with embarrassing results. About AD 843, a student at the Chinese National College slept late into the morning and dreamt that he was leaning idly against the doorpost of the college when he was accosted by a man dressed in yellow and carrying a hold-all. The stranger asked him his name, and when he told it smiled knowingly and said, 'You'll get through your examinations all right next spring.' The student then asked how several of his friends at the college would get on, and the man at once told him which of them would be successful and which of them would fail. 'Won't you come round with me to the pasty-shop in the Ch'ang-hsing Ward?' said the student. He often went there, for it lay only a few minutes' walk to the south of the college. The pasties for which the shop was famous were bought, but they had not been eating long when, in his dream, a dog-fight began just outside the shop, and he woke with a start. He jumped up and called out to his friends that he wanted to tell them a dream. He had hardly begun telling it when the proprietor of the pasty-shop appeared at the door. 'Are you aware,' he said, 'that you and your friend ordered two pounds of pasty and then went off without settling for them?' The student was very upset, for it so happened that at the moment he had run through his allowance, and had not a penny. Accompanied by the proprietor of the shop he went to a pawnbroker's and pawned his coat. Then he followed the shop-keeper back to the pasty-shop, curious to see whether the place where he was alleged to have sat corresponded with his dream. Everything, the stools, the dishes, the chopsticks, were just the same. 'My companion and I,' he said to the shop-keeper, 'were only your customers in a dream. You're not surely going to say that we actually consumed your pasties? 'You ordered them,' said the shop-keeper, 'and that is what matters. But come to think of it, I did notice that though you seemed to be eating them, the pasties did not get any smaller. I thought that perhaps you weren't getting on with them because you didn't like garlic. I did put a little in.'

Next spring the student and the three friends whom the stranger had named all took their degrees.

Sometimes one person's dream appears to another as a waking vision, and this is particularly so between people who are very intimate. In about AD 700, the famous Chinese statesman Liu Yu-ch'iu, then still only a small provincial official, was compelled to leave home for a while on an official mission. On his way back he was surprised to hear a noise of singing and loud laughter coming from a Buddhist shrine that stood by the wayside. He peeped through a chink in the wall and saw a number of gay young people picnicking in the courtyard. Among them he was astonished to see his young wife, to whom he was deeply attached, chattering and laughing. Amazed to see her so far from home and in such company and having tugged at the door and found that it was locked he did the first thing that came into his head – picked up a piece of broken tile and threw it over the wall. There was a tremendous crash, followed by a noise of rushing water, and peeping through his hole, he saw that he had hit the big earthenware bowl which the picnickers had brought to do their washing-up in. The people within were fleeing in every direction and had soon all disappeared. He then managed to climb the wall and searched the whole place. Not a soul could he find, though the one door which led into the premises was still locked as before. Utterly bewildered he hurried home. He was told that his wife was in bed. She soon came out to meet him and after a while she said, 'I have just had such an odd dream. I dreamt I was picnicking with a lot of other young people at a wayside shrine. I had no idea who they were. Suddenly someone threw a tile over the wall. It landed right in the middle of the cups and dishes, causing the wildest confusion, and I woke with a start.'

This became a classic dream-story and there are many later variants of it.

In AD 759 (these strange stories are very punctilious about dates) an official called Hsieh Wei had been lying sick of a fever for many days, tossing sleepless on his bed when he fell at last into a feverish doze. 'What is the use,' he said to himself in his dream, quite forgetting that he was weak and ill, 'what is the use of lying here in this hot bed? Surely it would be better to get up and go into the fresh air.' So he picked up his walking-stick and in his dream set out for a stroll along the river-bank. He came to a deep, clear pool in which the autumn leaves were reflected, and the idea came to him that it would be refreshing to have a bathe. As a boy he had been fond of swimming, but he was now very much out of practice, and seeing the fish glide swiftly past him he said to himself in his dream, 'We men make a very poor show of it, at best. If only I could get a temporary job as a fish and really swim to some effect.' 'You have only to apply for it,' said a voice near him. 'Even a permanent job might not be out of the question, but a temporary job can easily be arranged. I'll see about it for you.' Presently a giant with a fish's head appeared, riding on a leviathan, escorted by a band of fish attendants. He took out a scroll and read out the following proclamation:

'Though it is fit that denizens of the waves and dwellers on the land above should for the most part go their separate ways, it has been brought to Our notice that the human official Hsieh Wei shows an unusual partiality for the watery element and has applied for permission to serve us. We, the River Lord, in accordance with his desire, do hereby appoint him to the office of Temporary Red Carp in the eastern pool, giving him at the same time the warning, necessary to one embarking on this career, that bait attached to a hook is on no account to be approached.'

Glancing at himself while he listened, Hsieh Wei saw that he was already covered with scales.

He was told that he must report every evening at the eastern pool. But apart from that he was free to wander where he pleased, and he made many long excursions up stream and down, explored countless lakes and tributaries, and soon there was no creak or channel where he had not twisted and gambolled to his heart's content. On one of these occasions he could find nothing to eat and feeling very weak and hungry he followed a fishing-boat in the hope of picking up some scrap that the fisherman threw overboard. Coming closer he saw that the fisherman was Chao Kan, whom he knew very well. Presently Chao cast his line, and the bait smelt very good. But he remembered the warning, and reluctantly swam away. Soon, however, his hunger became unendurable and he said to himself, 'After all, although I have taken a temporary job in the fish-world, I did not resign my human post, and Chao Kan, if I tell him who I am, will certainly not dare to kill an official. He will no doubt take me back to my bureau, and all will be well.' So he swallowed the bait and Chao Kan hauled him in. He began to explain matters, but Chao Kan seemed not to be listening and having passed a string through his gills took him ashore and tied him up in a hidden place among the bullrushes. Presently a servant came, saying that the Senior Clerk was going to entertain some friends and wanted a large carp. 'I have plenty of small ones,' said the fisherman, hoping to sell Hsieh Wei for a higher price in the market, 'but I have not caught any big ones today.' 'I know your tricks,' said the servant, and beating about among the bullrushes he soon found a very big fish indeed. 'I am the Registrar Hsieh Wei,' the fish explained. 'I have been seconded to a fish-post, but I still hold my rank as a human official and you ought to make your obeisance to me.' But the servant did not seem to hear what he was saying and carried him off to the Government house. Several of his colleagues were sitting near the gate playing draughts. He called out to them, but all they said was, 'That's a fine big fish.' Wang the fish-cook was sent for and taking Hsieh Wei to the kitchen stood over him knife in hand. 'My good Wang,' cried Hsieh, 'I have never employed any one but you as my fish-cook ever since I came here. Surely you will not be so ungrateful as to kill me.' But Wang seemed unaware that anything had been said. He laid Hsieh's head on the chopper-board and was just bringing down his knife, when

Hsieh woke with a start. He was quite cured of his fever, and when his colleagues came to congratulate him, he told them of his dream. To his astonishment he learnt that everything had happened just as he had dreamed it. 'We saw your lips moving,' they said, 'but no sound came out, and we had not the faintest idea that the fish was you.' Neither Hsieh nor his colleagues could ever bring themselves to eat carp again.

A very convincing dream is recorded in the diary of the Japanese monk Jojin who visited China about AD 1070. After crossing the famous Stone Bridge that leads to the T'ien-t'ai Monastery in eastern China, he writes: 'Looking through my Dream Record I see that on the 30th of the 7th month in the fourth year of Kohyo (1061) I dreamt I was crossing over a great river by a stone bridge. Before I was across, the bridge broke; but some one else got across by stepping along my bed, and eventually got me across in the same way. Even in my dream I felt sure that the bridge was the Stone Bridge at T'ien-t'ai in China, about which it is said that only one who has attained to the Highest Enlightenment can get safely across.

'Now, long afterwards, I was delighted that my dream had come true and that I had succeeded in crossing the bridge. I examined its construction carefully, and it corresponded in every way to the bridge in my dream.'

The passage is interesting because it shows that Jojin (and probably other people too) carried about with him on his travels a record of dreams covering a period of many years.

Dreams can be bought and sold, or stolen. The Japanese Regent Masatoki, who lived in the twelfth century, had two daughters, who were step-sisters. The younger dreamt that the sun and moon fell into her lap. 'I must go and ask Masako what this means,' she thought. Masako was the name of the elder sister, who was learned in history, mythology and dream-interpretation. 'This would be a strange enough dream for a man to have,' thought the elder sister, 'and it is stranger still that it should come to a woman.' For she knew such a dream meant that the person concerned would become ruler of the land. Being herself of a masterful and ambitious character she determined to get hold of the dream and said deceitfully to the younger sister, 'This is a terribly unlucky dream. You had better get rid of it as quickly as possible.' 'How can one get rid of a dream?' asked the younger sister. 'Sell it!' said Masako. 'But who is there that would buy a bad dream?' 'I will buy it from you,' said Masako.

'But, dear sister, how could I bear to escape from misfortune, only to see it descend upon you?'

'That does not happen,' said Masako. 'A dream that is bought brings neither fortune nor misfortune.' The price paid was an ancient Chinese mirror. The young sister went back to her room saying, 'It has happened at last. The mirror that I have always wanted is mine.' Only long afterwards when Masako became the virtual ruler of Japan (1220–5) did the young sister realize what she had lost by selling her dream.

It is dangerous to tell one's dream except to an accredited interpreter. Anyone who hears a dream and has a good enough memory to repeat it word for word can rob the dreamer of its benefits. Mabi, the son of a provincial clerk in Japan, at the end of the seventh century, had a strange dream and went to have it interpreted by a woman dream interpreter. Before he had time to tell it the sons of the Governor arrived with a great troupe of attendants. Mabi was hustled away to a back room and asked to wait till the distinguished client had been attended to. Just to pass the time he put his ear to the key-hole and listened. 'I am afraid your dream won't come up to that young man's,' said the interpreter. 'You did not happen to hear any of it?' Mabi then repeated the dream word for word. 'Listen!' said the woman, who had taken a fancy to Mabi. 'As you have repeated the dream without my mistake, it is yours, if you care to have it. It means that you will be a great scholar and will rise to be a Minister of State.' Sure enough Mabi was chosen, from among all the youths of the kingdom, to go and study in China. He remained there for eighteen years and when he came back was made Minister of the Right. He is the great Kibi no Mabi whose name every Japanese schoolchild knows.

Psycho-analytical patients today sometimes claim to have hoaxed their doctor by telling him fictitious dreams. The doctor, not at all put out, explains that bogus dreams are for him quite as interesting as real ones. What the doctor probably does not know is that this view can be traced back to the third century AD, in China. At that time a famous interpreter of dreams called Chou Hsüan was more than once given bogus dreams by people who fondly imagined that they were scoring off him. Seeing that the prediction he based on such dreams always came true a client asked him if it really made any difference whether a dream was real or concocted, 'None at all,' he answered. 'For real dreams and false are both alike products of the soul.'

(*Listener*, May 1955.)

# THE POETRY OF CHINESE MIRRORS

Mirrors, made of polished metal, not of glass, have played an immense part in Chinese literature and popular belief. Here are some poems, stories and inscriptions in which those beliefs are referred to. I will begin with a poem by Po Chü-i, who lived in the ninth century:

My fair one when she parted from me
Left with me her mirror, lying in its box,
Which, now that her face is seen in it no more,
Is an autumn lake where no lotus grows.
After more than a year, today I opened the box;
A pink dust lay on the green bronze.
And now when I flick it and rub the dust away
All that I see is my own withered face.
I turn it over and am sadder than before;
On the back are carved two twining dragons.

The lady who gave Po Chü-i this mirror was probably a concubine whom he was obliged by the rites of mourning to dismiss when his mother died in AD 811.

On the back of a mirror dating from about the first century AD is the inscription:

You have your journey; I, my sadness:
The day of your going is fixed, but not the time of your return.
Please be sure to have good meals:
Take great pains about this.
I look up to Heaven and sighing deeply I say:
'Oh may he think tenderly of me forever.'

Sometimes a wife would send a mirror to an absent husband. There is an old song that says:

I meant by this messenger to send to you my news;
But all is blank – I cannot command my thoughts.
So I send instead this mirror bright as the moon,
Which truly reflects the image of my heart.

There was a belief that if a wife carried into the street at night the mirror that she had worn to protect her against evil influences at the time of her marriage, stray words of passers-by in the dark street would give her news of her husband. But on her way out she must worship the Stove-god in the kitchen, and no one must see her leave the house. The Stove-god is lord of human destinies.

'Sighing softly,' says a poem of the ninth century, she goes down the steps from the hall:

All alone in front of the stove she kneels and makes her bow;
Then goes into the street hoping she will hear no sound of
    sadness or weeping.
'If only he is alive what does it matter if he comes back now
    or later?'
Along the bright moonlit street no one any longer passes.
She has heard good words, again and again
Voices spoke of 'Coming'.

She rolls up the curtain and climbs into bed but is too
 excited to sleep.
She cuts out a dress to give him when he comes, but cuts it
 all awry.
'Will he be in time for us to pass together the three days'
 holiday?'
With its double-stitch brocade bag she wipes the face of the
 mirror.

The favourite, though not the only time for mirror-
divination was the last day of the year. The first three days of the
year were kept as a holiday, all shops and offices being closed,
and the mention of the three days' holiday here shows that this
was a New Year divination. In later times the holiday was
extended to five days.

In another poem of the same date a lady says to her mirror:

Slip of bronze, slip of bronze, if you have any magic
Let me see in you the image of my man that is a thousand
 miles away.

There is a story dating from early in the seventh century,
called *The Old Mirror*, which is in effect a catalogue of the
magic powers attributed to mirrors by the Chinese. This
mirror, since it reflected only reality, could show in their true
form evil spirits that had assumed human shape. It had a
special affinity with the sun and moon and always grew dim
during eclipses. It could rob a magic sword, that shone in the
darkness, of its magic; arrogate to itself all the sword's
brightness, and fill a whole room with light. If smeared with
'metal grease', rubbed with powdered pearl and exposed to the
sun, it could reflect things on the other side of a thick wall. If
rubbed 'with a certain herb very hard to get' it could be used

by doctors to see what was going on inside their patients. It could still storms and arrest the onward rush of a tidal wave.

What was meant by 'metal grease'? We do not know; but it is certain that the invention of metal mirrors consisted largely in the discovery of how to polish bronze; as also, of course, in the discovery that mirrors needed a high proportion of tin in the bronze. The Chinese were technically able to cast pieces of metal with a flat surface at least as early as the fourteenth century BC. But the earliest metal mirrors seem to date from some 900 years later. It was at that time presumably, in about the fifth century BC or somewhat earlier, that a suitable polishing agent was discovered. In early times it was called 'the mysterious tin'; it was a powder, and is usually taken to be oxide of mercury. The mediaeval Japanese used a substance with many ingredients – quicksilver, grindstone powder, burnt alum and a decoction of smoked unripe plums. To the boy who went round from house to house polishing people's mirrors some of the same mystery attached as to the chimney sweep in European popular belief.

The practical use of mirrors as an assistance in dressing the hair, powdering the face and so on, is occasionally mentioned in early mirror-inscriptions. But usually such inscriptions deal with the mirror's magic uses, as a talisman for ensuring numerous posterity, a successful career and peace and prosperity in the land.

All this is in great contrast with the attitude towards mirrors in classical times in the West. Greek and Etruscan mirrors are decorated with mythological themes that are usually quite unconnected with the mirror as such; and in Classical literature there are hardly any allusions to the mirror except as an adjunct to women's toilet. In this respect there is another contrast to the Chinese world, where men wore elaborate head-gears that often needed tidying and straightening. In the Story of the Old Mirror quoted above the hero, we are told, 'wanting to tidy his costume, took out his mirror and found to his surprise that its face had suddenly grown dull'. It was, I think, the requirements of men's toilet rather than those of women's that led to the use in China of polished metal mirrors. The earliest form of mirror in China was, it is generally agreed, a bowl of water, and a woman could very well powder her face with the aid of a bowl of water set upon a high stand. But a man needed a very small flat saucer of water that he could hold with one hand while he straightened his head-dress with the other. If he had stooped over a bowl, as ladies did, his head-dress would have gone askew again when he raised his head. These small flat metal saucers I imagine to have been the predecessors on the one hand of burning-mirrors, used with tinder to obtain fire, and on the other of small portable toilet-mirrors. A writer of the third century AD tells us that in his day the nomads to the west of China still used 'belt-pouch' mirrors (*P'an Ching*) and I imagine these to have been a survival of the kind of small water-mirror that was transitional between the large bowl-mirror and the polished metal mirror.

It is well known that mirrors are part of the equipment of shamans (intermediaries between man and the gods) in Mongolia and Siberia, and these mirrors are generally imported from China. Indeed, Chinese mirrors of the first century BC have been found in tombs as far away as Western Siberia. Probably some of the early Chinese mirrors in our collections were used by Chinese shamans. We possess some early Chinese shaman songs in which the shaman is thought of as having a kind of love-affair with the deity on the day of the festival, only to be left love-lorn when the ritual is over. It is with this situation that a famous inscription, repeated (often in mutilated forms) on a score of extant mirrors, must surely deal.

The shaman (according to my interpretation) says of the mirror (and addressing the deity):

Into it I put pure substances to reflect your brightness;
Their light was like the radiance of sun and moon,
That your heart might scorn dalliance and be forever true.
But it was not possible to keep them from flowing away.
I purified my soul to serve you;
But alas, idle pleasures have dimmed your light.
And as the mirror-polish spills its sheen
So you become estranged and day by day forget me.
I brood on the thought of my loved one in his perfect grace
Elsewhere receiving pleasures that make him gay.
I yearn for the god-like shadow of my fair one;
Would that he might love me forever without break!

Here we get the equation of the mirror with the sun and moon (often invoked as witnesses of love-vows) and with the heart (as in the story that I shall presently quote) and the dwindling of love compared to the oozing away of the quicksilver-sheen on the polished face of the mirror.

I have purposely left out, in this short survey of mirror-poetry and mirror-lore, one or two stories that have been quoted again and again in European studies of Chinese mirrors; as also all discussion of mirror beliefs in Japan, where most of the Chinese beliefs crop up again, alongside of a much more solemn cult of the mirror as the symbol of the Sun-goddess. I have left out too the symbolism of the mirror in Buddhist sayings and rites. But I must not leave out the strangest of all mirror-stories:

A pedlar once offered to Wang Tsung-shou, a high tenth-century official who was also a student of Taoist mysteries, an iron mirror, assuring him that it had great magic powers. It had a dull rusty surface in which nothing could be seen at all, and he was not much inclined to buy it. But the price was very low, and he eventually bought the mirror and began trying to polish it. He scrubbed and scrubbed, but still it remained sooty and lustreless. He put it away in a box and for a long while thought no more about it. Suddenly one day a light gleamed from the box. He opened it, and looking in the mirror saw the image of a boy, dressed in blue, sitting alone in the market-hall. Wang sent his servant to the market, and in a little while the man came back bringing with him the boy whose image had appeared in the mirror.

'That mirror is mine,' the boy said. 'I lost it long ago. You might as well hand it over to me; for if you do not, in any case it will fly away and cease to be yours.'

So saying, he took the mirror, slit open his body with a knife, put the mirror into his breast, and ran away.

'There are poems,' says a Chinese critic, 'that cannot be understood, yet are understood. The meaning is as intangible as a flower seen in a mirror or the moon reflected in the sea.' The story of Wang's mirror is like such poems. One feels its meaning, but to dissect the story would be to spoil it. This much one can say, that the mirror is not only a symbol of love, as we have seen already, but also a kind of magic heart.

(*Listener*, October 1954.)

# CHINESE STORIES ABOUT ACTORS

*S*everal speakers on this programme have mentioned the fondness of the Chinese for stories about ghostly hauntings and 'possessions'. They were in the old days, particularly in the eighteenth century, fond of stories about actors, and many of these stories turn upon the connection between actors and the world of the dead. For example, the door by which actors had access to the stage was called the Ghost Gate, and people explained this by saying that actors recreated in their plays the lives of those who lived long ago and were themselves, in a sense, ghosts or *revenants*.

Favourite among the heroes who lived again on the stage was Kuan Yü, worshipped as the. God of War. There was however also a cult of Yen Liang, the God of War's great enemy, whom he slew in single combat. At Lü-ch'eng in the province of Kiangsu there was a shrine in memory of the defeated hero. At this shrine a certain prefect of the district was rash enough to stage a play showing the slaying of Yen Liang by Kuan Yü, the God of War. The defeated hero, powerless in life to ward off the god's blows, was still in death a spirit strong enough to punish this re-enactment of his defeat. No sooner had the play begun than a great wind rose that carried the railings of the stage into the air and then let them fall with a crash on the stage, killing the actors who were playing the parts of Yen Liang's enemies.

Sometimes the names of the characters in plays had to be changed in order to avoid giving offence to the ancestors of the patron who was paying for the performance; and that no doubt is why many plays exist that are identical except for the names of the characters. There was no theatrical copyright, and what with name-changing and the insertion of new songs, dances, and turns of all kinds, a play as it travelled from province to province soon became almost unrecognizable. The author of *The Palace of Eternal Youth*, the famous play of which an excellent English translation has recently been published, complained that when this play reached south-east China it already bore hardly any relation to what he had written. A scene of mourning had been turned into one of rejoicing, and all kinds of gag and knockabout inserted. One alteration of which he complains strikes a familiar note. The southern actors had, to the author's horror, introduced an irrelevant 'lantern-dance'. One is reminded at once of certain stage vulgarities passed off as esoterically Oriental by European producers today.

Actors sometimes haunted the scene of their former triumphs long after those triumphs were over. There is a story of an actress in a female troupe, in which the male parts as well as the female ones were played by women, who, ousted by younger actresses from the girl-parts in which she had become famous, hanged herself in despair. But for long afterwards she used to be seen sitting among the audience, her eyes riveted upon the stage. 'She was there so often,' the story says, 'that people stopped taking any notice of her.'

In 1738, owing to a long drought, the waters of the Grand Canal became very low, and a transport boat, bringing grain to Peking, was stuck. The transport officer, hoping to get the local deities into a better humour, in which case they might send rain, hired a company of actors to give a play. The play chosen was one of what are called the four great plays of the Ming dynasty – *The Thorn Hairpin*. In this play the heroine, tricked into believing that her husband has disowned her, throws herself into the river. True, no great harm comes of this. She is fished out again, and after many vicissitudes she and her husband are reunited. In the scene where the heroine, Jade Ring, plunges into the river the boy actor impersonating her suddenly burst into floods of weeping and began making strange inarticulate sounds that seemed here and there like Fukhien dialect, but were quite unintelligible.

That the actor was possessed by some disembodied spirit was evident. The ghost was asked to name itself; but apparently it could not understand living speech. As a last resort paper and a writing-brush were given to it; but the 'possessed' boy shook his head, seeming to indicate, on the ghost's behalf, that it was illiterate. All he did was to point now at heaven and now at earth, as though calling upon them to right some great injury. The spectators could think of nothing for it but to carry the boy ashore. Here, however, he continued to fling himself about and groan hideously.

But when the people who had been standing round began to tire of staring and drifted away, the boy gradually came to. He finally regained his power of speech, and was able to tell those who had remained with him that while acting the river scene he had suddenly seen a girl advancing towards him. She was headless and carried her head in her hands. Horrified, he lost consciousness, and could remember nothing more. It was evident now that he had been 'possessed' in the middle of the play by the ghost of some girl who had been murdered and thrown into the stream. The subject of the play that had been staged drew her to the spot and, seeing officials in the audience, she had hoped to be able to tell them her story, get them to punish the murderer, and so avenge her death. But she had found, no doubt to her despair, that she could frame no living words in which to vent her wrong.

Divers were sent into the canal to see if they could discover a corpse, but none was found; nor could the local police discover that any girl bad been recently reported as missing. There was only one thing to do: the officials drew up a joint document giving a full account of what had happened and burned it on the altar of the municipal god. Four or five days later a member of the crew of the transport ship suddenly fell down dead. It then became obvious that it was he who had committed the murder, and the municipal god, having had his attention officially called to the matter, had after a few days' investigation duly punished the murderer.

In early days the principal part was that of the dignified hero or heroine. But in the seventeenth and eighteenth centuries the comic villain became more and more prominent, and was sometimes the main actor of the troupe. About 1700 one of the principal troupes at Soochow, having been summoned to give a play at the residence of a high official, found to their consternation that they had no one to take the part of the Wicked General who was the main character in the play they had been ordered to perform. The actor who usually played such roles had suddenly fallen ill. In such cases it was, by long tradition, the costume-manager's duty to find a substitute. The costume-manager accordingly went round to all the other troupes in Soochow, trying to borrow a 'villain', but none of them could spare one.

At last, a friend mentioned to him that a man who took 'villain' roles in rustic performances at a village near Soochow happened at the moment to be in town. The friend went off and returned with a very frail, undersized, depressed-looking, and tattered individual. When addressed, he spoke in so low a voice that he could hardly be heard. The 'villain', of course, is usually a large, immensely robust character, who bursts on to the stage thundering out his wicked intentions in a stentorian voice, leaping into the air and brandishing a gigantic wooden sword. But the costume-manager was completely worn out with rushing all over the huge city of Soochow seeking in vain for a 'villain'. Intensely relieved at being able to return not wholly empty-handed he hurried the queer little man to the theatre, hardly glancing at him lest he should prove to be too impossible.

'I've had an awful job finding anyone,' he said to the other members of the cast. 'I hope Mr Ch'en here will do.' The other actors, staring in amazement at the depressed little figure carrying an immense cloth bag, thought that the costume-manager was playing a joke upon them and began to curse him roundly. But it was too late to look for anyone else, and at last someone asked the ragged little man who was sitting gloomily alongside of his bag: 'Just tell us the truth. Have you ever in your life played the part of a villain?' 'That is the part I always play at home,' he murmured, just audibly. They decided that there was nothing to do but to let him try, and went into the green-room to have their meal. Usually a guest-actor was given the place of honour; but no one even made room for little Mr Ch'en, and when at last someone asked if he did not want something to eat, he did not reply. 'Well, I suppose we had better be getting into our costumes,' the head of the troupe said presently.

Suddenly assuming an active and business-like air, Mr Ch'en opened his bag, took out roll after roll of wool, and began stuffing it under his shirt, till he appeared to be of enormous girth. He then pulled out of the bag a pair of shoes with soles several inches thick. He stood up in them, and had the air of a veritable giant. Then, producing a hand-mirror and a painting-brush, he began making-up. When he turned round, his rat-like, timid little face had become a countenance of vast proportions and terrifying truculence. His entry when the play began was breathtaking. He leapt on to the stage flourishing his sword and bounding like an enraged tiger. The first words of his opening song came in such a thunderous crash of sound that the drums and gongs of the orchestra were inaudible. The rafters shook, raining dust upon the astonished spectators. Never had such a performance been seen.

In the green-room, after the first act of the play, the rest of the cast crowded round the villain, thanking him for having come so brilliantly to their rescue. Suddenly, however, Ch'en dashed towards a basin of water and began washing off his make-up. When he turned round, his portly, padded frame was surmounted by the small, timorous visage that they had seen at the start. 'I think I had better stop now,' he said. 'I'm not very good at the next act.' The actors implored him to forgive them for their uncivil treatment of him at supper. He took no notice, and began pulling yards and yards of padding from under his shirt. Only when they promised him a permanent place in the troupe did he begin laboriously re-padding himself and restoring his make-up. He finished the play with an even more boisterous energy than before. Next day the head of the troupe secured Ch'en's release from the village troupe, dismissed his usual 'villain', and installed Ch'en in his place. A few years later a performance by Ch'en was seen by the Emperor at Soochow; he was summoned to join one of the court troupes at Peking and for twenty years was the king of clowns in north China. He died at Soochow soon after 1750.

One cannot leave the actors of the eighteenth century without saying something about the most famous of them all – Wei Ch'ang-sheng. He was an actor of female roles who, having spent the first thirty years of his life far away in south-west China, came to Peking in 1779. Here he created a sensation by appearing on the stage dressed completely as a woman, with a feminine 'hair-do' and a woman's cramped and tilted shoes. Before this, actors playing female roles had merely thrown a scarf over their heads to conceal their male coiffure. He also played love-scenes with a detailed realism that fascinated his audiences but got him into trouble with the authorities. In the autumn of 1782 he was barred from appearing on the Peking stage. After wandering about in various parts of China he attempted long afterwards, in 1801, to make a come-back in Peking. He was now about fifty, venerable in appearance, and leading a nine-year-old grandson by the hand. His Rip Van Winkle reappearance caused a certain sensation, but his acting, now thoroughly respectable, was not a great success. He died suddenly a few months after his return.

We are told that when he was at the height of his fame he received a thousand ounces of silver (about £350) for appearing in a single scene at a theatre in Yangchow. When a rumour spread that he had gone out boating on the lake, hundreds of singing girls set out in pursuit of him, 'lashing the waves with their painted oars'. But he remained austerely unmoved. Indeed, like many Chinese actors of female roles he was in private life a perfectly normal family man, famous for his acts of generosity and loyalty.

I want to say something about the authors or collectors of these stories. The story about the transport ship that got stuck is from a book by the eighteenth-century bibliographer Chi Yün. It is sometimes evident in his works that he is using ghost-stories as a medium for disguised attacks upon the Confucian orthodoxy of his day. He was a subtle and complicated character. Particularly in the passage about the officials drawing up a report and burning it on the altar of the god in order to enlist his help in meting out justice, he may well have been gently laughing at popular beliefs about divine retribution. The story about the peasant-actor who became China's greatest clown is told by Chiao Hsün, a great

Confucian commentator, who died in 1820. He tells us that he made his collection of stories about the stage at a time when he was ill and not feeling strong enough to do serious work. But even on his sick-bed his habit of text-criticism and collation did not desert him. He conscientiously notes, for example, that the story about the clown exists in various forms, and he gives an alternative version.

Some of my Chinese friends feel that I pay too much attention to strange stories of the past and ought to be giving more attention to the spread of industrialism in China or some other current and concrete activity. I can only say in reply that I find in these stories touches of beauty and (in a profound sense) of truth, which draw me to them. There is nowhere else anything quite like them, whereas the monuments of industrialization are the same from Archangel to Tierra del Fuego.

(*Listener*, February 1957.)

# THE GREEN BOWER COLLECTION

*T*he 'Green Bower Collection' (*Ch'ing Lou Chi*) is a series of notes upon the careers of about a hundred singing-girls, of whom about half performed in *Tsa Chü*, which I shall henceforward refer to as 'regular drama'. This form of play seems to have come into existence in about 1260, at Peking. It has sometimes been called opera; but as prose dialogue generally occupies two-thirds of a play, the term is hardly appropriate. In regular drama almost invariably only one character, either the hero or the heroine, sang. The other characters spoke in prose or recited rhymed verse. There were four acts, all the songs of an act being in one key. There was also an additional quasi-act, the 'wedge', containing one or two short songs. Usually it came at the beginning of the play. Thus these Yüan dynasty regular plays were essentially star performances. The audience went in order to hear one actress (or actor) perform the extraordinary feat of singing forty to fifty arias, with only short intervals for rest while the prose dialogue proceeded. Several of the actresses in the *Green Bower* are said to have played male as well as female roles. The nucleus of acting, troupes at this period were a family unit consisting of father, mother, sons and daughters (real or adopted), sometimes a son-in-law or daughter-in-law and an occasional outsider who was likely to become a son-in-law or adopted son if he showed promise. Just as girls sometimes played male parts, boys presumably played female parts; but the only mention of this that I know is the case of Sun Tzŭ-kuei (*c.* 1260) a chief male-role actor who is said to have taken 'counterfeit woman-parts (*chuang-tan*)', probably meaning burlesque roles such as that of the old procuress who figures in so many plays and stories. The modern outcry (chiefly on the part of Westerners) against 'mixed' troupes on the Chinese stage on the ground that they are wholly untraditional is therefore in a sense ill-founded. In the thirteenth and fourteenth centuries the troupes were certainly often mixed. But it is true that from the seventeenth century (?) till modern times troupes have usually consisted exclusively of men or exclusively of women.

The performers not specifically mentioned as excelling in regular drama were experts in little-songs (*hsiao-ling*), that is to say short, detached arias, or again in *t'ao-shu*, song-suites in one key. One or two still sang *ch'u-kung-t'iao*, narrative ballads consisting of a number of song-suites in various keys, interspersed with passages of narrative prose, with string accompaniment. But this form was already dying out in the fourteenth century A few were performers in *Yüan Pên* ('Texts of the Courtyard'). This was the name given in the north to the standard type of play that existed before the rise of the regular drama. The earliest surviving specimen (*c.* 1420) and other, Ming dynasty, examples are short knock-about farces. The *Yüan Pên*, as may be seen from their titles, many of which survive, were of several different kinds, varying from mere variety turns to dramatizations of complicated stories. But it would seem that, after the rise of the regular drama, serious *Yüan Pên* dropped out and only the knock-about ones survived. If that is so, we must think of the ladies in the *Green Bower* who excelled in *Yüan Pên* as performers in knock-about farce. Several kinds of feminine role are distinguished. *Kuei-yüan* ('Boudoir Repinings') means upper-class ladies mourning the absence of their lover. The typical example would be the part of Ts'ui Ying-ying, parted from Mr Chang, in the *Hsi Hsiang Chi* (Mr Hsiung's *The Western Pavilion*). *Chia-t'ou* (Imperial Equipage) parts would presumably be roles such as that of Wang Chao-chün, the unhappy lady sent to be the bride of a barbarous Hun ruler in the first century BC. The best-known play on the subject was translated by Sir John Davis (*The Sorrows of Han*, 1829). Then there were *Hua-tan* ('Flowered Lady') parts. A note at the end of the book, obviously inserted in a blank space by a later hand, defines *Hua-tan* as meaning roles in which the actress's face was 'broken up with ink-blobs'. This does not, I think, refer to comic make-up, as has sometimes been suggested, but to ink-blobs like Chinese punctuation marks put on the face in imitation of tear-stains. That 'Green Forest' plays were about the Greenwood Tree and dealt with stories of Robin Hood type about sympathetic outlaws, seems an East-West correspondence too perfect to be true. Yet such was indeed the case. The subjects were taken from the cycle of outlaw-stories that ultimately became the novel *Shui Hu Chuan* (Pearl Buck's '*All Men are Brothers*').

Other accomplishments of those performers were dancing, playing the *p'i-p'a* and the *Yüan Hsien* (a smaller kind of lute), inventing riddles, playing backgammon and other games of chance, and exchanging witty repartees. Finally one actress (Fol. 11b) was good at reciting 'what are currently known as *hsiao-shuo* ("small stories")', which she did with a fluency 'like a ball rolling downhill or water pouring off the tiles.' These were presumably colloquial stories of the kind (to quote the most familiar example) now embodied in the *Chin Ku Ch'i Kuan* collection, almost all of which have been translated into European languages.

Most of the actresses worked at the capital, Peking; others in provinces ranging from Shantung to Kwangtung. The regular drama had evidently spread pretty well over China. The author is, however, only talking about the parts that he had knowledge of, and the fact that he does not mention Kansu, Szechwan or Yünnan does not necessarily mean that regular drama did not exist in these remoter provinces.

Often it is stated that the ladies were married to actors or musicians, whose names are given. In other cases where the husband's occupation is not specified the formation of his name makes it clear that he was an actor. During part at any rate of the period covered by this book (c. 1270–1364) it was illegal for actors and actresses to marry outside their own caste. A law of 1278 seems only to have applied to actors belonging to the Imperial Music Academy, and its object was to prevent trained performers from being carried off by officials, either as wives or concubines, to provincial posts. But in 1311 there was an Imperial Edict of a much more drastic kind: 'Henceforward *yüeh-jên* (public entertainers) are only to marry *yüeh-jên*. If any of those in close attendance upon me, or any official, or any one else takes a *yüen-jên* as his wife, it will be accounted a crime.' The penalty was apparently death, that at any rate was the fate of the Mongol Hsin Ha-erh-ti, in connection with whose offence the Edict was proclaimed. Unlike the Edict of 1278, the object of which, as we have seen, was to prevent performers trained for official festivities from drifting away into private hands, the Edict of 1311 aimed at maintaining the purity of upper-class legitimate blood, and nothing was said about concubines, whose children did not count as legitimate heirs. A large proportion of the ladies in the *Green Bower* who did not marry actors did in fact become the concubines of well-to-do theatre-patrons, thus achieving a relatively humble but perfectly respectable and recognized social position. Bringing with them their songs, dances and stories they formed a link between upper-class and popular culture, as indeed concubines had done since early times. A few of them were what we might call courtesans, 'selling their charms to serve men'. I think that is the meaning of the term *chio chi* (written, 'horn actress'). This, like most terms connected with the stage, is a colloquial expression written phonetically, and its origin is impossible to trace. The same is true, for example, of *mo-ni*, the name given to the role of the leading male actor. It ought to mean either 'jewel' or Mani, the founder of Manicheism; but it is not likely that either meaning supplies the real etymology. Similarly the clown-villain was called *Ching*, 'clean', 'pure', for which no convincing explanation has been given.

The girls seem to have been mostly illiterate; the fact that two or three of them had a certain amount of literary education is mentioned as though it were exceptional. They were not all good-looking. Several of those with wonderful voices were hunchbacked; others, blind in one eye, and so on. Their patrons, in the rough manner of the time, chaffed them ruthlessly about their physical defects and diseases. These patrons ranged from Chief Ministers Generals and high local officials who were mostly Mongols or Uighur Turks down to fairly well-to-do lovers of song, who held small posts or lived as private persons. All of them were deeply imbued with the new, vernacular culture which looked for a time like supplanting the old upper-class classical culture, so intimately bound up with the antiquated Civil Service examinations, which were abolished soon after the Mongols came into power, and were never revived. Appointment by examination was indeed restored in 1313, but the new examinations were based on the modern, straightforward explanations of Chu Hsi (died 1200) and bore little relation to the old system, founded on a complicated catena of ancient commentaries and sub-commentaries, that had been in force since the seventh century. The new examinations were in fact part of the new, popular culture that came into existence under the Mongols. There were, of course, scholars who still used the old literary forms, just as there are scholars who still write in classical Chinese today. But all the literary vitality of the time went into writing colloquial songs, song-suites, plays and stories.

One might expect in a book of this kind to find playwrights figuring largely. Actually, of the numerous literary men who are mentioned only three, I think (Po Jên-fu, Ch'iao Chi and Chung Ssu-ch'êng) are known to have written plays, and these three were all writers of songs or other works as well as being playwrights. Indeed, of the eighty or so Mongol dynasty playwrights only the few who also wrote songs or had some other claim to distinction seem to have been regarded with any interest by their contemporaries. Almost all the playwrights were humble literary craftsmen, as little known to the outside world as were craftsmen in general. I wonder, indeed, if their main task did not usually consist in reshaping existing old-style plays, ballads and puppet-texts, so as to make them conform with the exacting rules of the new regular drama. This may seem to be taking a poor view of the plays as dramatic literature. But it is the lyrics not the prose-dialogue that have always been regarded as the essential element in the plays, and even if we accept that the lyrics may often have been taken over from earlier works, this does not detract from their value.

Of Hsia Po-ho, the author of the *Green Bower Collection*, we know very little. He came of a family that had been prominent in Sungkiang (south-east of Soochow) for 200 years. He inherited a great fortune, but in his youth a fortune-teller warned him that twelve years hence there would be great upheavals in the south-east, in the course of which the rich would lose all their possessions. The sensible thing for him to do would be to spend on a scale that would leave him penniless when the trouble came. Acting on this advice he began to entertain lavishly, summoning to his parties all the best singers and musicians of the day and showering largesses on every one in the neighbourhood whom he saw to be in need. Exiled statesmen, poor scholars, peasants in difficulty all drew on his bounty. In 1356 rebels against the Mongol dynasty captured Sungkiang and every great house was looted, either by the rebels or by the Mongol troops sent to oppose them. Hsia Po-ho's calculated extravagance had left him with practically no possessions except 'several hundred volumes', all that remained of a once vast library. With these he and his family fled to a secluded village, where he spent his time jotting down notes about the singers whom he had known or heard about, teaching his children and roaming about the countryside. How this idyllic life was financed we are not told. He survived the overthrow of the Mongol dynasty (1368), but by how long we also do not know. He must have been born somewhere about 1320. The preface usually printed at the beginning of the book is dated 1364. Here are some extracts from the book; the information in brackets is added by me.

*Fol. 1a. Harmonious Cloud, with surname Chang, was good at both kinds of poem* [Shih and Tz'u] *and was witty in conversation. In her art she was supreme among her contemporaries, and had a great reputation in the Capital* [Peking]. *Chao Mêng-fu, Shang Tao and Kao K'o-kung all painted portraits of her and presented them; and so many famous people inscribed poems on them that there was hardly any room left. Yao Sui and Yen Fu constantly had small drinking parties at her house. One day when passing Bell Tower Street they met the Chief Minister Shih T'ien-tsê coming towards them. He dismounted and said with a smile 'I wonder if you two gentlemen would allow me to accompany you on your errand?' 'Excellency, get into your saddle,' said Yao Sui. Upon which the Chief Minister sent his servants back to his house to fetch wine and provisions as quickly as possible and rode with the other two to Harmonious Cloud's house, which looked over the lake. 'Look!' they cried, on arriving. 'We have brought you a wonderful guest. This is his lordship the Chief Minister. We two will help you to entertain him.' Harmonious Cloud first drank to the Minister's health and then sang one strophe of the song 'A grandee of Sung-kiang whose noble presence pervades the autumn', to the tune 'The Water Key Song', much to the delight of the Minister. After a time the wine and provisions for which he had sent arrived. He took two ingots of silver [representing something like £15?] and laid them on the singer's mat as a reward. When, later on, his servants were about to pack up the empty vessels which were all of gold or jade, the Minister said, 'Don't let us take those things away. They may come in handy next time these two gentlemen come here.' Such was the great Minister's appreciation of good music!*

Chao Mêng-fu (1254–1322), the great painter and calligrapher, who first came to the Capital in 1286, probably needs no introduction to readers of this journal, nor does the landscape painter Kao K'o-kung. The other three persons are likely to be less familiar. Shang Tao (*c.* 1200–72?) was a younger brother of Shang Hêng (1185–1231), a high official under the Chin Tartars and an uncle of Shang T'ing, a successful early Mongol dynasty official. He was famous as a song-writer and particularly for his 'Various Keys' ballad about the love of the poor student Shuang Chien for Su Hsiao-ch'ing, whose too prudent mother insisted upon marrying her to a rich tea-merchant. This was one of the most popular love-stories of the thirteenth and fourteenth centuries, being much more frequently alluded to even than the Western Pavilion (*Hsi Hsiang Chi*) story. Yao Sui (1239–1314) was the most admired prose-writer of his time; he also wrote many songs. Yen Fu (1236–1312) held high posts in the Han-lin Academy. He first came to Peking in 1271. Finally Shih T'ien-tsê (1202–75) was one of the few Chinese who held the post of Chief Minister under the Mongols, playing a role of immense importance as a mediator between the Chinese and their conquerors. His visit to Harmonious Cloud seems to have occurred *c.* 1272, when he was living in semi-retreat at Peking.

*Fol. 2b. Ts'ao Ê-hsiu was a famous singer of the Capital. She was extremely intelligent and, both in looks and in her art, unrivalled in her day. On one occasion Hsien-yü Shu, whose familiar name was Po-chi, gave a small party at which the guests were all gentlemen of high standing. Having occasion to go for a while into the inner room he asked Ts'ao to circulate the wine. When he came back, the wine had been the round. 'Po-chi, you have not had your drink,' the guests cried; and Ts'ao also exclaimed, 'Po-chi, you have not had your drink!' The guests were much amused and one of them said, 'So you too call him Po-chi! I had no idea you were on such intimate terms.' Hsien-yü, pretending to be angry, scolded her saying, 'You little devil, how dare you be so impertinent!' 'If I may not call you Po-chi,' she rejoined, 'it is only because you would not be content to be called anything but Wang Hsi-chih.' Everyone laughed heartily.*

Hsien-yü Shu (1257–1302) was a calligrapher, painter, poet, and song-writer who was also distinguished as a connoisseur. Wang Hsi-chih was China's greatest calligrapher. In her parting shot the girl adds to her impertinence by calling her host 'you' (êrh) instead of addressing him by some complimentary title.

*Fol. 6b. Sung Sixth Sister-in-law was the daughter of Chang Tsui-êrh, the* pi-li *player to whom Yüan Hao-wên once addressed a tz'ŭ-poem. Her duets with her husband were so marvellous as to seem hardly human. In these performances she sang, while her husband, who was a pupil of her father, accompanied her on the* pi-li.

Yüan Hao-wên (1190–1257) was the greatest poet of the Chin Tartar dynasty, which ruled over North China till extinguished by the Mongols in 1234. The *pi-li* was a reed instrument probably from Kucha in Central Asia.

*Fol. 8a. Natural Elegance [T'ien-jan-hsiu] had the surname Kao, and as she was the second in the family people called her Little Miss Two. Her mother Liu once served Shih T'ien-tsê. In appearance she was singularly distinguished and refined, and had a woodland air [i.e. of one detached from ordinary life]. In talent for her art she far surpassed her fellows. She was in her time the greatest exponent of 'boudoir-repining' play [see above, p. 89]. But she was also marvellous in 'flowered' female roles and Court scenes. She first married the actor Wang Yüan-ch'iao and then, after his death, the head-clerk Chiao T'ai-su. When he died she became an actress again. This loss of one who ranked as a leading beauty in good society was deeply regretted; but she continued to conduct herself with the most scrupulous propriety. Po Jên-fu and Li Hsiung greatly admired her.*

The Chief Minister Shih T'ien-tsê we have already encountered (see above, p. 93). Po Jên-fu (1226 till after 1306) was one of the few dramatists of the period who was a member of the ruling class and about whose life anything is known. He was a protégé of Shih T'ien-tsê, but refused Shih's offers to secure him an official post. His best-known play (No. 21 of the Hundred Plays) is 'Rain on the *wu-t'ung Tree*'. It deals with the story of the T'ang Emperor Ming-huang and his infatuation for his mistress Yang Kuei-fei. He is equally famous as a writer of songs.

Li Hsiung (1274–1332) was a high official in the Hanlin Academy, chiefly known for his part in the compilation of the *Ching Shih Ta Tien*, an official work on the fiscal administration of the Mongol dynasty. He was so excited at the prospect of taking part in this work that he struggled up from a sick-bed in order to do so. He was also known as a calligrapher and song-writer.

*Fol. 8a. Kuo Yü-ti was the wife of the assistant-director of the Music Academy, T'ung Kuan-kao. She was good at green-wood [outlaw] plays. She was particularly witty in conversation, and was well known for this at the Capital.*

The assistant-director of the Music Academy (*Chiao-fang*) was at this period usually an actor. He ranked as a fairly high officer (Fifth Class) in the Board of Rites and on Court occasions took his place along with other officers of his rank. There were numerous protests against this, and about 1341 officers of the Music Academy lost their status as members of the official hierarchy.

*Fol. 8b. Wang Golden Belt's real surname was Chang. She was sixth in her family. She was unrivalled both in beauty and as an artist. A certain Mr Wang, assistant to the governor of Teng-chou [in Honan] took her as his concubine and had a child by her. Someone spoke highly of her to the Grand Preceptor Bayan [1295–1340], who wanted to enter her as a performer at the Music Academy (at Peking). But Mr Wang obtained the good offices of a certain nun who appealed to Bayan's wife to interfere, and was thus able to keep his concubine.*

Bayan became Grand Preceptor in 1334. His wife was Buyan Tegin, a great-grand-daughter of Kublai Khan.

*Fol. 9a. Wei Tao-tao used at the theatre to perform the four movements of the Partridge dance, doing it as a solo, to serve as* ta-san. *Since the beginning of the dynasty onwards she had no successor…*

'The Partridge' was a Chin Tartar dance, with flute and drum accompaniment. A *ta-san* (dismissal) was a turn done to wind up the performance, after the play itself was over.

*Fol. 9a. Fan Shih-chên was famous singing-girl of the Capital. The Counsellor Chou Chung-hung took her as his concubine. When he went back to South China she drank farewell to him outside the Ch'i-hua Gate. He said to her, 'When I am gone keep close hold on yourself and do not get yourself into trouble.' She poured some wine on to the ground and took an oath, saying, 'If I am untrue to you, I will scoop out one eye, as forfeit to my lord.' Not long afterwards a rich and powerful man came along. Her mother was overawed by his high position and tempted by his wealth. But at first the girl was obdurate. After a time, however, much against her will, she gave in.*

*When at length Chou came back to Peking she said to him, 'After you went away I did my best to remain faithful. But in the end I had to yield to the advances of a rich and powerful man. However, the vow*

*I made when we parted was no idle one.' She then pulled out a golden hairpin and stabbed her left eye till the floor was covered with blood. This act so much impressed Chou that he loved her just as before. Someone who took an interest in this episode turned it into a play called, 'Fan Shih-chen stabs her eye with a golden pin.' The play is still current.*

I have not succeeded in finding out anything about Chou Chung-hung, or about the play.

*Fol. 9b. Sai Lien-hsiu was the wife of the [actor] Ch'ien Shua-ch'iao, who was the elder brother of the [actress] Chu Lien-hsiu. In middle life she lost the sight of both her eyes, yet when she went out at the gate or came in at the door the 'thread of her step' and the 'needle of her gait' were never out by a hair's breadth. Few people with sight could do better. Her voice 'stopped the journeying clouds'. Never in old times or now was there a better singer.*

*Fol. 10b. Wang Ch'iao-êrh was renowned in the Capital for her singing, dancing and beauty. Ch'ên Po was intimate with her and she hoped to become his concubine. But her mother privately arranged that one of the girl's fellow-singers should come and warn her, saying, 'Ch'en's wife is the Grand Preceptor Temüder's daughter. She is unspeakably jealous and if you were to be brought into the house, you would certainly be cruelly treated by her.' 'I am only a humble singer,' she replied, 'whom lord Ch'en has honoured by his intimacy. If only I can be his handmaid, come what may I shall not repine.' Her mother, seeing that she could not be dissuaded, moved house with her to a remote quarter of the town, where Ch'en would not be able to find her. But after ten days the girl managed to send a message to Ch'en, saying that her mother had a plan for her future and had carried her off to such-and-such a place, where on a certain day a rich merchant was to come and woo her. 'You must make some counterplan,' she said, 'to deal with this before it is too late.'*

*On the day in question the merchant duly arrived. The girl pleaded illness and weeping bitterly refused to see him. He sat drinking till midnight and then attempted to sleep with her. She resisted tooth and nail, and succeeded in warding him off. At the fifth watch [at dawn] Ch'en arrived. The Mongol grooms [ula-ghachi] with whom he had provided himself bound the merchant and were about to carry him off to the Board of Punishments to be tried, when the merchant in great panic said to Ch'en, 'I had no idea that she was a favourite of yours. If you will let the case drop I will pay you two hundred strings of cash as a contribution towards your expenses in the ceremony of installing her as your concubine.' 'There is no need for that,' said Ch'en laughing. He then gave a handsome present to the mother, and took the girl back with him to South China. After Ch'en's death she and the main wife [the great Temüder's daughter] devoted themselves successfully to keeping the family property intact, winning general approbation.*

The Mongol grandee Temüder was Chief Minister at intervals between 1311 and his death in 1322. Ch'ên Po (born *c.* 1279, died, 1339) was an eccentric poet who squandered a vast fortune. He was an authority on ritual vessels, and was at one time Grand Invoker in the Board of Worship.

*Fol. 12b. Grace of Twined Branches [Lien Chih Hsiu], whose surname was Sun, was a much-courted singing-girl of the Capital. The hermit Feng Kao Lao [Mad old Kao?] converted her and she became a Taoist nun. She wandered from place to place, and once turned up in Sung kiang [the author's home-town], accompanied by a female acolyte called Min-t'ung, who was good at singing and dancing. If any one asked her to have a drink, as soon as she had warmed up a little she would get up and dance and sing the 'Song of the Blue Sky'. Her companion danced too and joined in the song. It was indeed fairy music. She wanted to collect subscriptions and get herself a hermitage built, outside the eastern gate at Sung kiang. Lu Yu drew up for her an appeal, full of jokes at her expense. It contained, for example, the sentence 'This is no ordinary "hook". She has gone through a powerful lot of tweeking and hammering. A hundred smeltings could not subdue her; a host of husbands were no match for her.'*

*This upset her and she made off to Soochow, where she met a doctor called Li Ju-chai. The meeting revived her old inclinations. She returned to lay life and married the doctor. How she ended I do not know.*

Lu Yu, generally known as Lu Chai-chih, was the son of a cloth-merchant. He was a calligrapher, poet and authority on ink-slabs. The whole text of his mock appeal is given by T'ao Tsung-i in Book 12 of his *Cho Kêng Lu*. T'ao was a friend of the author of the *Green Bower* and they often, as in this case, tell the same stories. The conversion of a singing-girl is the subject of No. 77 in the Hundred Plays: *The Ordination of Liu Ts'ui.*

*Fol. 13b. Fan 'Fragrant-song' was a famous beauty of Nanking. She sang and danced marvellously and was witty in her conversation. She also had a considerable knowledge of books. Even the severest moralists of the Censorate were all enthusiastic about her. High officials used to come to her cottage and spend all day chatting and laughing there. Unfortunately she had a very short life, dying at the age of 22. She was buried outside the Southern Barrier and lovers of song and dance when their spring excursions took them that way always made libations of wine on her tomb – a custom that persists to this day.*

*Fol. 14b. Chang 'Jade-Lotus'…could sing old songs, the music of which had been forgotten. She could always find out the tune simply by. studying the words. She was equally proficient at string and wind instruments, there was no game of chance at which she was not expert, she was indefatigable in jest and elegant and refined to perfection. She could compose modern song-words to order, both in the northern and southern styles. In knowledge of music there was no one to compare with her. Her house was thronged by wealthy young grandees, and well-to-do families were delighted if they could secure her services. High officials cast their money at her as though it were dirt, thinking no price too high to pay. Secretary Lin [Lin Ch'üan-shêng, secretary to the administration of the sea port Ch'üan-*

chou; born 1299, died 1361, poet and Confucian scholar] *had her for a time as his concubine; but afterwards she returned to her profession... She had several daughters, among them Ch'ien-êrh and Fên-êrh, all artists of great distinction. But later they quitted the profession and scattered about in various directions. Jade-Lotus herself I saw in recent years at K'un-shan [between Soochow and Shanghai]. She was over sixty, but her hair was still black and her complexion fresh, nor was she any less dashing and witty than in her youth.*

*Fol. 16a. Lung-lou-ching ['Dragon Tower View'] and Tan-ch'ih-hsiu ['Cinnaber Courtyard Elegance'] were both daughters of [the actor?] Chin-mên Kao. They were very handsome. Both specialized in Southern Plays. Lung's voice was such as to wake echoes in the dust of the rafters. Tan's notes were rounded like the black dragon's pearl. Later on there was Fu-jung-hsiu ['Lotus-flower Elegance'] at Wu-chou [modern Kinhwa, in Chehkiang]. In the short songs of [southern] plays she was quite the equal of the other two. She also distinguished herself greatly in regular drama [northern style].*

This entry, not very thrilling for the general reader, is particularly interesting to the historian of Chinese drama. Southern Plays seemed to have belonged particularly to the triangle formed by Hangchow, Kinhwa and Wênchou, all in Chehkiang province, where they had a history that perhaps goes back to the twelfth century. They differed from the (northern) regular drama in that they consisted of a large number of very short acts, the songs in which (unlike those in one act of regular drama) could be in various keys. The singing was not confined to the main character, and several characters could sing in unison. They used more different musical modes than regular drama. It would be rash to generalize further about them, as only two or three pre-Ming examples survive. Overshadowed by northern drama from about 1280 to the end of the fourteenth century, they came into their own again in the fifteenth and finally drove the northern-style plays out of the field. My friend David Hawkes is working at a fourteenth-century (?) southern play, the *Yu Kuei Chi*.

*Fol. 16b. Sai 'Heavenly Scent' was the wife of [the actor] Li Fish-head. She was good at singing and dancing and had a fine presence. She had a mania for cleanliness and would never suffer the smallest speck of dust to pollute her 'jade bones and icy skin'. Ni Tsan of Wu-hsi had the same mania, and was greatly attached to her; a friendship which shows what sort of person she was.*

Ni Tsan (1301–74) needs no introduction to readers of this journal, being the greatest landscapist of the fourteenth century. He was in early life very well off, but at about the age of 40 he gave away all his possessions and spent his time paddling himself about on the lakes to the south-east of Soochow. He is also well known as a poet.

*Fol. 16b. Ts'ui-ho-hsiu had the surname Li. Her performances in regular drama were highly thought of in her day. From Yangchow she moved to Sung kiang, where Commander [Wan-hu] Shih made her his concubine. After Shih's death she swore to have no dealings with any one else. She spent all day burning incense and reciting the scriptures behind closed doors. Shih's son Commander Yün-bo and his grandson Commander Po-yü* [the office of Wan-hu was hereditary] *used to come at New Year and salute her. I saw her when she was over 70. Her eyebrows and hair were white as snow and her nails were over a foot long.*

She had perhaps vowed not to cut her nails. I cannot identify this Shih family.

*Fol. 17a. Ch'en P'o-hsi was good at playing [the lute] and singing... She was small and plain, but lively in conversation and swift in repartee. Many high officials admired her. She was one of the few girls who could sing Tartar [Mongol] songs, accompanying herself on the* p'i-p'a. *In the whole of north and south China there were only ten who could do this...*

*Fol. 17b. Wang Lien-lien was a much sought-after actress of Hu-chou [in Chehkiang]. She was handsome, and good in regular drama. Secretary Negübei fell in love with her. 'If you do not regard me as too poor and insignificant to be worthy of it,' she said to him, 'you ought to take me as your concubine.' Negübei then took her into his household with all the proper rites and she played the part of a 'wife' to perfection, nor did the arrangement meet with any criticism. After some years Negübei died, whereupon she shaved her head and became a nun. Many highly placed persons continued to visit her. To prevent them from having improper feelings towards her she arranged herself as unattractively as possible, and so ended her days.*

Negübei was a Mongol official who in 1311 was sent to Annam to announce the succession of the Emperor Ayurbarwada. He has some reputation as a poet. If we are to understand that he took this actress as his full wife, then he no doubt did so before the drastic legislation of 1311 referred to above (p. 100).

*Fol. 17b. Mi-li-ha was a Moslem girl who played leading female roles in drama. Her voice-production was clear and pure... Being nothing much to look at she specialized in plays where the leading woman was 'flowered' [made-up; see p. 90 above]. I once knew her [i.e. saw her act], and her reputation was certainly well-deserved.*

*Fol. 18a. Ku Shan-shan...came of a good family, but her father lost his free status, and she consequently lost hers along with him. She was very intelligent, and quite outstanding in her art. She first married the musician Li Hsiao-ta. After Li's death [The Mongol] Kharabukha, prefect of Hua-t'ing [in Kiangsu] made her his concubine. After some twelve years she again registered herself as a professional entertainer. She still works here in Sung-kiang and, though now old, in 'flowered' female parts she presents much the same appearance as in her youth. Younger performers who have studied under her speak highly of her as a teacher.*

*Fol. 18a. Li Ch'u-i was a famous singer of Yangchow. She specialized in short songs and was particularly good at slow-tempo [introductory] pieces. Wang Shih-hsi was very fond of her... Ch'iao Chi also addressed to her a large number of poems...*

Wang Shih-hsi (flourished *c.* 1312–30) besides holding a number of high official posts was well known as a landscape-painter, calligrapher and song-writer. Ch'iao Chi (died 1345) was one of the most famous dramatists and song-writers of the fourteenth century. His *Dream of Yangchow*, is No. 46 in the 'Hundred Plays of the Yüan Dynasty'. It tells the story of the infatuation of the ninth-century poet Tu Mu for the singer Chang Hao-hao.

Several of the songs addressed by Ch'iao Chi to Li Ch'u-i are preserved in the song-anthologies. They are not the sort of thing that survives in translation. The bare meaning of one of them is 'When she has washed off her make-up her skin shows bright as snow, with a texture like the lotus-leaf. She is reticent and meditative, restrained in all her gestures. How came she to leave the mists and rains of the River and be transplanted in this place of peach-blossom and plum? She completely outdoes the grace of the swallow and makes the oriole superfluous. She derides the falling blossoms and flying catkins as a mere damp mess. But the Hsiang river divides us, east and west. Gazing with longing I hoist my skirts; she, magnificent in mien, braves the autumn wind.' Such was the high-flown manner in which it was customary to address singers.

*Fol. 19a. Chên 'Phoenix Song' was a famous singer of Shantung, particularly good at short songs. When P'êng T'ing-chien [1312–54] was Associate Governor of I-chou [in Shantung] he was extremely strict in his behaviour. Chên however made sure that she could talk him out of his scruples and get on to good terms with him. One day when it was snowing heavily he gave a party which broke up late at night. Chên said it was too cold to go home. She then simply walked into his bedroom. He made no attempt to refuse, and after that they became very intimate.*

This must have happened in 1344. P'êng spent most of his life dealing with the numerous anti-Mongol revolts that were springing up on every side. He died in battle.

*Fol. 21b. Liu P'o-hsi was the wife of the musician Li Ssŭ. She performed in Kiangsi at the same period as Yang Ch'un-hsiu. She had some literary education and in joking, singing and dancing far surpassed her fellows. The great people of the time valued her highly. She first had an affair with C'ang Three, the son of Ch'ang the Police Commissioner at Fu-chou [in Kiangsi]. Her husband intervened, and one night she eloped with her lover. But they were discovered and she was condemned by the Court to a whipping. Humiliated by this she decided to go and live in Canton. On the way she passed through Kan-chou [southern Kiangsi]. Here at this time was Ch'üan P'u-an-sa-li (Turkish, Chöl Bunyansali?) whose style was Tzŭ–jên. He had been President of the Board of Rites, but a number of rebellions were going on, and he was chosen to go to Kan-chou as Defence Commissioner. He had shown complete incorruptibility as an official and had distinguished himself both in a literary way and in administration at the Censorate and on the Boards. But he had never divested himself of an inordinate love of flowers and wine. Every day when business was over he drank heavily with his colleagues, sang and made poems, always making it his pleasure to wear some flower tucked into his cap, or else some fruit or leaf – always something fresh every day.*

*When Liu P'o-hsi passed through Kan-chou she sent in word that she wanted to see him. He replied that he did not desire to have dealings with a woman who had been in trouble with the police. 'I am on my way to Canton,' she said to the doorkeeper, 'and I swear I will not come back here. But I have long heard of such remarkable accounts of the President's incorruptibility that my one desire is to meet him. That accomplished, I would die without repining.'*

*Ch'üan was touched by her insistence and said she might be shown in. He had a lot of guests with him, and was wearing a sprig of green plums on his cap. Wine was passed round and Ch'üan hummed the*

105

*words 'Green, so green the young fruit clusters on the bough', to the tune 'The Clear River'. He asked his guests to compose a continuation to the words; but no one responded. At last P'o-hsi, each hand demurely thrust into the opposite sleeve, came forward and said, 'May I venture to attempt it?' 'Certainly,' said Ch'üan. Whereupon she sang impromptu:*

> *Green, so green the young fruit clusters on the bough*
> *Hoping against hope that someone will be tempted to pluck it.*
> *But among them all only Ch'üan Tzŭ-jên*
> *Has a queer taste for what other palates reject.*
> *Just because you are sour, you interest him*
> *And he could not bring himself to cast you away.*

*Ch'üan was greatly impressed by this improvisation and henceforward she was a favourite, and soon became his concubine. Afterwards came the armed risings, and Ch'üan died doing his duty. Liu P'o-hsi remained true to his memory as though she had been a wife, and made a good end in his house.*

Ch'üan P'u-an-sa-li was from Turfan in Central Asia, which accounts for his strange, un-Chinese name. He committed suicide rather than surrender to the rebels in 1358. But for this passage we should know nothing about the lighter side of his life.

*Fol. 23a. Little Spring Feast's surname was Chang. She came from Wu-ch'ang [in Hupeh] to Chê-hsi [the Hangchow region]. She was by nature extremely intelligent and had an extraordinary memory. When she was to perform in the 'enclosure' [i.e. on the stage] a list of the parts she knew was always posted up at each corner of the railings, so that the spectators might choose a play and ask for it. In recent times few have equalled her in power of memory.*

(*Oriental Art*, New Series, 1957.)

# SHIBA KŌKAN, 1737–1818

*S*hiba Kōkan was the first person in Japan to feel that to be Far Eastern meant, in the world sense, to be provincial; to realize that his own country lay and had lain for centuries far aside from the main stream of human culture and discovery. Just at the moment when the Wisdom of the East was beginning to acquire its romantic prestige in Europe, this Oriental wrote: 'In China there is no natural philosophy; nor are we Japanese at all given to abstract enquiry. We trick out our writings with meretricious ornaments so as to make them seem cultured and literary; what we say has no bearing on realities. We all have minds like women. Women are in a state of perpetual muddle. They believe whatever they are told, and have no sense of fact.'

Kōkan set to work to divest himself of this Japanese frivolity; but in the long list of 'mistakes' that form the core of his Reminiscences he is obliged to confess that to stop being Japanese is after all not so easy: 'I was living in Japan, where no one else cared about the laws of the universe, nor took any interest in such subjects as astronomy or the different countries of the world. In trying to be different from my countrymen I made a great mistake.'

The first part of his life was spent in a series of endeavours to find in himself a talent that would make him famous after death; for he disbelieved in all other kinds of immortality, and at the same time longed passionately for some kind of survival.

'My first idea was to design swords. For these are the prime part of a warrior's equipment and are handed down in the family, so that the maker's name is remembered from generation to generation. But the government of the day was so strong that all opposition had disappeared. I found that swords had become mere fashionable ornaments, and those worn by the military class were all antiques. For new swords there was no demand at all. Moreover, I did not like the idea of making what, in intention, were instruments of carnage and slaughter. So I changed my mind and gave that profession up...

'I became acquainted with a certain Hiraga Gennai, a native of Sanuki, who was interested in the contrivances of the Dutch. The number of scholars in Japan who knew anything of Dutch learning was then very small. There were Sugita Genpaku[1] and Nakagawa Junan,[2] but practically no one else. Gennai possessed the Dutch book called *Yonsutonsu*,[3] which cost him fifty or sixty pieces of gold. To pay for it he was obliged to sell everything in his house, down to his very bed-clothes and washing-things. This book gives pictures, drawn from nature, of all the live things in the world, including creatures such as lions and dragons, which one cannot see in Japan. Nowadays there are several people who have the book; but at that time it was quite unknown. Afterwards, when he

---

1 1725–1809. Student of European medicine.

2 Dates uncertain. He and Hiraga Gennai experimented together in the manufacture of asbestos.

3 J Jonstons: *Beschrijving van de...viervoetige dieren...slangen en draken*. Amsterdam 1660. The author was known in England as 'John Jonston of Poland'.

went to Nagasaki he procured a book that the Dutch had sent up to the Shōgun as a present. It had been returned to Nagasaki as useless and had knocked about in the interpreter's house, getting more and more damaged, till it was found by Gennai and brought back to Yedo. After several days of deep cogitation he completely mastered the subject, which was the machine that we now call the "electer". The daimyōs and small lords were all agog to see this instrument and Gennai became a hero. But the electer could do nothing better than make bits of paper jump into the air and send sparks flying. It had no effect on the human frame. There is also a thing called the "glass jar"; but I am not sure what it is supposed to do. It came from Holland after Gennai's death, and is still exhibited as a curiosity, even quite uneducated people coming to look at it. Gennai also believed that when a mountain contained gold, silver, copper or iron, a particular projection like a kind of rock or stone at the top of the mountain signified what lay within, and he attempted to interpret these signs.

'I was involved with him in his researches. But in the end I decided it had all been a great mistake and waste of time.'

[Hiraga Gennai was born in 1732. In 1759 he refounded the Bussan Kwai or 'Products Society', a corporation the principal business of which was to protect the merchants of Japan against imposture by the Dutch. Gennai had an extraordinary knowledge of medicinal herbs and was employed by the importers to examine and identify those which the foreigners offered for sale. In 1763 he published his *Butsurui Hinshitsu*, 'On the Distinction of Species'; also two fantastic novels (one, a sort of *Gulliver's Travels*). In 1764 he brought out his treatise on asbestos, and in 1770 built his famous 'electric machine'. In the same year he wrote a puppet-play in Yedo dialect. These plays had always been written in the dialect of Ōsaka, the home of the puppet-theatre, and were consequently difficult for Yedo people to follow. *The Ghost at the Ford of Yaguchi* was a tremendous success. In 1779 he was arrested on a charge of manslaughter (an innkeeper had been killed in the course of a drunken brawl) and died in the Demma-chō prison. But according to some accounts the story of his death was invented by the prison authorities in order to facilitate his escape, and several persons claim to have encountered him nearly forty years later.]

But to return to Shiba Kōkan:

'I think there were painters among my ancestors,' he writes. 'Certainly my uncle (my father's elder brother) had a natural talent for painting. This I seem to have inherited, for at the age of 6, seeing a design of sparrows on a bowl, I copied it on to paper and showed it to my uncle. At 10 I was fond of painting Darumas,[1] which I produced in quantities and always brought to my uncle. When I grew up I became a pupil of Kanō Furunobu.[2] But I thought the native style vulgar and went to Sō Shiseki.[3] At that time there was a painter of the Popular School called Suzuki Harunobu, who excelled in illustrating the female modes and manners of his day. He died suddenly,[4] when he was not much over 40. I made imitations of his work and engraved them on woodblocks. No one knew that those prints were by me and not by Harunobu; indeed, I was actually supposed to be Harunobu. It seemed to me that I was behaving with disloyalty to his memory [and I stopped].

'Next I did what are called spring pictures,[5] colouring them in the style of the Chinese painters Ch'iu Ying[6] and Chou

1 In Sanskrit, Bodhidharma, reputed originator of the Zen sect.

2 This is a misprint, for Furunobu died in 1724.

3 Painter in the Chinese style, 1715–80.

4 In 1770.

5 Erotic pictures.

6 Sixteenth century.

Ch'én.[1]... It was about this time that ladies began using the instrument called *binzashi*,[2] which soon altered the whole method of doing the hair. This I showed to the life in my pictures, which consequently enjoyed a great vogue. But I feared that such work would damage my reputation, and I gave it up.

'There was a Confucian scholar...called Karahashi Seisai.[3] He often came to the house of my neighbour, the doctor Sōgen, and read with him, sometimes making dissertations on the text. I used to join them, in order to learn what I could. Seisai would give out themes, and we had to write Chinese poems on them. It seemed to me that it would look better if I had a Chinese form of name to sign under such poems. So I took...the surname Shiba[4]...and the pen-name Kōkan.[5]... But afterwards I met a Mr Nyorai, who said it did not do to use two characters that were both names of rivers, and he laughed at my ignorance. By that time however I was generally known as Kōkan, and Kōkan I have remained. But this was another of my mistakes.'

To remain unmarried after the age of 20 was very unusual in Japan. Kōkan held out till he was over 40.[6] His intention was to avoid marriage altogether. In this he was influenced by his admiration for the old *hokku*-poet Matsuki Tantan,[7] who lived for 88 years without wife or children, 'but always kept round

1 *c.*1500.

2 An instrument made of bone or metal that held out the hair flat on each side.

3 1736–1800.

4 A common Chinese surname. Cf. the Han poet Ssŭ-ma (pronounced in Japan 'Shiba') Hsiang-ju, the historians Ssŭ-ma Ch'ien and Ssu-ma Kuang.

5 'The River Han', or 'The Yangtze [and] the Han'.

6 'Over 30' says the text of his book; but other sources say '40' and evidence points to about 1790 as the date.

7 1674–1761. The *hokku* is a diminutive poem in three lines.

him a great number of young girls about 12 years old, who saved him all trouble. That is why it is so hard to obtain any specimen of his handwriting, for he dictated everything to these children.

'When my mother died... I meant to leave home and go off by myself, wandering from place to place till I had seen all the mountains in Japan. But my relations kept on showing me passages in the writings of the Sage, to the effect that Man's duty is to marry and found a family and that to act otherwise is inhuman. In the end I allowed them to prevail upon me, which was a great mistake.

'Again, as to children, a childless man misses an important part of life's emotion.[1] It is through love of one's own children that one arrives at love of young people in general, and this feeling is a very deep and important one, that cannot be expressed in any essay or book. But as soon as children grow up they begin to have ideas of their own which are bound to conflict with those of their parents...and whereas to a parent the child is always a child and his feelings towards it remain as deep as before, with the children themselves it is quite otherwise. As often as not they feel towards their parents no sort of natural affection at all.

'I now see that it would have been better for me not to have children.

'I had a passionate longing for fame and wealth, and it was in pursuit of these two things that I muddled away my time for ten years. As I see it now, fame is merely an inconvenience. It means that if one commits the slightest indiscretion, the whole world immediately knows; whereas if an obscure person does the same thing, no one hears about it. In the end I realized what a mistake fame is, and have come to wish that I had never

1 *Mono no aware*, 'the movingness of things', *lacrimae rerum*.

112

pursued it. And what after all does it amount to? Heaven and earth will go on forever. One may succeed in being famous for a few centuries. But what is that set against ten, a hundred thousand years?

'Measured with the small instrument of our human understanding, life seems a long dream; contrasted with the huge operations of the universe, it is a very short dream; nor can our thoughts ever extend beyond the limit of this dream-world till we ourselves know that we dream. And suppose we should begin to wake and all our delusions melt away; I do not know that we should be best pleased at what we discovered. And suppose we succeeded in getting ourselves wide awake, did not like it, and found that, try as we might, we could not get to sleep again...

'Granted then that the things of this world are the bewildered imaginings of sleep: we are dream-men and those about us are dream-men too. Even among the phantoms and unrealities that encompass us, some are painful, others pleasing; some gloomy, others gay. We had better settle down quietly to life's sleep; then there will be some chance that we shall not frighten ourselves with evil dreams.

'And this we may take as our sleeper's-rule, that too pleasant a dream will be followed always by a distressing nightmare. Fame and wealth – these two, of all phantoms and beguilements, I would warn the sleeper to avoid.'

And with this philosophy Kōkan, despite family ties, spent much of his life in wandering from place to place. It is difficult to reconstruct the history of those tours, for the entries in the *Shunparō Nikki* are seldom dated. We know, however, that he visited Nagasaki in 1788, for he published a description[1] of his

1 The *Seiyu Ryodan*, published 1803, four chapters. A new edition with a fifth chapter by Kōkan's pupil Ranko was published *c.* 1820.

journey, illustrating it with sketches made on the tour. This book contains some very brief notes about the Dutch and Chinese traders at Nagasaki; but its most interesting section, as regards both pictures and text, is the description of the whale-fishery at Ikitsuki, an island lying north-west of the Kyūshū coast. Here he spent thirty days, minutely noting every stage of the whaler's craft.

His experience of the actual fishing, as is common in such cases, was not fortunate. He went out several times with the fleet. Whales were repeatedly sighted, but never caught. He relates these experiences with the slightly mournful candour that is typical of him.

The following extracts from the *Shunparō Nikki* further illustrate the wide range of Kōkan's curiosity.

It is well known that the Japanese islands are scattered with Megalithic chambered mounds, stone circles and menhirs. Their origin remains as obscure as it was in Kōkan's time, when all such monuments were regarded as the work of gods. Particularly famous was the Ama no Saka-hoko or 'Heavenly reversed halberd', left upon the top of Mount Kirishima by the God Kuni-toko-tachi. All such stories, says Kōkan, are 'stuff and nonsense' (*rachi mo naki koto*). The 'Heavenly halberd' is a 'natural, spontaneous formation that happens to resemble a spear. In our country we have no written records that go back even as far as the Heroic Age, and we do not know what strange race may have lived here earlier still. In the province of Harima there is the place they call the stone treasure-hall. It is a room four *ken* square, carved out of the rock, and cannot be anything but the work of man. Again, in Inaba Province there is the Holy Place of the Bear. It is all paved with flat stones and is obviously the work of man. But what its purpose was we do not know. The peasants say that it is part of a bridge made in ancient days by some god who wanted to cross this stretch of the sea.

'Again, in the Ainu country there is a place called Tasarichi. Here there is a great number of six-sided flat stones. But one finds such stones all along that coast, and they are certainly not artificial....

'The world is full of all kinds of things far stranger than this. The Dutch books show the most unexpected and astonishing natural scenes and spectacles; and if we Japanese are taken aback by so simple a thing as the rock which they call the Halberd of Heaven, it is because we are ignorant of the world's greater marvels.'

### The weather

'With my cold-hot rise-sink[1] I can measure the temperature. In an ordinary winter it stands at twelve or thirteen, with an extreme of eight or nine. But in the sixth year of the Bunkwa (1809) there was a remarkable spell of cold. The instrument stood at five on the ninth day of the eleventh month. At five again on the twenty-fifth day. At two and a half on the twenty-sixth day... Two and a half on the tenth day of the New Year, accompanied by heavy snow. Indeed, such a spell of cold as does not occur once in ten years. It lasted for more than forty days.'

### The recession of the sea

'If you look at a map of Yedo in the Yeiroku periods[2]...you will see that Temple of Kwannon at Asakusa was then entirely surrounded by water. The Shiba-dōri (?Shiba-ura) and the quarters adjoining the Nihon-bashi, the Ogawa chō, Shitaya, Honjo, Fukagawa – were then all under shallow water, forming a sort of lake. "Asakusa" is in itself the name of a marine plant.

1 Thermometer, recently imported by the Dutch.
2 1558–69.

Since then the ocean has gradually receded, and in ten million years one will be able to walk dry-foot to America.'

*Vaccination*

'It is because Japanese civilization is recent that our capacities are so limited. In the Imperially Compiled Mirror for Doctors[1] and in the Dutch books there is a method (of dealing with smallpox) called "planting the poison". When this is used deaths do not occur, there is no disfigurement and no serious disturbance of the system. When the disease is prevalent those who harbour a large quantity of the poison die. But even those who are born with the poison in their system, can lessen it by vaccination, which must be performed twice. Some relations of mine have a small child. I told them of this method, but they would not give their consent. They said it seemed like going out of one's way to have a disease.'

*The Groot Historie*

'The Dutch book *Groot Historie* contains an account of the beginnings of the world. Before heaven and earth were separated there were no men and we have therefore no means of actually knowing what existed. We can only guess, and it is such guesses that the *Historie* contains. In the beginning the wheel of the sun appeared in the sky and the sun-spirit produced water-spirit, which became solid and turned into this earth...'

*Reply of the Lord of Shirakawa to Russian traders who in 1793 arrived at Nemoro in the entrance north of Japan, wishing to purchase Japanese rice*

'Permission for one Russian boat to proceed to Nagasaki. Take note that the doctrine of the Christians is entirely prohibited in

1 A Chinese work.

116

this country. Christian images, vessels, books and the like cannot be brought on shore, under pain of severe penalties. You must understand this perfectly. At Nagasaki you will undergo another examination before you are allowed to land. This permit is only provisional.'

Kōkan's comment upon this letter is:

'The Lord of Shirakawa may be a very learned and very intelligent man; but he evidently knows nothing about geography. Why send them all the way to Nagasaki, which is a thousand leagues further on? Far better to let them open up a centre of trade in the Ainu country, which would then begin to lose its present barbarity. And as for this panic about Christianity – I really see no reason for it.'

*Buddhism*

'Not many years ago I was at Kamakura during the tenth month and chanced to pass the Kōmyōji. It was the fourteenth day of the month and the whole building was crammed with men and women young and old, who had come to hear the service. Suddenly I noticed that in the portico outside the building a number of men were lying, huddled under rush-plaited cloaks. I asked them why they were there; for the night was cold and stormy. They answered that peasants were not allowed into the temple, but must catch what they could of the service from outside and get Buddhahood by such fragments of doctrine as they could thus acquire.

'The priests of the present day constitute a sort of "idle proletariat"; their calling no longer involves any activity. Even Buddhism might have a certain utility as an aid to peace and good order among the people. But priests today cannot even conduct their own lives in a respectable way... In old days any one who wished to become a priest had to engage in a course of rigorous austerities. There was a "national temple" in each province and anyone who wanted to be a priest had to go there first and receive his training. These studies enabled him to understand not only the superficial and apparent sense of the scriptures, but also the deeper meanings that lie hidden under anecdote and parable. Thus equipped they were able so to play upon the feelings of the poor and ignorant as really to improve their conduct; so that figures of speech, such as Hell and Heaven, were actually of some use. In those days there was at the capital an office called the Gembaryō, where examinations were held, and there were also in many places institutions called Ordination Altars. To these the successful candidate went for his licence; and only then was he allowed to receive the tonsure and become a priest. Henceforward he might call himself a qualified Doctrinal Professor.

'Nowadays the priest regards a temple as his private house, concentrates all his ambition upon rank and advancement, and would not know how to lead the common people into good ways even should he desire to do so. He can in no way be regarded as a national asset, and it is most desirable that henceforth entries into the priesthood should be in some way restricted. At present even the poorest yokel if he has several sons will send the youngest to a temple while it is still a child, "for the family's salvation".[1]

'Many of these children grow up into very indifferent priests. On the other hand if any one in middle age shows a disposition towards Buddhist life and thought, there is no harm in his becoming a priest. He may indeed very well distinguish himself by his learning and piety. The old method of admission had the advantage of keeping the numbers down.

'Nowadays the clergy do nothing whatever except occasionally read the burial service.'

1 One priest in a family was supposed to save all the members from Hell.

118

*Kōkan's ghost-story*

'This happened about forty years ago. Someone who had formerly learnt painting from me ran a dye-works at Gōchi.[1] One autumn, towards the end of the ninth month, he took me with him to Gōchi, and as very bad weather came on I stayed four or five days. At that time, a mile or two aside from the road, there lived a certain writing-master who was said to come from Yedo, and my pupil took me to call on him. It was late at night when we returned. On the way we passed a temple called the Senso-kuji (Foot-washing Temple). The story is that when His Highness the first Shōgun[2] made an August Progress through this place, he saw an old woman washing, and gave orders that the temple should henceforward bear this name, which is indeed a very odd one.

'We did not know it, but that afternoon there had been a funeral there. It was about midnight when the dyer and I reached what in the darkness appeared to be the gateway of the temple. Here we were astonished to see a figure clad all in white. It seemed to be raised above the level of the ground, and thus suspended was rocking to and fro. In my childhood I had heard many stories about ghosts, but had never seen one. This time there seemed to be no doubt about the matter. We were both very much frightened. Near at hand was a wine-house, and though it was all locked up and everybody asleep, we roused the landlord, who greeted us with a six-foot bludgeon in his hand. "Ghosts?" he cried. "We'll soon see to that," and led the way, while we crept cautiously behind.

'It turned out that during the funeral white paper flags had been hung upon the boughs of a tree, and left there afterwards. The entrance to the temple was overshadowed by dense foliage, and even by day the place was always in a sort of

---

1 Not far from Yedo, in Musashi Province.
2 Tokugawa Iyeyasu, 1542–1616.

twilight. It was therefore quite natural that on a dark night we should make the strange error that I have described.'

*The fortune-teller*
'In the Mishima-chō at Shiba[1] there lives an old phrenologist called Master Stone Dragon. He is a native of Ikeda in the province of Settsu. With him lives a certain Kōan, who is not his son, but came with his first wife, and was adopted at the age of 5. Kōan must now be about 30. This first wife fell ill and died, but Stone Dragon married again, and the three of them still live together. The old man is well over 70, but very vigorous. Kōan is a noble character. Despite the fact that his stepmother is a most disagreeable woman he humours her in everything, and indeed treats her with just such a reverence and humility as the Canons of the Sage require.

'Yet at the same time he is quite ready to take 100 *sen* for reading people's "signs" and hardly a day passes that he does not swindle several score of clients, rich and poor. In favourable seasons, like the third month of spring, he will have as many as fifty or sixty of them coming to him. And on ordinary days he usually has anything from fourteen to twenty-eight. He also takes pupils in the art of phrenology. That is to say, people have interviews with him at which he reads and comments upon a printed book called *The True Meaning of the Divine Art of Phrenology, Part I*. For the privilege of entering themselves as his pupils they pay as much as 500 pieces of gold. He also possesses a book called *The Secret Tradition of the Extreme*, and for communication of this work he charges seven *ryō* two *bun* of gold; and in the case of important clients as much as twenty or thirty flat pieces of silver.

1 A quarter of Yedo.

'The father, old Stone Dragon, can neither read nor write, mixes as little as possible with the rest of humanity, and has about as much notion of manners as a sailor on the high seas. The only people he ever speaks to are a couple of his son's pupils. One of these kept a seed shop in the Kiridōshi at Shiba. On the eleventh day of the second month of the eighth year of Bunkwa (1811) a fire broke out and raged in the whole space between Ichitani and the Akabane Bridge in Shiba. The seedsman's shop was burnt down and he with it. Despite the large fees that he had paid for lessons in prognostication, he was quite unaware that he was going to be roasted alive. I myself once consulted Stone Dragon and his son. They told me that I had only three years to live. But I am not dead yet.

'These phrenologists identify the various features and parts of the head with different natural bodies. Thus, they call the eyes "The Sun and Moon", and there are other parts that they identify with each of the five great mountains of China. They then proceed like the Diagram[1] diviners, who lay out their rods, and if a wind-symbol comes under an earth-symbol say that "wind-earth" spells "pleasure", and consequently predict good fortune. In reality the phrenologists depend on the silliest sort of guess-work. They tell anyone who does not look very strong that he has not long to live. A person who is obviously short of cash is told that he "lacks the bump of wealth". The rest of their clients – soldiers, citizens, peasants, are not difficult to recognize as such and cater for accordingly.

'I once heard Kōan say to his father: "Life is slipping by and there is no time to lose. Surely it would not be a bad thing to have a little enjoyment occasionally. We sit here all day interviewing dupes and fools. In spring the blossom comes to the trees, but we know nothing of it. In summer there are

1 Diviners who use the diagrams of the Chinese *Book of Changes*.

places where one can escape the heat, but we stay here and broil. I should like sometimes to read a book, but even for such distractions as that I never get the time. What sense is there in such a life?" Old Stone Dragon answered: "As far as I am concerned, if I can get 100 *sen* for reading someone's signs and put it by, knowing that it will grow into silver and then into gold, that is all the pleasure I need. For the rest, I ask no more than that I should get my rice three times a day." '

*Collectors*

'In this country things are valued simply for their rarity, and fools give 10,000 pieces of gold for something that has no merit save that it is unique. A second example is discovered, and the price goes down to nothing. A Chinese picture that is all blackened and broken, so that one cannot make out anything at all, is talked of with bated breath and scrambled for by the connoisseurs simply because it is supposed to be the only example of some famous master. Even if it were genuine it could not, in that defaced condition, be of any interest.'

*The English ship*

'An English ship…was in harbour at Hirato. At that time a certain Matsura Hōgen, a retired official, had been put in charge of the place. One day he brought his wife on board the English ship. Inside there were a lot of paintings on panels. One of them was a *shungwa*.[1] Without examining it closely the lady at once prostrated herself before it… They supposed she must think it was a Buddha. She was then asked to play on the *samisen*. The English said they had no such instrument in their country, and took notes about its shape and construction. Among other things they had copies of papers signed by the

1 'Spring painting', see above, p. 110

122

first Shōgun, Lord Iyeyasu, with translations into the language of their own country.

'When the English came to Yedo and saw the mansions of the nobility...they were astonished to find that no "crystal" was used in the windows... Their country is very cold and all the walls are made of stone. For the windows they use *biidoro* (i.e. Portuguese *vidro* "glass") just as we use paper.

'On the fifth day of the sixth month (1811) I met a peasant near Kumagai – a man of about 60. He said to me that he had heard I possessed a map of the heavens. A certain relative of his called Mr Yoshida had told him so. "And I have heard, Sir," said the man, "that every morning you make an offering of water to this map and say your prayers to it. That is why your family is so prosperous. I should take it as very kind if you would teach me this way of keeping out of trouble." At this I laughed and said "I will gladly give you a map of the stars, and you shall say your prayers to it or not, exactly as you please. But I assure you that good or bad fortune are not controlled by stars." "I hope you don't mind my having mentioned it," he said and went away.'

*Fires*

'Fires are always due to someone's negligence, but the person who starts them is never brought to book. This is because they generally start in the big houses of influential people. Such places teem with irresponsible underlings, to whom it is of no consequence whether the city burns or not. Most of them are hired by the year. They have no houses of their own, nor property of any kind. They wear very thin clothing and in winter feel the cold so much that it is only by keeping close to the brazier that they can get along at all. So far from dreading a conflagration, such people, I believe, many of them positively welcome it. Not to speak of carpenters, plasterers, roofers and their subordinates, who pray for a house-on-fire as the greatest boon that Heaven can bestow.

'In Yedo, at the beginning of the present Shōgunate[1] there were 808 blocks of houses; there are now something like 1,808. The total number of hearths must be prodigious and it is natural that in winter there should be outbreaks of fire…

'Someone told me the story of a certain small official called Tomi who went into the country with four companions and at the house of the village headman had some rice to eat for his lunch, which poisoned all five of them, so that they died immediately. An enquiry was held and it was found that there was a lizard in the rice. It had apparently dropped from the rafters while the rice was being ladled into the bowl. The meal was prepared by a girl of 16 to 17 years old who, simply because the five men were in the employment of the government, was put to death, though no evil intention was proved against her. In my opinion, to be unaware that a reptile has got into the rice-pot implies not carelessness but sheer imbecility.

'The fire in Bull Street at Shiba was due to a tobacco-smoker's negligence, and the fire at Shitaya began by someone lighting a fire and then going off to his neighbour's and forgetting about it. It need hardly be said that at times when the typhoon is blowing, to be careless about fire is criminal.

'In contrast to the people of Kyōto, those of Yedo are in general very slap-dash. The town is full of countrymen from the neighbouring provinces who come here to take service in gentlemen's houses. That is the sort of fellow who sets the fires going. Invariably it is one individual who is to blame. If trouble were taken to detect him and inflict a heavy punishment, I am certain that fewer fires would take place.'

1 Sixteenth century.

*His interview with the Lord of Ku*

'The first time that I was summoned to wait upon the Lord of Kii,[1] his secretary said to me, "Please understand that this is not an audience with His Highness the Lord Councillor. You will converse with us and His Lordship will, if he chooses, overhear the conversation at a suitable distance." I signified my humble acquiescence in this arrangement and went to fetch the celestial sphere and globe of the world that I had recently constructed. These I brought into the Presence and laid before His Highness with a deep bow. "Kōkan," he at once said, "I have heard a great deal about you and am delighted that we have met at last." I then explained my sphere and globe to the secretary. Presently His Highness interposed, saying: "I have myself possessed a globe and sphere for some time. But there is much about them that I do not understand. Bring yours over here, so that I may examine them carefully while you are speaking."

I brought them to him and said quietly: "In Japan there is no one but myself who understands the revolution of the earth; to demonstrate its principle, I have made a special contrivance."[2] Then, of course, I explained to him why part of the year is cold, and the cause of thunder and lightning, and about auras, and how the spectrum is created out of the two principles of fire and water, and the "five flavours" out of salt and sulphur. I also told him about the specific gravity of liquids, and how gases liquefy and liquids evaporate into gas.[3]

---

1 The Lords of Kii were descended from Yorinobu, eighth son of the first Shōgun, Iyeyasu. Kōkan's patron may have been Harusada, the ninth lord.

2 Showing the earth and the five planets. It was actually constructcd by Kōkan's pupil Oku Kisaburō.

3 The text is in the whole of the above passage obviously somewhat corrupt and I am not sure that I have always caught Kōkan's meaning.

'Then I painted for him, doing a view of the coast at Waka no Ura and several other landscapes; and after this display of my talents, I withdrew to a respectful distance. I heard his lordship say to the secretary, "I have seldom passed so instructive a day".

'I have since been told that his lordship had for years past been devoted to astronomy. At one time he sent for Mr Yoshida, assistant in the Astronomical Board, for Yamaji Saisuke and some others of that sort, to question them about the stars. But he could get nothing out of them. And no wonder; for they were subordinate officials who were in such a panic at appearing before so exalted a personage that even if they had been able, after desperate cogitations, to arrive at some idea, they would never have summoned up courage enough to produce it. Moreover they were almanack-makers rather than natural philosophers. The only result of questioning such people was that they scuttled away biting their tongues and hanging their heads, which greatly irritated his Lordship.

'I, on the other hand, was not in the least nervous when I appeared before him. I am quite used to dealing with these great people and I think no more of an audience with this or that prince than of a talk with one of my own colleagues. Consequently, when confronted with His Lordship of Kii I treated him to such a discourse about the heavens as has not been heard since the days of Ch'in Fu,[1] and my lord was much gratified. He was very anxious that I should enter his service. But at the time I was already over 50 and had never been

---

1 See *Romance of the Three Kingdoms*, ch. 86. In this Chinese novel, Ch'in Fu bursts drunk into a party and, chiefly in order to impress an envoy from the kingdom of Wu, makes a speech about Heaven, in which he proves that Heaven has a head, ears, feet and a surname. He becomes very excited, and 'his words pour out like a river in flood'.

under anyone else's orders, so I told him I intended that such powers of mind and body as I still possessed should remain at my own disposition to do my own work with, rather than be used by others; and I persistently declined his offers.

'Now I am 75. I do nothing that I do not feel inclined to, and if all the princes in Japan were to demand my attendance, I would not budge. Even my own work I have dropped. In winter I lie about in the sunshine and in summer sit under the trees. I have always been fond of nature, and make many excursions. When I find a hill or scene that pleases me I have a good look at it, and afterwards when I am at home amuse myself by turning it into a picture. I am still interested in natural philosophy and perhaps my greatest pleasure of all consists in discussing such matters with those who have been friendly to my theories, particularly as regards astronomy and the revolutions of the earth... Men are like clothes and furniture. There comes a time when they are so worn and damaged that they are no longer any use.

'Not long ago there was a certain Sakuzō who was 107 years of age. Many great lords and gentlemen tried to get him to their houses in the absurd idea that they could learn from him some secret of longevity. Small good it would do them to be like Sakuzo, who is played out and no use to anybody.'

The above was written in the winter of 1811. Kōkan died on the twenty-first day of the tenth month, 1818, at the age of 82. He was buried in the Jigenji, at Saruye in Fukagawa, Yedo; but his tombstone has been removed to a temple outside the town.

(*Ostasiatische Zeitschrift*, 1927.)

127

# SOME POEMS FROM THE
## *MANYŌSHŪ* AND *RYŌJIN HISSHŌ*

I. *Manyō*. Of the 4,100 short poems in the *Manyōshū*, about 200 have been translated, by Florenz,[1] Aston,[2] Dickins,[3] and others.[4] Many more deserve translation, particularly the dialect-songs, which have been avoided by previous translators. A few of these (noted as such when they occur), and some fifty other songs not hitherto translated, will be found below, with text and rendering.

For general information with regard to the *Manyō*, I must refer my reader to the works mentioned at the foot of this page. The order of the poems is that of the *Manyō*; the numbers, those of the *Kokka Daikwan*.

95. *Ware wa mo yo*     I have got her,
     *Yasumiko etari,*     Have got Yasumiko;
     *Mina hito no*     She who for any man
     *Egate ni su tou*     Was thought hard to get,
     *Yasumiko etari!*     Yasumiko I have got!

1 *Geschichte der japanischen Literatur.*
2 *History of Japanese Literature.*
3 *Japanese Texts.*
4 e.g. Waley, *Japanese Poetry* (Clarendon Press, 1919).

By Fujiwara no Kamatari (AD 614–59). This song, astounding in its simplicity, was made by Kamatari when he married the lady-in-waiting Yasumiko.

| | | |
|---|---|---|
| 123. | *Takeba nure;* | When it is put up, it straggles; |
| | *Takaneba nagaki* | When it is let down, it is too long, |
| | *Imo ga kami,* | My lady's hair! |
| | *Kono-goro minu ni* | This great while that I have not seen her |
| | *Midare tsuramu ka?* | How tangled it must have grown! |

By Mikata no Sami.[1]

| | | |
|---|---|---|
| 124. | *Hito mina wa* | Every one is saying |
| | *'Ima wa nagashi' to,* | 'Now it is too long' |
| | *'Take' to iyedo,* | And 'Put it up'; |
| | *Kimi ga mishi kami* | But the hair that you used to look at, |
| | *Midaritari to mo –* | However tangled it may grow – |

(Reply to above.)

| | | |
|---|---|---|
| 125. | *Tachibana no* | What longing fills my heart |
| | *Kage fumu michi no* | When at the meeting of the ways that tread |
| | *Ya-chimata ni* | The shadow of orange-trees |
| | *Mono wo zo omou* | I meet not with my love! |
| | *Imo ni awazute!* | |

By Mikata no Sami.

1 Where no date is given it may be assumed that the writer lived *c.* 700. In cases where no writer's name is given the poems are anonymous.

130

142.  *Iye ni areba*        My rice that when I was at
                                   home
      *Ki ni moru ii wo,*    I ate from a wooden bowl,
      *Kusamakura*         Now that I wander
      *Tabi ni shi areba*    On grass-pillowed journey
      *Shii no ha ni moru.*  In an oak-leaf is served!
    By the Prince of Arima, seventh century.

607.  *Mina hito wo*       Though now to all men
      *'Neyo' to no kane wa*  'Go sleep!' the evening bell
      *Utsunaredo,*        Its warning tolls;
      *Kimi wo shi omoyeba*  Yet I that am longing for my
                                   lord,
      *Inegatenu kamo!*    Alas, I sleep not!
    By Lady Kasa, died 733.

1158. *Sumiyoshi no*      Of onward-creeping waves
      *Kishi no matsu ga ne* That bleach the pine-tree
                                   roots
      *Uchisarashi*        How very clean the sound,
      *Yorikuru nami no*    At Sumiyoshi shore!
      *Oto shi kiyoshi mo!*

1165. *Yūnagi ni*        That crane who in the evening
                                   breeze
      *Asarisuru tazu*     Searches the shore for food,
      *Shio miteba,*       Because the tide grows high
      *Okinami takami*    And the waves of the offing
                                   rise
      *Ono go tsuma yobu.*  Calls warning to his mate.

1235. *Nami takashi.*     The waves are high.
      *Ika ni, kajitori,*   How now, helmsman,
      *Mizudori no*      Shall we like water-birds

| | |
|---|---|
| *Ukine ya subeki,* | Sleep a floating sleep, |
| *Nao ya kogubeki?* | Or go on rowing?[1] |

1257. *Michi no be no* — Only because you smiled on me

*Kusafuke yuri no* — With a smile like the lily which grows

*Hana emi ni* — In the grass-clump by the wayside,

*Emashishi kara ni* — Am I to call you bride?
*Tsuma to iubeshi ya?*

1263. *'Aka toki' to* — 'The time is dawn'

*Yo-garasu nakedo,* — The crows of night are calling;

*Kono mine no* — But round the tree-tops of yonder mountain

*Konure go uye wa* — All yet is still.[2]
*Imada shizukeshi*

1777. *Kimi nakuba* — Were it not for you,

*Nado ni yosowamu?* — Why should I adorn my body?

*Kushige taru* — Even the little combs of box-wood

*Tsuge no okushi mo* — That are in my comb-box
*Toramu to mo* — I think I should not use.
*omowazu.*

By the Lady of Harima.

1796. *Momijiba no* — How sad to gaze upon the shore

*Suginishi kora to* — Where hand in hand I wandered

*Tazusawari* — With a maiden vanished

---

1 A satirical appeal to the oarsmen to row hard through the storm.

2 Addressed by a lady to a lover leaving her at dawn.

| | |
|---|---|
| *Asobishi iso wo* | As leaves fall from the trees! |
| *Mireba kanashi mo!* | |

By Hitomaro.

1885. | *Mono mina wa* | All other things |
|---|---|
| *Atarashiki yoshi;* | Find ways to be young again; |
| *Tada hito wa* | Man only with staying old |
| *Furitaru nomi shi* | Must rest content. |
| *Yoroshikarubeshi.* | |

1892. | *Haruyama no* | Even the nightingale |
|---|---|
| *Kiri ni madoyeru* | That has lost its way |
| *Uguisu mo* | In the mist of the spring hills |
| *Ware ni masarite* | Not more baffled is |
| *Mono omowame ya mo.* | Than I by the maze of love. |

By Hitomaro.

1949. | *Hototogisu* | The cuckoo's cry |
|---|---|
| *Kesa no asake ni* | That at the daybreak of today |
| *Nakitsuru wa* | I heard to ring – |
| *Kimi kikikemu ka,* | Did you hear it, or were you sleeping |
| *Asa i ka nuramu?* | Your morning sleep, my lord? |

2368. | *Tarachine no* | Since first I left the hands |
|---|---|
| *Haha ga te karete* | Of the mother who suckled me, |
| *Kaku bakari* | Never by plight so helpless |
| *Sube naki koto wa* | Was I yet perplexed! |
| *Imada senaku ni.* | |

By Hitomaro.

2495. | *Tarachine no* | Oh that I might get sight |
|---|---|
| *Haha ga kauko no* | Of my lady hidden away |
| *Mayu-gomori* | Like silkworms in their cocoons, |

133

*Komoreru imo wo*      The silkworms that her
*Mimu yoshi mo gamo!*      mother breeds!
By Hitomaro.

2550. *Tachite omoi,*      Abroad I dream,
    *Ite mo zo omou*      At home forever dream,
    *Kurenai no*      Of a form that vanished, trailing
    *Aka mosuso hiki*      Petticoats crimson-dyed.
    *Inishi sugata wo.*

2564. *Nubatama no*      My lady's hair that is black
    *Imo ga kurokami*      As the whortleberry –
    *Koyoi mo ka*      Tonight, too, when I am far
                        away,
    *Ware naki toko ni*      Does she trail it in sleep
    *Nabikete nuramu?*      across the bed?

2687. *Sakurao no*      On the under-leaves of the
                       thicket
    *Ou no shitagusa*      Of hemp close-growing
    *Tsuyu shi areba*      Fast falls the dew;
    *Akashite iyuke,*      Do not leave me till the dawn
                       breaks,
    *Haha wa shiru to mo.*      Even should my mother know –

2841. *Waga seko ga*      Because but dimly
    *Asake no sugata*      At the break of morning
    *Yoku mizute*      I saw my lover's form,
    *Kefu no aida wo*      All the hours of today
    *Koi ya kurasamu.*      In longing I shall spend.

2855. *Niibari no*      Clear as gleams the road
    *Ima tsukuru michi no*      That today the workmen were
                       digging
    *Savaka ni mo*      I have heard it at last,

Kikinikeru kamo,        The tale that of my lady is
Imo ga uye no koto wo.      told.

2859. *Asukagawa*        Asuka River
*Takagawa yogashi*       Right to its source I mounted
*Koyete kitsu.*          And came back hither;
*Makoto koyoi wa*        Tonight, I swear it,
*Akezu yukame ya.*       I will not leave you till dawn.

2869. *Ima wa a wa*      Now, now shall I
*Shinamu yo, wagimo!*    Die, lo my lord!
*Awazushite*             Because we met not
*Omoiwatareba*           Being in mind so troubled
*Yasukeke mo nashi.*     That I cannot rest.

3149. *Tsukubane no*     Though on new mulberry-
                             leaves
*Niiguwa mayo no*        Of Tsukubane the silkworms
                             were fed
*Kinu wa aredo,*         From whose silk my dress is
                             spun,
*Kimi ga mikeshi shi*    Thy splendid garment
*Aya ni kihoshi mo*      Rashly would I wear!

3350. *Shinanu ji wa*    On the Shinano way
*Ima no hari michi*      Where they are making the
                             new path,
*Karibaka ni*            Upon the spikes
*Ashi fumashimu na,*     Do not tread with bare feet;
*Kutsu hake, waga se!*   Put on your shoes, my
                             Brother![1]

---

1 Addressed by a rustic lady to a fine lord. To 'share a garment' means to lie under
the same cloak.

3455. *Koishikeba*     Because I am longing,
      *Kimase, waga seko!*    Come, O my Brother!
      *Kaki tsu yagi*    The willows of the hedge –
      *Ure tsumikarashi*    Their tops I will trim,
      *Ware tachimatamu.*    And wait for you there.

3459. *Ine tsukeba*     My hand that is sore
      Kagaru aga te wo    With pounding the rice,
      *Koyoi mo ka*    Tonight again
      *Tono no waku ko ga*    The young lord's son –
      *Torite nagekamu?*    Will he take it and sigh?

3476. *Ube kona wa* [1]     Well may my beloved
      *Wanu ni kounamo!*    Be pining for me;
      *Tato tsuku no*    For while of months that pass
      *Nuganaye yukeba*    The stream flows by
      *Koishikarunamo.*    How dear she grows!

*Kona = kora, wanu = ware, kounamo = kouramu, tato tsuku =*
*tatsu tsuki, nuganaye = nagaraye.*

3517. *Shirakumo no*     Like a white cloud
      *Tayenishi imo we*    Has my lady vanished.
      *Aze sero to?*    Oh, what shall I do?
      *Kokoro ni norite*    She rides upon my heart,
      *Kokoba kanashike.*    And I am thus dispirited.

*Ase sero = ikani semu.*

3873. *Waga kado ni*     At my house door
      *Chidori shiba naku;*    Loudly the curlews cry;
      *Oki yo, oki yo,*    Rise up, rise up,
      *Waga hito-yo tsuma!*    My one night's bride!
      *Hito ni shirayu na!*    Lest our love be known to men.

---

1 The remaining songs are, to a varying degree, in the Eastern dialect.

4285. *Yuko saki ni*    Where I must go
    *Nami oto erai;*    The noise of waves resounds;
    *Shirube ni wa*    In the place from whence I
        come

  *Ko wo ra, tsuma wo ra*  Children and wife I have left.
  *Okite ra mo kinu.*

By Sasaibe no Isoshima.

*Yuko = yuku; ra*, a particle much used in the Eastern Dialect.

4389. *Shiobune no*    With the swiftness of a white
        wave
    *He kosu shire nami*    That suddenly whelms the stern
    *Niwashikumo*    Of a ship at sea
    *Ōse-tamao ka*    Has come the King's command,
    *Omowaye naku ni*    At an hour when I expected it
        not.

By Hasebe Ōtoshi.

4405. *Waga imoko ga*    The sash that, saying
    *'Shinubi ni seyo' to*    'For remembrance wear it',
    *Tsukeshi himo*    My lady put on me –
    *Ito ni naru to mo*    Though it wear to a thread
    *Wa wa tokaji to yo.*    Never will I untie it!

By Asakura Masuhito.

4431. *Sasa ga ha no*    On this frosty night when clash
    *Sayagu shimo-yo ni*    The bamboo leaves in the wind,
    *Nanaye karu*    Better than these nine coats I
        wear
    *Koromo ni maseru*    My lady's limbs would warm
    *Koro ga hada wa mo.*    me.

*Koro=ko ra.*

## II. Ryōjin Hisshō.

The priest Kenkō speaks in his *Tsurezuregusa* (*c.* 1336) of a song-book called the *Ryōjin Hisshō*. Even in the words of these rustic tunes, he says, there are many charming passages. The songs were supposed to have been collected in the middle of the twelfth century under the auspices of the Emperor Goshirakawa. Soon after Kenkō's time the book disappeared and was not rediscovered till 1911, when Mr Wada Hidematsu unearthed the MS. in a second-hand bookshop. It was published by Mr Sasaki Nobutsuna in the following year. Most of the songs are crude paraphrases of passages from the Buddhist scriptures, and are of no interest as literature; others are adaptations of well-known classical poems. But there remains a residuum of true folk-poetry, which is of the greatest interest.

The book has not, so far as I know, been even alluded to by any European writer; I have therefore translated a few of the folk-poems.

1. *Ware wo tanomete konu otoko*
   *Tsuno mitsu oitaru oni ni nare;*
   *Sate hito ni utomare yo!*
   *Shimo yuki azare furu*

   *Mizuta no tori to nare;*
   *Sate ashi tsumetakare!*

   *Ike no ukigusa to narine kashi!*
   *To-yuni, kau-yuri yurare arike!*

   May he that bade me trust him but did not come,
   Turn into a demon with three horns on his head,
   That all men may fly from him!
   May he become a bird of the waterfields
   Where frost, snow, and hail fall,
   That his feet may be frozen to ice!
   Oh may he become a weed afloat on the pond!
   May he tremble as he walks with the trembling of the hare, with the trembling of the doe!

2.  *Bijo uchimireba,* — When I look at my lovely lady
    *Hito moto kazura* — 'Oh that I might become a
    *narinaba ya to zo* — clinging vine', I yearn,
    *omou;*
    *Moto yori suye made* — 'That from toe to tip I might be
    *yorarebaya!* — twined about her'.
    *Kiru to mo kizamu to mo* — Then though they should cut,
    though they should carve
    *Hanaregataki wa waga* — Our fates could not be severed.
    *sukuse!*

3.  *Kimi ga aiseshi aya-i-gasa* — The hat you loved, the damask
    *aya-i-gasa* — trimmed reed-hat
    *Ochinikeri, ochinikeri!* — Has fallen, fallen!
    *Kamogawa ni, kawa* — Into Kamo River, into the
    *naka ni.* — middle of the river.
    *Sore wo motomu to tazune* — And while I searched and while
    *to seshi hodo ni* — I sought
    *Akenikeri, akenikeri;* — Day dawned, day dawned;
    *Sara sara to ike no aki no* — Oh the rustling rustling of that
    *vo wa.* — autumn night by the pools!

4.  *Wage koi wa* — As for my love –
    *Ototohi miyezu, kinou* — Yesterday he came not, nor the
    *kozu;* — day before was seen.
    *Kefu otozure nakuba,* — If today there is no news
    *Asu no tsurezure* — With tomorrow's idle hours
    *Ike ni semu!* — Oh what shall I do?

5.  *Yamabushi no* — The conch-shell fastened
    *Koshi ni tsuketaru* — At the pilgrim's thigh,
    *Horagai no* — The pilgrim mountain-faring –
    *Cho to ochi,* — With a *chō* it has fallen,
    *Tei to ware:* — With a *tei* it has cracked.

139

    *Kudakete mono wo*    Even so my heart is shattered
    *Omou koro!*      By this torment of love.

6. *Azuma yori*     But yesterday
  *Kinou kitareba*    I came from the East, and brought
  *Me mo motazu;*    No bride with me;
  *Kono kitaru*     I pray you, take
  *Kon no kariao ni*   This purple hunting-cloak I wear
  *Musume kaye tabe!*  And buy for me a maid!

7. *Yama-osa ga*    Like the rattan-whip
  *Koshi ni saitaru*   That the headsman of the mountain
  *Tsuzura-fuchi*    Wears fastened at his thigh,
  *Omowamu hito no*   To the limbs of one that should love me
  *Koshi ni sasasemu!*  Would that I were pressed!

8. *Kaze ni nabiku mono –* Things that bend in the wind –
  *Matsu no kozuye no*  The tall branches of pine-tree tops,
   *takaki eda,*
  *Take no kozuye to ka,* Or the little twigs of bamboos,
  *Umi ni ho kakete*   Boats that run with spread sails on the sea,
   *hashiru fune,*
  *Sora ni wa ukigumo,* Floating clouds in the sky,
  *Nobe ni wa hana-susuki.* And in the fields the flowering *susuki.*

9. *Tsukushi no Moji no Seki* The Warden of the barrier,
  *Seki no sekimori oinikeri;* The Barrier of the Gatemen in Tsukushi Land

| | |
|---|---|
| *Bin shiroshi.* | Has grown old and the hair of his temples is white. |
| *Nani tote suyetaru* | He that in his Ward-house is warden |
| *Seki no sekiya no sekimori nareba,* | Of the barrier that bars the road |
| *Toshi no yukuye wo ba* | How comes it that he cannot tarry |
| *Todomezaramu?* | The passage of the years? |

| | |
|---|---|
| 10. *Tsuki mo, tsuki* | Even the moon – |
| *Tatsu-tsuki gate ni* | The moon at each new-moon is |
| *Wakaki kana.* | young again. |
| *Tsukuzuku oi wo suru waga mi* | But of me that am forever ageing, |
| *Nani naruramu?* | Oh what will the end be? |

| | |
|---|---|
| 11. *Asobi wo semu to ya* | For sport and play |
| *Umarekemu;* | I think that we are born; |
| *Tawabure semu to ya* | For jesting and laughter |
| *Mumarekemu.* | I doubt not we are born. |
| *Asobu kodomo no* | For when I hear |
| *Koye kikeba* | The voices of children at their play, |
| *Waga mi saye koso* | My limbs, even my |
| *Yurugarure.* | Stiff limbs, are stirred. |

| | |
|---|---|
| 12. *Maye, maye, katatsuburi!* | Dance, dance, Mr Snail! |
| *Mawanu mono naraba* | If you won't, I shall leave you |
| *Uma no ko ya* | For the little horse, |
| *Ushi no ko ni* | For the little ox, |
| *Kuyesasetemu;* | To tread under his hoof, |
| *Fumi-warasetemu.* | To trample to bits. |
| *Makoto ni utsuhushiku* | But if quite prettily |

| | |
|---|---|
| *Mautaraba,* | You dance your dance, |
| *Hana no sono made* | To a garden of flowers |
| *Asobasemu!* | I will carry you to play. |

3. *Chihayaburu kami*      Oh gods almighty!
   *Kami ni mashimasu*    If gods indeed you are,
   *Mono naraba,*           Take pity on me;
   *Aware to oboshimese!*    For even the gods were once
   *Kami mo mukashi wa*    Such men as we.
   *Hito zo kashi.*

14. *Obotsukana*           In the unexplored
    *Tori dani nakanu*     Deep hills where even of bird
    *Okuyama ni*         There is no song –
    *Hito koso oto su nare.*   Voices of men I hear.
    *Ana! Tōto*          Who can these be? It is the
                                passing
    *Shugyōja no*        Of the holy pilgrims on their
    *Tōru narikeri!*       way.

    (*Journal of the Royal Asiatic Society*, April 1921.)

# Kono Tabi:
# A little-known Japanese Religion

*J*n 1802 Kino, a middle-aged Japanese peasant woman in a remote country place, declared that God, having many times tried unsuccessfully to manifest himself in saints and prophets, had 'this time' (*kono tabi*) managed at last to find in her a vehicle for the delivery of his full and final message. From 1802 till 1826 (the year of her death) God, through his intermediary Kompira[1] (who plays the part that the archangel Gabriel plays in the Koran), inspired this illiterate peasant with a continuous flow of communications, which from 1811 onwards were taken down in writing and are preserved in some 300 rolls. On the strength of this revelation she founded a sect that despite prosecution in the nineteenth century today numbers about 40,000 followers, and which, though its ways of life owes something to Buddhist monasticism, can only be described as a separate religion.

Kino was born in Hataya-machi, Atsuta, province of Owari, in 1756, the third of three daughters. Left an orphan at the age of eight, she was looked after by an uncle till 1768, when at the age of twelve she went into domestic service. In 1778 she

---

1 Sanskrit, Kumbhīra. A minor Indian deity, incorporated in the Buddhist pantheon.

married an agricultural labourer in a neighbouring village. He treated her badly, and before long she returned to domestic service. In 1795 she went back to her native village and lived alone, on the produce of her cottage garden. Seven years later, in the summer of 1802, she felt an inspiration descend upon her, and began to preach daily. Her audience at first no doubt consisted chiefly of people of her own class. But before long it included persons of education and refinement, among them some of the provincial Governor's retinue.

The manner in which her utterances were taken down is of some interest. Four 'recorders' wrote down what she said, while a fifth listened and memorized. The four versions were then compared and a fair copy made, which was checked by the listener. Another copy was then made, embodying his corrections, and read out to Kino. Finally her corrections were made in a third copy. Of the enormous body of literature thus scrupulously edited the greater part has never been seen except by members of the sect. The only extracts that have been printed are those contained in Dr Ishibashi Tomonobu's pamphlet *Nyorai-kyō no oshie*.[1]

Kino died on the second day of the fifth month, 1826, at the age of seventy. She was then living in a hut at Shinkawa, which is still preserved and venerated by the sect; as is also the cottage in which she was born, at Hataya-machi, which has become the headquarters of 'Kono Tabi'.

In the organization of the sect there is no hierarchy of ranks and grades such as exists in Buddhism and other religions. To manage its affairs two elders are chosen by lot each year, and most of the sixty-two branch-settlements (distributed over all

---

1 I owe all my knowledge of the subject to Professor Anesaki, who sent me this pamphlet and put me into communication with the authorities of the sect. A very short summary of Dr Ishibashi's work was printed in German in the *Proceedings of the Imperial Academy*, Tōkyō, 1928.

parts of Japan) have a head, chosen in the same manner. These posts can be filled by men or women. All members of the sect, of whatever sex or status, wear a black cotton garment, of the dressing-gown type. At the beginning of the cold season all members of the sect (in practice, several thousands) collect at the headquarters in Hataya-machi, and exchange their summer dress for a slightly thicker winter one, the discarded dresses being washed, mended, and put by at Hataya-machi till they are needed again. The beginning of summer sees a second gathering, at which the light garments are distributed. At meals the men sit on one side of a long mat, the women on the other. Buddhism, of course, has never allowed monks and nuns to eat together. The services are held at 3 a.m. in summer and 3.30 in winter. There is no image or altar, but only a panel inscribed with Kino's 'name in religion', Ryūzen, before which the worshippers prostrate themselves. Then follows a reading from *O-kyō-sama*, the cursive text of the foundress's utterances, the only book of devotion that the sect employs.

The deity of Kino's system is called Nyorai, a term borrowed from Buddhism; but since he is omnipotent, omniscient, made the Universe and stands in the relation of a father to mankind, I think one is justified in using the term God. The existence of the Buddhas and Shintō (native Japanese) gods is not denied, but they are represented as being completely subject to Nyorai. God created the first man, causing him to spring out suddenly from the face of a rock, at the sight of which the Shintō *kami* (deities), God's subjects, burst into laughter. The man complained after a time that he had nothing to eat. 'Lick my skin,' said God. 'Is it good to lick?' said man, and licked it with his tongue. 'Is it sweet?' asked God. 'Sweet!' exclaimed man. 'I only wish I had known about it from the start.' 'No wonder you find it good,' said God, 'it is nectar (*kanro*), the sweetest of all things.' 'What a pity I did not know that before,' the man said again. Then

God ordered the man to clap his hands three times. Whereupon a small man hopped out of the first man's mouth. The process was repeated till there were seventy-five men. At this point all the deities (including God?) said: 'That's all right now', and went up to Heaven. As the seventy-five men had eaten nothing, but only licked God's flesh, they, too, were pure enough to ascend to Heaven, and the earth was left unpopulated save for a *kami* whom the great god of the Ise Shrine left behind as temple-keeper. This *kami*, presumably wishing also to be free to escape to Heaven, took upon himself to create five new men, from whom mankind is descended.

But elsewhere Kino varies the myth, saying that after the deities had retired to Heaven, the Devil (*Ma-dō* 'Demon-path') visited the earth and created a woman to be his wife. It is from their offspring that the human race is descended. According to another version the Devil, seeing that the god of Ise and his temple-guardian were going off to Heaven, leaving the five newly created men behind, asked if he might take charge of them. The evils of the world result from the fact that it was thus handed over to the devil. God labours to mitigate these ills. Why he permitted the situation to arise we are not told, and the problem is hardly one that we should expect Kino to tackle.

Man is thus in a state of original sin, though he is not himself aware of it. He believes himself indeed to be clean of heart and fair of form.

But God is able to see the horns that man has inherited from the Devil, his forefather. The sight fills God's eyes with tears, and he labours to abolish man's spiritual and bodily disfigurements. The task is one which he alone can accomplish.

Good works, on man's part, are utterly insufficient. 'You believe and constantly assert that those who do good go to the Good Place. But they do not go to the Good Place. On the contrary, they go to a very Bad Place. How often I hear you speak of your ancestors as being in a lovely place! "How glad we are that our ancestors are in a good place!" Why you should be confident of this I do not know. It breaks God's heart to hear men talk so, and fills him daily with the deepest pity.'

God is deeply wounded by the refusal of mankind to let him help them out of their predicament. 'You smite my head. "God, you fool," you say, "we don't want any of your interference." But gently, poor fellows. I am glad that you should smite my head. Beat me, bang me, twist me, spit upon me, so long as you do not shun me I rejoice no less than if you did good to me. So long as your thoughts hang upon me, I do not care whether you chop me in pieces. Indeed, I should count it a blessing that you should chop me in pieces, and not as an affliction.'

The words are nominally those of God, as reported by Kompira. Several passages, however, show that Kino regarded herself not merely as a prophetess, but as a transformation (*kawari-mi*) of God, and the sufferings here described may be considered hers no less than God's. Like the Buddhist saint Vimalakirti and like Christ himself Kino vicariously suffered all the woes of mankind.

'I cannot bear it. Put me out of my pain. Will not one of you do as I bid, and put me out of my pain? All the miseries of mankind are being laid on me alone. It is so, it is so. Were I not suffering in the place of all mankind, why should a single person suffer such pain as this? It is so. I have many daughters, and endure the punishment of their many sins. Come, God, come and do away with their sins. Do away with them.'

Such were Kino's last words, spoken on the second day of the fifth month, 1826. Needless to say, the daughters of whom she speaks were not her daughters in the flesh.

Most of the other published extracts deal with God's love and pity. They do little but transfer the characteristics of Kwannon, in Japan (at any rate, in popular religion) a maternal deity, to Nyorai, who figures as a universal father. In tone they approach very closely not merely to Buddhist but also to Christian conceptions, the resemblance to the latter being enhanced by the fact that, as in Christianity, God figures as a father.

Professor Anesaki, in his *History of Japanese Religion*, has suggested that Kino may have been indirectly influenced by Christianity, though the Christian missions had, of course, been suppressed centuries before her time. As one proof of this he instances the name Ryūzen by which Kino is known to her followers. This he compares with names of the type 'Lucena' and the like which occur on the graves of Japanese converted to Christianity by the Spanish and Portuguese missions. The subject is one upon which Professor Anesaki is a great authority; but until a definite Christian influence on Kino's doctrines can be proved, the origin of this name must remain an open question.[1] Her debt to Buddhism, born as she was in a Buddhist country, cannot fail to be large. As regards certain exterior aspects of Kono Tabi, there has been a quite recent borrowing from Buddhism. In 1884, in consequence of the law which sought to put an end to the fusion of Shintōism and Buddhism, Kino's followers, in order to avoid the suspicion that their faith was an amalgam of this kind, enrolled themselves nominally as members of Zen Buddhist temples. This obliged them to adopt the tonsure and other outward features of Buddhist monasticism. Moreover, one of the most influential elders of the sect, Daisetsu who had died in 1912, had been a Zen monk before he became converted to Kino's doctrines, and brought with him many Buddhist habits and ideas.

---

1 In 1858 the sect was suspected of being connected with Christianity and was temporarily suppressed. But this happened at a time of anti-European panic, and the fact that the sect was not recognizably either Buddhist or Shintō was enough at such a moment to bring it under suspicion.

Nevertheless, the chief interest of Kino Tabi lies in the fact that Kino was, in a small way, a religious founder like Buddha or Muhammad and not a reformer, like Nāgārjuna or St Benedict. A hundred years after her death the miniature Church that she had established still continues to flourish, and though a faith confined to the country of its origin and claiming a relatively small number of adherents has not, for the student of comparative religion, the same importance as the religions that have spread over half the world, the fact that we can trace the whole history of Kono Tabi and its scriptures from the beginning gives it a peculiar interest. Linguistically, too, Kino's utterances, so laboriously transcribed, form an important document for the study of Owari dialect in the eighteenth century.

(*Bulletin of the School of Oriental Studies*, Vol 7, 1953.)

# THE CHINESE CINDERELLA STORY

*T*he earliest datable version of the Cinderella story anywhere in the world occurs in a Chinese book written about AD 850–860. As this version has hitherto been only very inadequately translated and commented upon, I have thought it worth while to make a fresh translation and to furnish such information as is necessary for a proper understanding of it. I shall also say rather more than is usual in such cases about the book in which the story is preserved and the circumstances under which a Chinese official came to write down a story which was, in fact, not Chinese, but which belonged to certain aborigines in the extreme south of China.

The author of the book in which the story occurs lived from about AD 800 to 863. He belonged to an influential family. His father, Tuan Wên-ch'ang, held many high posts both at the Capital and in the provinces, and acquired the reputation of having a special gift for managing the aborigines of the south. He died in 835, while serving as Controller of a large district in Sechwan. His son, Tuan Ch'eng-shih, had two passions: book-collecting and hunting. When the father held a high post in Sechwan, Tuan Ch'eng-shih, who was supposed to be helping his father in his official work, was always away on hunting expeditions. A secretary was sent to explain to him that this sort of thing could not be allowed to continue. Next day a present of pheasants or hares arrived for every member of his father's staff. Along with each present of game was a document recounting some story of former generations connected with the bird or beast in question; and no two recipients got the same story. Thus Tuan Ch'êng-shih proved that his devotion to sport was coupled with a great zest for acquiring out-of-the-way information. He afterwards held various posts at the Capital, was prefect of Chi-chou in Kiangsi, and finally held a position in the T'ai-ch'ang Ssu, the office which arranged the rites connected with imperial ancestor-worship. He wrote a book called *Yu Yang Tsa Tsu*, which might be translated *Miscellany of Forgotten Lore*. It is named after a mountain in Hunan to which some scholars are supposed to have retreated at the time when the wicked Emperor Shih-huang 'burnt the books'. According to this legend, they brought with them texts which no longer survive anywhere else and the cave where these are stored has sometimes been explored by adventurous travellers, who have come back with a store of out-of-the-way information.

The book shows a great interest in foreign things. There is a section on foreign plants, perfumes, etc., which was much used by Laufer in his book on Persian products imported into China. There are also many foreign stories – Korean, Persian, Turkic, Indian and Central Asiatic. He appears to give these stories just as they were told to him, without any attempt to adapt them to Chinese taste or ideas. The stories he tells deal almost exclusively with the supernatural. Some of them he quotes from books, others he got orally (and in such cases he often names his informant); occasionally he draws on his own experience. But the strange things actually witnessed by Tuan were not half so strange as those that he reports as having happened to his friends or to friends of his friends. His interest in such stories is of quite a different kind from that of modern European folklorists. He knows nothing of our fads, such as 'matriarchy', rites of passage, sun myths or the like. He is grieved, not thrilled, by intriguing instances of wide diffusion. Thus when he finds that a story commonly told about an eighth-century Chinese alchemist had previously been told in Benares about an Indian alchemist, he merely regards the later story as false information about the Chinese alchemist Ku Hsüan-chi, and warns his readers against accepting it, in a section of his book specially devoted to the correction of current mistakes.

Tuan, in fact, values the strange stories he tells not as literature nor as exotic samples of human fantasy, but as contributions to our knowledge of the hidden powers and influences that are all the time at work behind the stolid façade of everyday existence.

His Cinderella story runs as follows:

'Among the people of the south there is a tradition that before the Ch'in and Han dynasties there was a cave-master called Wu. The aborigines called the place the Wu cave. He married two wives. One wife died. She had a daughter called Yeh-hsien, who from childhood was intelligent and good at making pottery on the wheel. Her father loved her. After some years the father died, and she was ill-treated by her stepmother, who always made her collect firewood in dangerous places and draw water from deep pools. She once got a fish about two inches long, with red fins and golden eyes. She put it into a bowl of water. It grew bigger every day, and after she had changed the bowl several times she could find no bowl big enough for it, so she threw it into the back pond. Whatever food was left over from meals she put into the water to feed it. When she came to the pond, the fish always exposed its head and pillowed it on the bank; but when anyone else came, it did not come out. The stepmother knew about this, but when she watched for it, it did not once appear. So she tricked the girl, saying, "Haven't you worked hard! I am going to give you a new dress". She then made the girl change out of her tattered clothing. Afterwards she sent her to get water from another spring and, reckoning that it was several hundred leagues, the stepmother at her leisure put on her daughter's clothes, hid a sharp blade up her sleeve, and went to the pond. She called to the fish. The fish at once put its head out, and she chopped it off and killed it. The fish was now more than 10 feet long. She served it up and it tasted twice as good as an ordinary fish. She hid the bones under the dung-hill. Next day, when the girl came to the pond, no fish appeared. She howled with grief in the open countryside, and suddenly there appeared a man with his hair loose over his shoulders and coarse clothes. He came down from the sky. He consoled her, saying, "Don't howl! Your stepmother has killed the fish and its bones are under the dung. You go back, take the fish's bones and hide them in your room. Whatever you want, you have only to pray to them for it. It is bound to be granted." The girl followed his advice, and was able to provide herself with gold, pearls, dresses and food whenever she wanted them.

'When the time came for the cave-festival, the stepmother went, leaving the girl to keep watch over the fruit-trees in the garden. She waited till the stepmother was some way off, and then went herself, wearing a cloak of stuff spun from kingfisher feathers and shoes of gold. Her stepsister recognized her and said to the stepmother, "That's very like my sister". The stepmother suspected the same thing. The girl was aware of this and went away in such a hurry that she lost one shoe. It was picked up by one of the people in the cave. When the stepmother got home, she found the girl asleep, with her arms round one of the trees in the garden, and thought no more about it.

'This cave was near to an island in the sea. On this island was a kingdom called T'o-han. Its soldiers had subdued twenty or thirty other islands and it had a coast-line of several thousand leagues. The cave-man sold the shoe in T'o-han, and the ruler of T'o-han got it. He told those about him to put it on; but it was an inch too small even for the one among them that had the smallest foot. He ordered all the women in his kingdom to try it on; but there was not one that it fitted. It was light as down and made no noise even when treading on stone. The king of T'o-han thought the cave-man had got it unlawfully. He put him in prison and tortured him, but did not end by finding out where it had come from. So he throw it down at the wayside. Then they went everywhere[1] through all the people's houses and arrested them. If there was a woman's shoe, they arrested them and told the king of T'o-han. He thought it strange, searched the inner-rooms and found Yeh-hsien. He made her put on the shoe, and it was true.

'Yeh-hsien then came forward, wearing her cloak spun from halcyon feathers and her shoes. She was as beautiful as a heavenly being. She now began to render service to the king, and he took the fish-bones and Yeh-hsien, and brought them back to his country.

'The stepmother and stepsister were shortly afterwards struck by flying stones, and died. The cave people were sorry for them and buried them in a stone-pit, which was called the Tomb of the Distressed Women. The men of the cave made mating-offerings there; any girl they prayed for there, they got. The king of T'o-han, when he got back to his kingdom, made Yeh-hsien his chief wife. The first year the king was very greedy and by his prayers to the fish-bones got treasures and jade without limit. Next year, there was no response, so the

---

1 Something here seems to have gone slightly wrong with the text.

king buried the fish-bones on the seashore. He covered them with a hundred bushels of pearls and bordered them with gold. Later there was a mutiny of some soldiers who had been conscripted and their general opened (the hiding-place) in order to make better provision for his army. One night they (the bones) were washed away by the tide.

'This story was told me by Li Shih-yüan, who has been in the service of my family a long while. He was himself originally a man from the caves of Yung-chou and remembers many strange things of the South.'

It is evident that certain passages in this story need comment or explanation. I will deal with them in the order in which they occur. We are told that the events of the story took place 'before the Han and Ch'in dynasties'. This is merely a way of saying 'in the good old days' before the Chinese conquest of Hsi-yüan, the area with which the story deals. And here a slight digression is necessary. We must turn to the end of the story, where it is said that it was told to the author by an old family servant who was himself 'a man from the caves of Yung-chou'. Yung-chou corresponds to the modern Nan-ning, in the province of Kwangsi, about 100 miles north of the frontiers of Annam. It lay in a district that in the ninth century was called Hsi-yüan and the *New T'ang History* has a whole section devoted to the 'aborigines of Hsi-yüan'. In our story, Cinderella's father is referred to as a 'cave-owner', and the aborigines of this district are described by another T'ang writer in 821 as 'living in precipitous places on the mountain side' and 'calling themselves cave-owners'. It is possible that in the ninth century they still lived chiefly in caves. But in Sung times (tenth to thirteenth centuries) 'cave' had come simply to mean 'native settlement'. The *Sung History* enumerates eleven 'caves' ('native settlements') near Nan-ning. It is evident from the story that Cinderella lived in a house, not a cave, and that the term 'cave-owner' is applied to her father in an ethnic, not a literal, sense. We are told that his surname was Wu, and this was a well-known name in those parts. In AD 759 the poet Yüan Chieh, some of whose poems I translated in *170 Chinese Poems*, was prefect of Tao-chou, which lay just north of the district with which we are here concerned. The town was besieged by rebellious aborigines, one of whose leaders was called Wu Kung-ts'ao. He had, that is to say, the same surname as the cave-owner Wu of our story, and was at the head of the Hsi-yüan aborigines, whom he brought up from farther south. Wu Kung-ts'ao was eventually captured alive and the rebellion was suppressed. There is little doubt that it was to this same Wu family that Cinderella belonged.

The next point that arrests our attention is the statement that Cinderella's father had two wives. Chinese, of course, could only have one wife, though they might have several concubines. Some modern aborigines of southern China have more than one wife if they can afford to; but it is not clear in this story whether the father had two wives at once or merely took a second wife after the first died.

I do not think we can extract any information from Yeh-hsien's name, which is written with Chinese characters meaning Leaf Limit. It certainly does not look like a Chinese girl's name. The contemporary pronunciation would have been something like Zyap-han. Unfortunately we do not know what language the Hsi-yüan aborigines spoke, and consequently we cannot etymologize her name.

Yeh-hsien's skill in pottery is another non-Chinese trait. Pottery is usually regarded in China as man's work. Modern writers, both Chinese and European, about aborigines in this part of China are curiously silent about their pottery; if pottery were still women's work they would probably have noted it.

In connection with Yeh-hsien's fish, it is worth noting that in the Annamite and Sham versions there is a fishing competition between the two sisters. In some modern Chinese versions the friendly animal is a cow, which is a reincarnation of Cinderella's mother.

The 'festival' of this story corresponds, of course, to the ball of our English Cinderella story. The great festival of many of the aborigines in southern China took place in the spring. Among the aborigines of Kwangsi, however, it happened at the beginning of the Chinese tenth month (i.e. round about December 1st). It is a ceremony of ancestor-worship and at the same time a mating festival.

We next come to the shoe, which is indeed the turning-point of all true Cinderella stories. One might regard the mention of shoes as a non-primitive trait. It is unlikely that the Hsi-yüan aborigines usually wore shoes; their modern counterparts certainly do not. But the moderns do use straw sandals on ceremonial occasions; such sandals are, for example, described as part of the outfit of the shaman. The fact that shoes were not generally worn would have made the story additionally impressive. Moreover, they were 'gold shoes'. This was perhaps rather less impressive to the natives of those parts than to us. Hsi-yüan was an important gold-mining centre. The *History of the Sung Dynasty* gives the situation of a number of gold-mines in this neighbourhood, and the modern aborigines were apparently still wearing gold ornaments late in the nineteenth century, though this does not seem to be the case today.

In our story Cinderella marries the king of T'o-han. I do not think there is any doubt that this is the T'o-huan (a transcription of something like Tavan) of the T'ang histories. This was an Indianized kingdom on an island off the northern shore of the gulf of Siam, politically dependent upon the great Mon kingdom of Dvaravati, which occupied the central part of what is now Siam. The story, of course, reads as though the kingdom of T'o-han were on an island off the coast of Kwangsi or Kwangtung, quite close to Cinderella's 'cave'. But T'o-han is obviously the transcription of a foreign word; and in any case there was never a great island kingdom off the coast of southern China. This leads us to the conclusion that the story in its present form did not originate with the natives of Kwangsi, who had no 'kingdom of T'o-han' lying off their shores, but with the people of Dvaravati, who had as their close neighbour an island kingdom called T'o-huan. Whether the story came by sea to Canton or by land through Cambodia and Annam we do not know.

You will remember that, at the point where Cinderella is identified as the owner of the shoe, something has gone slightly wrong with the text. It seems, however, that the king must have ordered his servants to put the shoe at the wayside and watch to see if anyone came to take it. Apparently Yeh-hsien came and took the shoe, was followed and seen to go into a certain house, where she was duly discovered and identified.

The 'robe of halcyon feathers' of course at once reminds us of swan-maiden stories. But it is important to note that for the teller of the story a robe of feathers did not necessarily have mythical connotations. We are told, for example, by a seventeenth-century writer that some of the aborigines in Kwangtung and Kwangsi wore robes made of goose-feather and leaves. Again, when the story says that Cinderella looked 'beautiful as a heavenly person', we are once more reminded of the swan-maiden motif, for in the Japanese Nō play, The Robe of Feathers (*Hagoromo*), which deals with a typical 'swan-maiden' theme, it is this exact expression 'heavenly person', written as here, that is used to describe the heavenly visitant whose robe of feathers is stolen by the fisherman. There is, however, a possibility that the term 'heavenly person' in our story refers to a special institution of the Kwangsi natives; for we are told by an eighteenth-century writer that among some of them (the T'ung), the chief's 'daughter' is called 'the Heavenly Lady' and that it is her business to counter the magic of sorceresses. It is not, however, certain that the term 'heavenly person' refers in our story to any such institution. It is quite a natural one in Chinese and to Tuan Ch'êng-shih, who wrote the story down, it would certainly have suggested a Buddhist Angel (*apsaras*), such as those that are often to be seen swooping down from the sky, more or less head first, their draperies all a-flutter, in Buddhist paintings and on Buddhist stone-reliefs.

The episode in which the stepmother and stepsister are struck by flying stones reminds one of the flying-stone motif in Chinese poltergeist stories. It may perhaps turn out to be a general rule that when, as here, hostile phantasies are expressed in a story, they can go to extremes; the stones actually kill the objects of the aggrieved girl's hostility; but when similar hostility is expressed not in a story but in concrete tricks and manipulations, as in poltergeist phenomena, it stops short of the killing. Poltergeists in China (and I think elsewhere) are mischievous and destructive but not homicidal.

The next episode comes as rather a shock, demanding as it does a complete shift in the reader's sympathies. The spirits of the two wicked persecutors became dispensers of love-magic. To us it seems that a fragment of cult-origin myth has been arbitrarily inserted in the story, though in the minds of the aborigines there may well have been connections that are not apparent to us. The tomb of the stepmother and stepsister was called 'The Tomb of the Distressed Women'. The word used for 'distressed' (*ao*) is a rather unexpected one, and I wonder whether there has not been a confusion with the Yao word *ao*, which means 'two'. A 'tomb of the two women' was one of the sights of Kweilin, capital of Kwangsi in the ninth century. It was a considerable tumulus, apparently some 500 yards in circumference. It too was associated with a stepchild story, for the Two Women were the two wives of the mythical Chinese emperor Shun, who was maltreated by but triumphed over his step-relatives.

It seems likely that the tumulus which the aborigines associated with the Cinderella story was connected by the Chinese with their own favourite stepchild story. The story ends with a reference to the narrator, an old family servant called Li Shih-yüan, who was an aborigine from Nan-ning in Kwangsi. A disaster, which may have some bearing on how Li came into Tuan Ch'êng-shih's service, befell the aborigines in 821. The local military commander asked the Government for support in carrying out a large scale campaign against the Hsi-yüan aborigines. And here another famous Chinese writer comes on to the scene. Han Yü (AD 768–824) sent a petition to the Throne opposing the expedition. He said the aborigines gave no trouble when left alone: 'only when in danger do they band together in self-defence… They live in caves or behind earth-works in wild and remote places. Even if we completely exterminated them and took over their land, in what way would our own national interests be forwarded?' He hinted that the commander was merely looking for an easy way of getting the rewards (lands, money, titles, etc.) always accorded to leaders of successful campaigns. The petition was ignored, and in the autumn of 821 the aborigines were heavily defeated. Li Shih-yüan may have been the son of an aborigine captured in this campaign and bought as a slave by Tuan Ch'êng-shih's father. Slaves and servants in general were great disseminators of stories.

*How stories circulated*

There was, of course, an upward and a downward process. Folk-stories reached the upper classes through servants (as in the present case), through wet-nurses, who were peasant women, and through singing girls. Literate 'upper-class people, if they were struck by a story, often wrote it down. The return journey (from the upper classes to the people) was, I think, very largely facilitated by the drama. Dramatists used the stories that literary people had written down and officials gave dramatic performances, to which the common people were admitted, on birthdays, at weddings and for other purposes, such as to aid navigation.[1] So the peasants finally got their stories back again in a new form, and such stories (though they might have passed through every phase of literary treatment and dramatization) were still believed in as current happenings, and might at any moment be related as having happened recently in the next village. As another story, that of the White Snake is a better example of diffusion than Cinderella, which never, so far as I know, was made into a ballad or a play. I will make a short digression concerning the history of the White Snake theme.

There are two T'ang stories about a man who meets a lovely lady dressed in white. He marries her and at last discovers to his horror that she is a white snake. In the first half of the sixteenth century a similar story was being told by the blind story-teller T'ao Chên, as an origin-legend of the Thunder Peak Pagoda near Hangchow, the capital of Chekiang. In the first half of the eighteenth century it was retold in a literary form; this is the version of which I published a translation in *Horizon* (August 1946). In the second half of the eighteenth

---

1 In 1738 the level of the Grand Canal sank and some transport barges got stuck. The scene where Jade Lotus, heroine of the fourteenth-century drama, *The Thorn Hairpin*, throws herself into the river, was played in order to appease the river spirit. (See Chi Yün's *Yüeh-wei-ts'ao-t'ang Pi-chi*, XV, 4. Also, p. 81 above.)

century the story was staged as *The Thunder Peak Pagoda* and has ever since been a favourite subject of plays. It was also the subject of a long narrative ballad and of a shadow play. Finally came, at the beginning of the nineteenth century, a longish novel on the subject, translated in 1834 by Stanislas Julien, under the title *Les Deux Couleuvres-Fées*.

But despite all these literary versions, a nineteenth-century author[1] tells as an actual occurrence (*c.* 1730), the story of a poor man from a village near Huchow (north of Hangchow) whose wife by her business acumen made him one of the richest men in the neighbourhood. But on the fifth of the fifth month she always hid herself, and it was discovered that on this day she was not a woman, but a snake. The village schoolmaster advised the husband (who was apparently unperturbed by the discovery) that snake-wives eventually brought ill-luck. The snake-woman resented the school-master's interference and that night she disappeared and was never seen again.

This is manifestly an echo of the stage-play, but it is an unconscious one, and the literary theme is well on its way towards being a folk-theme again.

### The modern Chinese Versions of Cinderella

I have not had access in the original to any of the current stories. One of them is translated in Eberhard's *Chinese Fairy Tales* (p. 17). Except for the stepchild situation and the slipper-motif, it has very little resemblance to the T'ang story. Eberhard also refers briefly in his *Typen Chinesischer Volksmärchen* (p. 52) to a number of other current oral versions. Where the provenance is known they all seem to come from near Canton, that is to say from the same part of

---

1 Ch'ien Yung in his *Li Yüan Ts'ung Hua*, p. 220.

China as the T'ang version. An example from Shantung in the north 'contains only one of the motifs'; Eberhard does not say which. But Professor R D Jameson speaks of 'the oral versions I have found in the north'.[1] Unfortunately he tells us nothing about them. Until the folk-stories of China have been more completely collected it would be rash to assert that the story belongs at present particularly to the extreme south of China.

It is not, however, the purpose of this paper to discuss either the distribution or the origin of the story. I have merely tried to put the T'ang version, the earliest datable version known to us, at the disposal of folk-lorists, paying rather more attention than is usual to the narrator and to the writer-down of the story.

## APPENDIX

*Other foreign stories recorded by Tuan Ch'êng-shih*

### 1. *A Korean Story*

The Chin family is the noblest lineage in Silla (a kingdom in south-eastern Korea). One of its members, Chin Ko, says that he had a remote ancestor called P'ang I. Pang I had a younger brother who was very rich; but the brothers lived separately and the elder brother P'ang I had to beg for his clothing and food. So one of the people of the country gave him a piece of spare land, an acre in extent, and he then asked his younger brother to give him silkworm-eggs and grain-seed. The younger brother boiled them before giving them to him; but P'ang I did not know of this. When the silkworm season came, only one egg hatched, somewhat over an inch long. In ten days it was as big as a cow. It ate the leaves of several trees and still

---

[1] *Three Lectures on Chinese Folklore*, Peking, 1932, p. 60.

had not enough. As the days went by the silkworms from a hundred leagues round came flying to settle near P'ang I's house. People called it the giant silkworm and said that it was the king of the silkworms. All the neighbours came and pulled silk from it.

[The younger brother, knowing of this, waited for an opportunity and killed the silkworm.][1]

Of the corn, only one stalk grew. Its ears were more than a foot long. P'ang I watched over it all the time; but suddenly it was broken off by a bird that carried it off in its beak. P'ang I followed the bird up a mountain for five or six leagues. The bird flew into a crevice in the rocks. The sun had set and it was now quite dark; so he stayed beside the rock. At midnight, the moon shone and he saw a lot of little boys dressed in red playing together. One little boy said, 'What thing would you like?' Another said, 'I should like some wine'. The first little boy then brought out a golden awl and struck the rock with it, whereupon wine and cups were both provided. Another said, 'I want something to eat'. He struck again, whereupon cakes, soup and broiled meat ranged themselves on top of the rock. When they had eaten and drunk for some time, they scattered, having first put the golden awl into a crevice in the rock. In great delight P'ang I took the awl and went home. By striking with it he got everything he wanted. In this way he became as rich as the most powerful man of the land. He often supplied his younger brother with pearls, and the younger brother began to regret the trick that he had played on P'ang I in the matter of the silkworms and corn. However, he said to P'ang I, 'Try that trick about the silkworms and corn on me. Perhaps I shall then get a golden awl like yours.' P'ang I thought this silly and remonstrated with him. But it was no good; so he did

[1] This sentence has become displaced in the text.

as his brother asked. From the eggs the brother only got one silkworm, of the usual size. From the corn-seed he only got one stalk that grew. It was almost ripe when it too was carried off by a bird. The brother was delighted and followed the bird into the mountain. At the place where the bird went into [a crack], he met a lot of demons. They were very angry and said, 'This is the man who stole our golden awl'. They then seized the brother and said to him, 'Would you rather build us a wall of chaff 3 *pan* (about 20 English feet) high or have a nose 10 feet long?' The brother said he would rather build the wall of chaff. For three days he toiled, with nothing to eat. But he had no success, and at last he begged the demons to have mercy on him. But they pulled his nose, and it became as long as an elephant's trunk. When he went home, the people of the land were amazed and gathered round to stare at him. He was so embarrassed that he died. Afterwards one of [P'ang I's] descendants for a joke struck with the awl and asked for wolf's dung. At this, thunder rolled, the earth shook and the awl disappeared.

## 2. *Turkic Story*

The ancestor of the Turks was Shê-mo. The lake-spirit Shê-li displayed his divinity to the west of the cave called A-shih-tê. To Shê-mo a divine wonder happened; every day at dusk the lake-spirit's daughter sent a white deer to fetch him. Shê-mo went with it into the lake; at dawn it escorted him out (of the water). This went on for twenty or thirty years. One night when the tribe was going to have a great hunt, the lake-spirit ('s daughter) said to Shê-mo, 'Tomorrow during the hunt a white deer with golden horns will come out of the cave where your ancestors were born. If your arrow hits this deer's wondrous form you will be able to go on visiting me. But if you do not hit the deer, it is all over between us.'

When day came and he entered the beaters' ring a white deer with golden horns did indeed start up in the birth-cave. Shê-mo told his servants to make the ring secure; but just as the deer was bounding out, one of the beaters killed it. Shê-mo was angry and with his own hand slew the headman A-jo and as he did so swore, saying, 'For ever afterwards, now that this (deer) has been killed, there must be human sacrifices offered up to Heaven.' He took A-jo's sons and grandsons and slew them in sacrifice. Till this day when the Turks perform human sacrifice they use men of the A-Jo tribe.

So Shê-mo slew A-jo and in the evening went back to the lake-spirit's daughter. But she told Shê-mo, 'With your hand you have slain a man. You stink with the smell of blood. All is over between us.'

### 3. *The King of Persia's Daughter*

The city of Vadiya[1] in Tukhara was built by an ancient king of Persia called Ghushtashp. The first time he built this city, no sooner had he finished it than it fell to pieces. The king sighed over and over again, asking himself, 'What sin have I done that Heaven should unmake the city I have built?'

The king had a young daughter called Najek, who seeing that her father was unhappy said to him, 'King, have you enemies on your frontiers?' The king shook his head. 'I am the king of Persia,' he said, 'and more than a thousand kingdoms are subject to me. But now I have come to Tukhara and want to build this city, that I may be remembered for ten thousand generations; but I cannot do it. That is why I am sad.' 'Do not be sad,' she said, 'but tomorrow tell your workmen to follow me, and I will show them where to build.'

1 This seems to be a name for Balkh. This is the only known reference in Chinese literature to one of the legendary early Persian kings of the *Shah-nameh* epic.

Next morning she rose and walked to the North-East and cut the little finger of her right hand. All day she walked, till the plan of the city was drawn on the ground by the blood that fell from her hand. They built the city where she showed, and this time it did not fall.

Then she turned into a lake-spirit, and the lake she haunted is still there, near to the city walls, its water clear as a mirror. It is a small lake; you can go all round it by walking five hundred steps.

(*Folklore*, 1947)

# CHINA'S GREATEST WRITER

*I* am going to try to interest you in China's greatest prose-writer. This does not sound as though it ought to be a difficult thing to do. It is, of course, a handicap that I cannot quote him to you in the original, and the picture I shall present will inevitably tend to be that of the man rather than the writer. But fortunately Han Yü, quite apart from his literary eminence, is of singular interest as a human being and this will compensate, I hope, for the special difficulties presented by both the form and the content of his best-known works.

Han Yü (who was born in AD 768) is famous above all as a great master of style. The style so much admired is that of a thousand years before his time, which he succeeded in more or less convincingly imitating. I do not think that we in Europe today would be inclined to give him many marks for that. It is not possible to cite an exact parallel, because English is a young language compared with Chinese. But if we picked up a contemporary author and thought at first we were reading Sir Thomas Browne, we should regard the writer as a clever pasticheur; but we do not consider such imitations as very difficult things to achieve and do not accord a high place to those who can produce them.

It was not however a case of mere archaism. The language that Han Yü successfully imitated was that of the Confucian Classics, and the nearest parallel in our culture is that of writers, such as Doughty, who have been highly thought of because their style resembled that of the Bible. We are likely then to be a little grudging about Han Yü's form; when we come to his content even more formidable difficulties, this time of an intellectual rather than an aesthetic nature, obstruct our appreciation. Briefly, Han Yü's position is this:

In the dim past there was a series of Supermen who invented morals, civilization and culture in general. This was the Way of the Supermen, and when they ceased to appear in the world it was handed down in some unexplained way to a series of Inspired Teachers. The greatest of these was Confucius; then came Mencius, who lived more than 100 years later, and last of all came Yang Hsiung, who died in AD 18. Yang Hsiung's only claim to figure in the series is that he produced a book called *Model Sayings*, which is a clever imitation of the style of the *Analects* of Confucius. No one, I think, has ever pretended that the content of the sayings is of any interest. After Yang Hsiung there was a complete blank for nearly 800 years. No one transmitted the Way of the Supermen; there were plenty of Inspired Teachers, but they were occupied (and this seemed deplorable to Han Yü) in transmitting the Way of a foreigner called Buddha. Was it possible, after the lapse of so many centuries, to pick up the thread?

Han Yü became convinced at the age of about 30 that it was; he became convinced that Heaven had entrusted him with a mission to transmit the Way of the Supermen, and he set up as a teacher in the old style, not indeed claiming to be as great as Confucius and Mencius, but definitely regarding himself as being on the same lines. The claim was ridiculed; it was pointed out that Mencius himself had said, 'The trouble about people is that they are always wanting to set up as other people's teachers'; and another writer of the period says in a letter dating from 813 that everyone now regarded Han Yü as completely mad. Even his little circle of followers saw difficulties. One of them wrote suggesting that he would fill his role more convincingly if he gave up gambling, and also raised objection to the frivolous and fanciful nature of his general conversation. About the gambling he was inclined to agree; but he would not admit that jokes were inconsistent with his calling. Even in the Confucian Classics, he said, joking is mentioned, and he quoted the poem from the *Book of Songs* in which it is said:

> How free, how easy
> He leant over his chariot-rail!
> How cleverly he chaffed and joked
> And yet was never rude.

Much that he wrote and did still causes similar uneasiness. He lived in an age when the writing of toadying letters to people in power was the normal means of obtaining a job; but Han Yü rose to heights of cadging and toadying which even to the recipients of his applications must have seemed rather far-fetched. Pious Confucians who have always been deadly enemies of the palace eunuchs are shocked to find him addressing in terms of unctuous respect a eunuch who afterwards became notorious for deeds of ferocious cruelty. He at any rate had the courage to change his mind. An official, a relative of the Emperor's, whose tender regard for the welfare of the people he eulogized in 803, is depicted by him in 813 as having been a monster of stony-hearted extortion and oppression. On several occasions he showed great physical courage, as when in 821 he insisted on risking his life in order to carry out a mission to the camp of a rebel commander, whom he boldly denounced in front of all his troops. On the other hand there was an unfortunate incident when he got stuck on the Hua Shan, China's most precipitous mountain, and was too frightened to go either up or down. He had already resigned himself to his doom and dropped a letter of farewell to his family into the fearful abyss, when his companions succeeded in coaxing him down into safety.

The same friend who objected to his jokes (which, judging from the one humorous essay that survives, may well have been rather ponderous) also urged him to reinstate the Way of the Supermen and deal a final death-blow to Buddhism by writing a book; otherwise his influence would never extend beyond a small circle of friends and admirers. He replied that he agreed in principle but that there was no hurry; he would write the book in his old age. He did, however, when he was about 35, write a series of short essays (on The Way, on Inborn Qualities, on Man, and on Spirits); and it is these, together with the great attack on Buddhism written some fifteen years later, that were destined to become the most famous models of Chinese prose. They are, as I have said, written in the language of the fourth and third centuries BC. Han Yü regarded himself as a 'transmitter', but his conception of transmission is a rather curious one. For example, the question 'Is human nature good?' was one of the main problems of early Chinese philosophy. I think that even some of us who are not Logical Positivists may well doubt whether such a question has any meaning. But every Chinese thinker was expected to answer it, and Mencius had stoutly maintained that human nature is good.

As Han Yü claimed to be the modern representative of the line of orthodox tradition to which Mencius belonged, one would have expected him, at any rate on such a vital issue as this, to be more or less in agreement with Mencius. But not at all. He tells us, without any attempt to reconcile the contradiction, that there are three kinds of nature: good, bad and indifferent. In the essay on 'The Way he maintains that what he means by the expression 'The Way and its Power' was what any ordinary person would mean by it; whereas the Taoists used this expression in a private sense of their own. As a matter of fact, just the opposite is the case. The expression 'The Way and its Power', enshrined in the title of the famous Taoist scripture, the *Tao Tê Ching*, i.e. 'Book of The Way and its Power', had in Han Yü's day come to be inseparably connected with Taoism, and it was Han Yü himself who insisted on using it in a 'private sense' of his own.

Let us follow out the main events of his life a little farther. In 804 he protested courageously against the terrorization practised by the palace eunuchs upon the population of the capital and also against the crushing burdens of over-taxation. He was banished to a place about 100 miles north-west of Canton. Recalled to the capital in 806 he became a university professor there and at the secondary capital at Lo-yang. In 813 by a curious irony (for no man can ever have had less sense of historic fact) he was made an official historian and called upon to write the history of the Emperor Shun Tsung, who reigned during the one year 805. Such works were, of course, written in current, modern language. The great master of archaism had, so to speak, to appear in mufti. The effect was electric; suddenly, writing about events he had lived through in the language of his own day, Han Yü displays a brilliant and pungent anecdotal gift. *The Record of Shun Tsung's Reign* is one of the liveliest books that China has ever produced. Though nominally dealing with only one year, it frequently carries the story well back into the eighth century, and passages taken from it enliven large stretches of the complete histories written in later times.

A haunting figure in the book is Wei Ch'h-i, the timorous nonentity whom the clique in power had raised to the position of Prime Minister. After the fall of this clique, Wei lingered on as Prime Minister. But he and everyone knew that he only held the post on sufferance. 'He was still Prime Minister', writes Han Yü, 'but felt so unsure of his position that he hardly dared to breathe and every footfall he heard made him turn pale with fright. Even in the days of his early obscurity he was obsessed by the idea that his career would end in banishment, and he had a horror of mentioning the name of any place south of the mountains. Later on it was noticed that when he and his fellow secretaries were looking at maps of China, so soon as they came to a map of the south, Wei shut his eyes and would not look. When he became Prime Minister and took over his new official quarters, he noticed at once that there was a map on the wall. For a week he could not bring himself to examine it. When at last he screwed up his courage and looked, he found it was a map of Yai-chou. And sure enough it was to Yai-chou that he was banished in the end, and at Yai-chou that he died when not much over 40.' Yai-chou was in the island of Hainan; it was in T'ang times the remotest and most dreaded place of banishment.

It will have struck you that his methods are here those of the dramatist rather than of the historian. It was indeed complained, when he first presented his history, that he had not taken enough trouble to get his facts right. He puts the blame, rather meanly as we should be inclined to think, on collaborators who had helped him to collect information.

Leaving out perforce many episodes in his middle life, I will come at once to the famous affair of 'Buddha's bones'. It was a custom that once every so many years a Buddha relic kept at a temple near the capital should be brought to the Emperor's palace. The occasion was a great popular festival and huge crowds witnessed the magnificent processions to and from the palace. In 819, Han Yü protested against this practice in what is perhaps the most celebrated of his writings. The basis of his attack was that Buddhism was a foreign religion. He thus takes up a narrow, nationalistic standpoint that is quite alien to the liberal, humanistic spirit typical of Confucianism at its best. His other main argument was that imperial patronage of Buddhism had always been followed by disaster. This was simply untrue; incidentally it was equivalent to the *lèse-majesté* of saying that the present Emperor was heading for disaster. Han Yü was banished once more, wrote an abject apology to the Emperor, and in less than a year was recalled. In 824 he died at the age of 56.

Han Yü was adored by a small group of followers and intimate friends; but what strikes me most is his own boundless admiration for these disciples. He did not found a school; several of his followers were older than himself, and only one, his nephew by marriage, Li Ao, long survived him. But Li Ao disgraced himself by smuggling Buddhist ideas into his theories about human nature, and became the one black sheep among the disciples.

(*Listener*, May 1947.)

# BLAKE THE TAOIST

Some twenty years ago the Chinese poet Hsü Chih-mo took down a book from my shelves and after reading a few lines he exclaimed, 'This man is a Taoist!' The book was the long prophetic poem *Milton*, by William Blake. In his excitement he bent back the pages of the book at the place where he had opened it, and even today the book still opens of itself at the page which made Hsü cry out in astonishment, 'This man is a Taoist!' The words he had read were these: 'There is a place where contrarities are equally true. This place is called Beulah. It is a pleasant lovely shadow where no dispute can come.' We both thought at once of the second chapter of the Taoist book *Chuang Tzu*, which bears the title *Chi Wu Lun*, rendered in the standard English translation 'Discourse on the Identity of Contraries'. When *Chuang Tzu* was written the old beliefs, centering round sacrifice to the ancestors, were fading away. It was a time of bitter controversy – the so-called 'warring of the Hundred Schools'. Each School sought continually for fresh arguments by which to convert its adversaries, but the adversaries remained unconvinced. From this empty strife the Taoists escaped in vision (*ming*) to the realm of Tao, in which 'Is' and 'Is not', 'So' and 'Not So' are smoothed away. Blake too lived at a time when traditional beliefs and the forms of society from which they sprang were crumbling, and controversy raged. He, too, through imagination, which corresponds to what the Taoists call 'vision' sought a realm 'where no disputes can come'. In the passage of *Milton* that follows the words I have quoted already ('There is a place where contrarieties are equally true') Blake conveys through the simile of a lovely morning, the transcendent bliss of escape from the realm of contradiction:

Thou hearest the nightingale begin the song of spring.
The lark sitting upon his earthy bed, just as the morn
Appears, listens silent; then springing from the waving
    cornfield, loud
He leads the choir of day: trill, trill, trill, trill,
Mounting upon the wings of light into the great expanse,
Re-echoing against the lovely blue and shining heavenly shell,
His little throat labours with inspiration; every feather
On throat and breast and wings vibrates with the effluence
    divine.
All Nature listens silent to him, and the awful sun
Stands still upon the mountain looking on this little bird
With eyes of soft humility and wonder, love and awe.
Then loud from their green covert: all the birds begin their
    song;
The thrush, the linnet and the goldfinch, robin and the wren
Awake the sun from his sweet reverie upon the mountain.
The nightingale again assays his song, and through the day
And through the night warbles luxuriant, every bird of song
Attending his loud harmony with admiration and love...
Thou perceivest the flowers put forth their precious odours,
And none can tell how from so small a centre come such
    sweets,
Forgetting that within that centre Eternity expands
Its ever-during doors...

First, e'er the morning breaks, joy opens in the flowery
    bosoms,
Joy even to tears, which the sun rising dries, first the wild
    thyme
And meadowsweet, downy and soft waving among the reeds,
Light-springing on the air lead the sweet dance; they wake
The honeysuckle sleeping on the oak, the flaunting beauty
Revels along upon the wind; the whitethorn, lovely may,
Opens her many lovely eyes, listening, the rose still sleeps,
None dare to wake her. Soon she bursts her crimson-
    curtained bed
And comes forth in the majesty of beauty; every flower,
The pink, the jessamine, the wall-flower, the carnation,
The jonquil, the mild lily opes her heavens, every tree
And flower and herb soon fill the air with an innumerable
    dance,
Yet all in order sweet and lovely. Men are sick with love.

The Taoists believed that truth could only be seen through
'vision', through what Blake calls Imagination. Their bugbears
were the intellectualists of the day – the logician Hui Tzu and
the eclectic Kung-sun Lung, who claimed to have 'mastered
all the philosophies'. 'Abandon learning and there will be no
more grieving,' says Lao Tzu. Blake had the same distrust of
purely intellectual processes and of those who exalted such
processes at the expense of Imagination. His particular
bugbears were the French philosophers Voltaire and
Rousseau:

        Mock on, mock on Voltaire, Rousseau;
        Mock on, mock on, 'tis all in vain!
        You throw the sand against the wind,
        And the wind throws it back again.
        And every sand becomes a gem

Reflected in the beams divine;
Blown back they blind the mocking eye,
But still in Israel's paths they shine.

The atoms of Democritus
And Newton's particles of light
Are sands upon the Red Sea shore,
Where Israel's tents do shine so bright.

'Prisons,' says Blake, 'are built with the stones of Law.' Here, too, the Taoists are on his side, for they believed that the legendary sages of antiquity and the Confucians who honoured them had, by the invention of law and morality, destroyed the natural happiness of men, and not only their happiness, but also their 'natural powers' and 'inborn faculties'. The prohibitions and restraints that the moralists imposed created criminality: 'Saintliness and wisdom,' says a Taoist writer, 'were the clasp and catch that fastened the prisoner's cangue; goodness and duty were the bolt and eye that fastened his gyves.' The 'Sages and Confucians' of the Taoists are the kings and priests of Blake's poems – sanctimonious busybodies who write 'Thou shalt not!' over the door of Life. Here is Blake's poem called *The Garden of Love*:

I went to the Garden of Love
And saw what I never had seen:
A chapel was built in the midst,
Where I used to play in the green.

And the gates of this chapel were shut
And 'Thou shalt not' writ over the door;
So I turned to the Garden of Love

That so many sweet flowers bore.

And I saw it was filled with graves
And tombstones, where flowers should be,
And priests in black gowns were walking their
    rounds
And binding with briars my joys and desires.

The Taoists were fond of paradoxes. 'The greatest traveller does not know where he has got to; the greatest sight-seer does not know what he is looking at,' says Lieh Tzu. 'The perfect door has neither bolt nor bar,' says Lao Tzu. Blake used the same method, as in his proverbs, 'The road of excess leads to the palace of wisdom'; 'If the fool would persist in his folly he would become wise'. Let me, as I have mentioned Blake's proverbs, quote some more of them to you, for they lead us to the very heart of Blake's philosophy. I will begin with some that deal with imagination or what the Taoists call Vision (*ming*):

What is now proved was once only imagined.
Eternity is in love with the productions of Time,
One thought fills immensity.
Everything possible to be believed is an image of truth.
No bird soars too high if he soars with his own wings.

And here are some of the ethical as opposed to the metaphysical proverbs:

Exuberance is beauty.
He who desires but acts not breeds pestilence.
You never know what is enough unless you know what is more than enough.

This doctrine of 'exuberance' is definitely un-Taoist; but in his proverb 'The most sublime act is to set another before you' Blake reminds us of many Taoist maxims about the importance, both for states and individuals, of 'getting behind' and 'getting underneath'.

And finally, here is a prose passage from *The Last Judgment*, written about 1810:

'The Last Judgment is an overwhelming of bad art and science. Mental things alone are real; what is called corporeal, nobody knows of its dwelling-place, it is in fallacy and its existence an imposture. Where is the existence, outside of mind or thought? Where is it but in the mind of a fool? Some people flatter themselves that there will be no Last Judgment and that bad art will be adopted and mixed with good art, that error or experiment will make a part of Truth… I will not flatter them; error is created, Truth is eternal. Error, or creation, will be burnt up and then, and not till then, Truth and Eternity will appear. It is burnt up the moment men cease to behold it. I assert for myself that I do not behold the outward Creation and that to me it is hindrance, not action. It is as dirt upon my feet – no part of me. "What?" it will be questioned, "when the sun rises do you not see a disc of fire somewhat like a guinea?" O no, no, I see an innumerable company of the heavenly host crying, "Holy, holy, holy is the Lord God Almighty". I question not my corporeal or vegetative eye any more than I would question a window concerning a sight. I look through it and not with it.' Is not all this summed up in Chuang Tzu's one saying: 'The eye envies the mind'?

I have said enough to show that Blake's philosophy has very strong affinities with Taoism. Could he, you will ask have actually been influenced by Taoist texts? The only such text to which he could possibly have had access was the *Tao Tê Ching*. A Latin version of this, made by a Portuguese in the second half of the eighteenth century, was acquire by the Royal Society of London in 1788. It had belonged to Matthew Raper, who was Chief of Council of the East India Company's establishment at Canton from 1777 till 1781 Raper, in turn, acquired it from the Jesuit missionary Joseph de Grammont, who was at Canton from 1785 to 1790. The work of this anonymous Portuguese is far more than a translation. It is a detailed attempt, founded upon the early seventeenth-century edition of the *Tao Tê Ching* called *Lao Tzu I* ('Wings of Lao Tzu'), to interpret the book in terms of Western mysticism. This manuscript would have excited Blake profoundly. But it is doubtful if he knew enough Latin to read it; and if he had read it he would almost certainly have left some record of the fact. But it is not impossible that some knowledge of Lao Tzu's ideas had reached him in an indirect way, through conversation with someone who had read the manuscript. Blake knew several members of the Royal Society, including Joseph Priestley, the discoverer of oxygen. He may well have questioned them about the manuscript, the acquisition of which by the Royal Society was prominently announced in *Philosophical Transactions*, the journal in which the Society published its proceedings.

Thus a Taoist text may have influenced Blake, though this is very uncertain. It is on the other hand quite certain that Blake's works could throw a very important light on Taoist texts. It has often been said that different parts of such works, for example, of *Chuang Tzu*, cannot be by the same hand because they express contradictory ideas. Now Blake's works, about the authenticity of which there is not the slightest doubt, constantly show the most surprising contradictions, both in his use of terms and symbols, and in his ideas. 'Satan', for example, sometimes stands for what Blake regards as good and sometimes for all that is evil. Terms like 'God' and 'Angel' he uses sometimes in their ordinary sense and sometimes in a meaning peculiar to his own system. In short, the study of Blake proves (what we might in any case have suspected) that mystics are not always consistent, and that if in a given work Confucius is sometimes derided and sometimes treated as the fountain of all wisdom, this does not necessarily mean that the book in question is by a number of different hands.

(*Broadcast*, January 1948.)

# HISTORY AND RELIGION

his is a belated note on the exchange of views published by D T Suzuki and Hu Shih in the April 1953 number of *Philosophy East and West*. I write it because I believe it is possible to go even further than Van Meter Ames (in his article of April 1954) toward making these two ardent workers understand one another. I take it that the aim of Suzuki's many works in English has been to draw the West toward Zen and the non-rational approach which, like all forms of religious experience, Zen demands. No one could deny that in this task he has been eminently successful. The current interest in and comfort derived from Zen in America and Europe are due almost solely to his long series of writings. None of the defects in them which scholars have noted in any way detract from their efficacy as propaganda (and I am not using the word in any derogatory sense) for the Zen attitude to life. Hu, on the other hand, writes primarily as a historian, as one who is passionately interested not only in finding out what really happened but also in discovering the sequence in which things happened. Religious writers are sometimes apt to forget how much they owe to secular scholars. In the present case it was Hu, after all, who first discovered the T'ang Dynasty Zen writings in the Pelliot collection and who set going the whole train of research which has made clear to us what the early history of the Zen sect in China, long falsified by Zen writers themselves, really was. The influence of these discoveries is apparent in many of Suzuki's later writings, despite the fact that to him 'Zen is above space-time relations and naturally above historical facts'. If this were really so, the proper course for Suzuki to take would seem to be to avoid history altogether. Even to say 'once upon a time', as in the fairy stories, would from his point of view be too historical, for it would imply a past and a present. Instead, he has always given the reader a great deal of history. But a writer who is hostile to history (at any rate, in connection with the subject about which he writes) is not likely to be a very good historian. An instance occurs to me in which Suzuki breaks an obvious and elementary rule of historical research, namely, that evidence is valuable in proportion as it dates from a time near the event in question and valueless if it is separated from this event by hundreds of years. In *The Zen Doctrine of No-Mind*[1] he gives as his authority for the dates of Bodhidharma (sixth century AD) an author called Ch'i-sung, who lived in the eleventh century.

But is the attitude that Zen is 'above historical facts' really a Zen attitude at all and not, rather, a personal prejudice? It seems to me that this separation of the mundane and the transcendental, of the finite from the infinite, comes of an attitude that almost every one of the old Zen writers has warned us against. Surely the whole burden of their teaching is that Buddha does not exist apart from the World, nor the World apart from Buddha. Again and again, when a disciple asks for a definition of 'Buddha' the Master replies by diyerting his attention to some commonplace object or some

---

1 D T Suzuki, *The Zen Doctrine of No-Mind*, The Significance of the Sutra of Hui-neng (Wei Lang) (London: Rider and Company, 1949), p. 9.

banal activity of daily life. 'What is Buddha?' 'Let's have a cup of tea!'

'To set up what you like against what you dislike – this is the disease of the mind,' says Sêng-ts'an whom I quote in Suzuki's own translation. Suzuki dislikes history (at any rate, when it is applied to Zen) and likes legends. He even seems to feel it to be a kind of blasphemy to disentangle fact from fiction. Hu has (it appears) pointed out that most of what we are told about the culture-hero Fu Ta-shih (AD 497–569, according to tradition, and inventor of the prayer-wheel) belongs to popular legend, and the poems attributed to him are in reality of much later date. Suzuki is moved to say: Fu Ta-shih 'does not vanish even when thickly enveloped in the heavy fogs over New York these winter mornings… Hu Shih kills Fu Ta-shih with his *gāthā*, which however remains quite eloquent even to this day'. If Zen is 'above history', why should it matter so much to Suzuki whether the songs in question are by a Mr Fu in the sixth century or by an anonymous poet in the eighth century? Why should it move him to this display of what, on the analogy of pyrotechnics, I can only call *prajñā*-technics? As for the verses themselves, the one about 'the bridge flows, but the water stands still', referred to by Suzuki, seems to me one of those lapses into mechanical paradox to which in China Taoists and Buddhists alike were rather too prone. For strangeness I much prefer his landscape where

> The fiercest wind does not stir the trees,
> A drum is beaten but no sound is heard,
> The sun rises, but the trees cast no shadow

Incidentally if we accept the legend of Fu Ta-shih as history we are placed in a dilemma. On the one hand, we can then accept as fact the story about Fu and the nun. One day he caught a nun stealing vegctables from his garden. In her greed she took more than she could carry in her arms and began to drop them in her flight. Fu went to the house, fetched a basket and caught her up, saying, 'Wouldn't this be a help to you?' But, on the other hand, we have to admit that in order to raise funds for repairing a monastery he sold his wife and two children by auction. I do not think Suzuki has ever discussed the subject, but I have a feeling he would (to use his own term) 'kill' the second story and keep the first, which, one cannot deny, 'remains quite eloquent even to this day', though it is in a tradition of Chinese super-goodness that originated in Confucianism rather than in Buddhism.

Where I feel that Hu, in his inveterate love of the reasonable, goes too far is in his contention that Zen sayings in general have a rational meaning. He produces a handful of cases where this is so, but, if one reads through several hundred *kung-an* (Japanese, kōan), questions for meditation, of the tenth century onward, it seems to me it is very seldom true that there is any rational meaning at all. They are in most cases simply verbal devices for breaking down the commonsense everyday view of things, in order to make room for what Suzuki calls '*prajñā*-intuition'.

Obviously the antinomy revealed in the April 1953 discussion is not one that is confined to the two distinguished people there concerned. Some of us remember the difficulties in which the Ligue des Fois, originally founded, I think, as the League of Faiths by Younghusband in England, became involved when it was discovered that some of its members regarded it as an organization for carrying on historical research, while others were only concerned with introducing into Europe the religious ideas of the East or with using a supposed basic identity of all religions as a lever to international goodwill. Well known, too, is the disquiet caused in some circles at Oxford when Radhakrishnan, whose role had been essentially that of an interpreter of the East to the

West, was succeeded in the Spalding Chair by a scholar who announced his intention of functioning simply as a scholar. But, to parody Han-shan:

> Water and ice do one another no harm;
> History and religion – both alike are good.

After all, every Zen Master who has ever existed lived in time and space, was a man of T'ang or Sung or Ashikaga times, a man of Honan or Kuangtung or Kyoto, and it was not in some transcendental existence, but to working and sleeping, eating his rice and sipping his tea, that his *satori*, enlightenment, could be incorporated. And surely the case of the artist is much the same. One cannot communicate Beethoven's musical *satori* by tracing his movements in time and space. Yet, no one thinks it 'sinful' or even irrelevant to inquire into the history of his life and relate it to what was going on in the world around. Some modern Zenists would think this analogy between Zen and music frivolous. But it certainly would not have been thought so in ancient China, for example, at Hangchow in the thirteenth century, when art was so often discussed in terms of Zen. Suzuki need not feel that he is a 'sinner' (he actually uses this word) if he has sometimes dabbled in history, for apart from the mundane there is no transcendental. Still less need he ask Hu to join him in his *peccavi*, for if there were no Hus there would be no Suzukis.

*(Philosophy East and West*, April 1955.)

# NOTES ON TRANSLATION

*I* shall begin by saying something that seems obvious, but that cannot really be so obvious or it would not be so often ignored and even contradicted. Different kinds of translation are needed for different purposes. If one is translating a legal document all one needs to do is to convey the meaning; but if one is translating literature one has to convey feeling as well as grammatical sense. The author puts his feelings – exasperation, pity, delight – into the original. They are there in his rhythm, his emphasis, his exact choice of words, and if the translator does not *feel* while he reads, and simply gives a series of rhythmless dictionary meanings, he may think he is being 'faithful', but in fact he is totally misrepresenting the original.

Almost at the end of the *Bhagavad Gita* there is a passage of great power and beauty in which, instructed by the God, the warrior Arjuna at last overcomes all his scruples. There is a war on, he is a soldier and must fight even though the enemy are his friends and kinsmen. This is what various standard translations make him say:

(1) O Unfallen One! By your favour has my ignorance been destroyed, and I have gained memory (of my duties); I

am (now) free from doubt; I shall now do (fight) as told by you!

(2) Destroyed is my delusion; through Thy grace, O Achutya, knowledge is gained by me. I stand forth free from doubt. I will act according to Thy word.

(3) My bewilderment has vanished away; I have gotten remembrance by Thy Grace, O Never-Falling. I stand free from doubt. I will do Thy word.

(4) My bewilderment is destroyed; I have gained memory through thy favour, O stable one. I am established; my doubt is gone; I will do thy word.

In addition to being totally without rhythm No. 1 has the disadvantage of a pointless inversion of word order and of quite unnecessary explanations in brackets. If any reader has got as far as this in the poem and yet still needs to be told what it is that Arjuna now remembers and what it is that he proposes to do, he must be so exceptionally inattentive as not to be worth catering for. No. 2 is better; but as the title Achutya will convey nothing to the mind of the reader, it seems better to translate it, as the other three translators have done. And is there any point in trying to preserve, as all the translators do, the Sanskrit idiom 'get memory' for 'to remember'? In No. 3 the rhythm would be better without the 'away' after 'vanished', and 'away' adds nothing to the sense. But I think No. 3 (by Professor Barnett) is the best of the four. No. 4 is spoiled by 'I am established', which, though a correct etymological gloss on the original, is not a possible way of saying 'I have taken my stand' – that is to say, 'I am resolved'.

I suggest something of this kind:

> You, god imperishable,
> Have broken my illusion;
> By your grace I have remembered.

I take my stand, I doubt no longer.
I will do your bidding.

I don't pretend that this is more than a pale echo of the original; but I think it has a shade more force and rhythm than the four other versions. No doubt all four translators were aware that they were tackling the finest moment of a fine poem, but this feeling does not seem to me to come through in their translations.

There are indeed in anything one translates certain key passages or lines about which one feels from the start that it is going to be of vital importance to get them exactly right. No makeshift or approximation will do. Such a passage comes at the end of the chapter 'Ukifune' in *The Tale of Genji*. Ukifune, unable to decide between her two lovers, has made up her mind to throw herself into the river. Her maid Ukon pesters her with good advice.

Literally translated the passage runs: 'Ukon, space-nearly lying, that doing: "Thus only when one thinks about things, because the soul of the person who thinks about things goes astray there are indeed likely to be frightening dreams. Having decided one way or the other, oh that you may somehow get on!" So she sighed. [Ukifune] pressing the soft clothes against her face, lay; that indeed.' The dream referred to is evidently (as commentators have recognized) the dream 'too terrible to mention' which Ukifune's mother had had the night before. I translated the passage: 'Ukon now came to sit with her for a little. "When a person goes on tormenting herself as you are doing, we all know what happens: the soul gets loose from the body and goes wandering about by itself. That's why your mother has been having these bad dreams. There's nothing to worry about. Just make up your mind one way or the other, and it will be all right. At least I hope so," she said with a sigh.'

'Ukifune lay with the soft bed clothes pressed tight against her face.'

Ukon, of course, is not a peasant. But she is on an infinitely lower rung of the social scale than Ukifune, and this (though I have not attempted to bring it out even in my literal translation) is expressed in the verb forms that she uses. One must make her talk as a maid might conceivably talk to a mistress, but remember that she is the daughter of Ukifune's old nurse and is an intimate as well as a servant. Then one must make it clear that she is being aggravating and that it is just this continual flow of well-meant and quite useless advice that is driving Ukifune to desperation. Have I elaborated too much, to the point of spoiling the poignancy of the passage? I don't think so; looking at it some twenty-five years later I do not want to alter it, and even feel that if Ukon had been speaking English, this is more or less what she would have said.

There is not any other translation of the passage with which I can compare mine. If there were, I might suddenly feel that I did, after all, make rather a mess of it. In saying this I have in mind a passage in the No play *Sotoba Komachi*:

> Oh how fell she from splendour,
> How came the white of winter
> To crown her head?
> Where are gone the lovely locks, double-twined,
> The coils of jet?
> Lank wisps, scant curls wither now
> On wilted flesh,
> And twin-arches, moth-brows, tinge no more
> With the hue of far hills.

That was the way I translated It in 1921, and it is not bad verse. But I must confess that when recently I read Sam Houston Brock's translation of *Sotoba Komachi* in Donald

Keene's anthology, I was rather shaken. His translation of this passage is:

> How was ever such loveliness lost?
> When did she change?
> Her hair a tangle of frosted grass
> Where the black curls lay in her neck
> And the colour lost from the twin arched peaks
> Of her brow.

I felt at once that my translation was hopelessly overladen and wordy and that it tried in a quite unwarrantable way to improve upon the original. Not that I am altogether satisfied with Mr Brock's. If mine is too poetical, his I think is a shade too prosy, and nothing will convince me that 'Of her brow' makes a very good line of verse.

There is a wonderful passage in the Chinese novel *Monkey* where Tripitaka after his Illumination sees his discarded earthly body drifting downstream: 'Tripitaka stared at it in consternation. Monkey laughed. "Don't be frightened, Master," he said, "that's you." And Pigsy said, "It's you, it's you." Sandy clapped his hands. "It's you, it's you," he cried. The ferryman too joined in the chorus, "There *you* go," he cried. "My best congratulations." In her paraphrase of the book (1930) Helen Hayes says, 'A dead body drifted by them, and the Master saw it with fear. But the Monkey, ever before him, said: "Master, do not be alarmed. It is none other than your own!" The Pilot also rejoiced as he turned to say "This body was your own! May you know joy!" '

Vital (in the original) is the repetition of the two simple words *shih ni*, 'It's you', and if one gets bored with the repetition and represents the words as only having been spoken by two people, it seems to me that one spoils the whole passage. The second thing to note is that when the ferryman says 'My best congratulations' (*k'o ho*) he is using the ordinary everyday formula of congratulation that one would use if one met an official who had had a rise, and that it is with whimsical intention that it is applied to Tripitaka's advance from ordinary human status to Buddhahood. Helen Hayes' 'May you know joy!' so far from being a banal formula (which is what is required) is something that no one has ever said to anybody.

This brings us to the question of voices. When translating prose dialogue one ought to make the characters say things that people talking English could conceivably say. One ought to hear them talking, just as a novelist hears his characters talk. That sounds obvious and undeniable. But it does not seem to be the principle upon which translators, whether from Far Eastern or European languages, generally work.

Take for example Beatrice Lane's translation of the No play *Tsuchigumo*. A concubine called Kocho (Butterfly) is made to say 'Bearing medicine given by the doctor, I, Kocho, have come. Pray tell him so.' Can you hear anyone saying that? A literal translation would be 'Please tell his Honour that Butterfly has come with some medicine for him from the Chief Physician.'

One does not have to be a literary genius in order to avoid translator's pidgin of the kind I have just quoted. One simply has to develop the habit of hearing voices talk. The reader who cannot consult the original will of course tend to think that 'queer' English is the result of a praiseworthy fidelity to the author's idiom and may have a comforting sense that he is getting right inside the author's mind. I have even been told that translations which read well cannot possibly give a true idea of the original. But as a matter of fact when, as in the case quoted above, one compares bits of queer translation with the text, one generally finds that the oddity is completely arbitrary and represents no native idiom at all. People, in fact, who write very well when expressing their own ideas tend (unless they have been to some extent schooled in translation) to lose all power of normal expression when faced with a foreign text. I once edited a volume in which a number of archaeologists, all of them excellent writers when expressing their own ideas, undertook to translate articles by German colleagues. The matter of the articles was purely technical and concrete; the translators knew exactly what had to be said. But one and all they were unable to produce anything but the most abject translator's pidgin. The sight of German sentences put them completely out of their stride.

I have used the expression 'schooled in translation' because I believe that even if it is a question of translating literature (and not merely technical information) there is a lot that could be learned. It is not, after all, as though a translator has to be or even had better be a creative genius. His role is rather like that of the executant in music, as contrasted with the composer. He must start with a certain degree of sensibility to words and rhythm. But I am sure that this sensibility could be enormously stimulated and increased, just as musical sensibility obviously can be.

A French scholar (whom I greatly admire) wrote recently with regard to translators: 'Qu'ils s'effacent derrière les textes et ceux-ci, s'ils ont été vraiment compris, parleront d'eux-mêmes.' Except in the rather rare case of plain concrete statements such as 'The cat chases the mouse' there are seldom sentences that have exact word-for-word equivalents in another language. It becomes a question of choosing between various approximations. One can't, for example, say in English, 'Let them efface themselves behind the texts.' One has to say something like, 'They should efface themselves, leaving it to the texts to speak', and so on. I have always found that it was I, not the texts, that had to do the talking. Hundreds of times I have sat for hours in front of texts the meaning of which I understood perfectly, and yet been unable to see how they ought to be put into English in such a way as to re-embody not merely a series of correct dictionary meanings, but also the emphasis, the tone, the eloquence of the original.

'Toute recherche esthétique,' the French scholar continues, 'va contre la bonne foi du traducteur.' I would rather say that the true work of the translator begins with 'recherche esthétique'. What comes before that – knowledge of the foreign language – is of course essential as a foundation, but it is a matter of linguistics and has nothing to do with the art that I am discussing. There do of course exist texts in which only logical meaning, and not feeling, is expressed. But particularly in the Far East they are exceedingly rare. The appeal, even in philosophical texts, has always been to emotion rather than to logic.

When I had been translating Chinese poetry for about six years, guided metrically by instinct alone, I discovered that I had been unconsciously obeying a certain rule. This was: to have one stress to each Chinese syllable. The stressed syllables could come side by side, as in

On the hígh hílls nó creature stírs

or they could be separated by anything up to three unstressed syllables, as in

I have stíll to trável in my sólitáry bóat.

This gave something which Gerard Manley Hopkins (whom I had not then read) called, I think, 'sprung rhythm'. I did not use rhyme because I found that to do so carries one too far away from the original. But exactly what sounds one uses at the end of a line is as important if one is not rhyming as it is if one is using rhyme, and a proper rhythmical relation between the lines is as important in free verse as it is in standard, traditional meters. It is true, however, that the tangles into which rhymers get themselves are sometimes almost incredible. A translator who shall be nameless has the two lines:

> This little grandchild, five years short of twelve,
> As yet can neither spin nor deeply delve.

Believe it or not – all that the original says is

> The little children cannot yet help with the plowing
> or weaving.

At the same time, though he has made such a mess here, I don't question that the translator was right in using rhyme, because all his experience and practice had been in writing rhymed poetry. The translator must use the tools that he knows best how to handle. And this reflection reminds me at once of what Lin Shu, the great early nineteenth-century translator of European fiction into Chinese, said when he was asked why he translated Dickens into ancient Chinese instead of into modern colloquial. His reply was: 'Because ancient Chinese is what I am good at.'

There are indeed so many lessons about translation to be learned from the story of this extraordinary man that I want to devote quite a bit of space to him. Let me introduce him to you by quoting from the preface to his translation of *The Old Curiosity Shop*:

'I once went into retreat, shutting myself up in one room for weeks on end. All day the people of the house passed to and fro outside, and although I could not see them I was soon able to distinguish their footsteps and know infallibly who was passing my door.

'I have a number of friends who from time to time bring me Western books. I cannot read any Western language, but these friends translate them aloud to me and I have come to be able to distinguish between the different styles of writing as surely as I recognized the footsteps of the people in my house.'

Lin Shu (1852–1924) was already famous as a writer of essays and criticism in a terse, clear, and vigorous style of literary Chinese when, more or less accidentally, his career as a translator began. In 1893 a young friend called Wang Tzu-jen, who had just returned from studying in France, brought him a copy of Dumas's novel *La Dame aux Camélias* and translated it to him viva voce, in ordinary Chinese colloquial. Lin Shu began turning this translation into literary Chinese. It was rather an odd thing to do because, although short stories were sometimes written in literary Chinese, no Chinese novel had ever been in anything but colloquial. The translation was published, and was an immense success.

During the next twenty-five years he published about 60 translations. Wang Tzu-jen, to whom he was deeply devoted, was never again available as a collaborator, and seems to have died rather young. But two of Wang's nephews knew French and collaborated in various works. One of them, twenty years later, helped Lin Shu to translate Bernardin de Saint-Pierre's *Paul et Virginie*. During the twenty-five years or so when he was translating he used at least sixteen different collaborators. Most of them were gifted and highly educated young men who had been sent abroad to study practical subjects, such as naval engineering. They soon became engrossed in their careers, diplomatic or governmental, and it was natural that they were not available as collaborators in translation for very long.

There were, of course, great disadvantages in Lin Shu's method of work. Knowing no foreign language he was, as he more or less confesses in his analogy about footsteps, rather in the position of a blind man at a picture gallery, whose friends are able to tell him everything about the pictures except what they actually look like. Naturally the method led to numerous small mistakes, and he continually received lists of errata from readers all over China. What made him so remarkable as a translator was the immense force and vivacity of his style and the intensity with which he *felt* the stories that were communicated to him. 'People in a book,' he writes in the preface to Charlotte Yonge's *The Eagle and the Dove*, 'at once become my nearest and dearest relations. When they are in difficulties I fall into despair; when they are successful, I am triumphant. I am no longer a human being, but a puppet whom the author dangles on his strings.'

He worked with immense rapidity. In 1907 alone he published translations of Scott's *The Talisman* and *The Betrothed*, Dickens' *The Old Curiosity Shop* and *Nicholas Nickleby*, Washington Irving's *Sketch Book*, Arthur Morrison's *The Hole in the Wall*, and a number of stories by Conan Doyle and other popular writers.

It is perhaps by his translation of Dickens that he is best known. He translated all the principal Dickens novels, and I have compared a number of passages with the original. To put Dickens into classical Chinese would on the face of it seem to be a grotesque undertaking. But the results are not at all grotesque. Dickens, inevitably, becomes a rather different and to my mind a better writer. All the over-elaboration, the overstatement and uncurbed garrulity disappear. The humour is there, but is transmuted by a precise, economical style; every point that Dickens spoils by uncontrolled exuberance, Lin Shu makes quietly and efficiently.

You may question at this point whether it is right to call him a translator at all. But at any rate in the case of the Dickens novels it would be misleading, I think, to use such terms as 'paraphrase' or 'adaptation'. In any case he was the transmitter, on the grandest possible scale of European fiction to China, and through him Chinese fiction (which had been tied down to ancient storytellers' conventions that no longer fitted what the contemporary novelist wanted to say) was revitalized when it was at its last gasp. I have spoken of the lessons that can be drawn from Lin Shu's achievement. First, then, what matters most is that the translator, whether working at first- or at second-hand, should be someone who delights in handling words. As another example of what a difference this makes I would cite the *Four Cautionary Tales* by Harold Acton and Lee Yi-hsieh, who worked together in much the same way as Lin Shu worked with his collaborators.

Whether the translator's style is contemporary or archaic does not matter. Some writers have been brought up on the Bible and handle a Biblical style with vigour and ease. I would cite as an instance Gordon Luce's *The Glass Palace Chronicle of the Kings of Burma*. There is all the difference in the world between the deliberate, consistent archaism of this translation and the pointless occasional Bilicisms (such as 'these twain' for 'these two') of unskillful translators.

The second point concerns the selection of books to translate. About 1950 the novelist and translator Tseng P'u called on Lin Shu at Peking and explained to him that all he was doing was to add to the already vast number of T'ang stories a whole series of new T'ang stories that differed from their predecessors only in the fact that their material was taken from foreign sources. Such a procedure, said Tseng P'u, could have no influence on the future course of Chinese literature. He advised him, among other things, to draw up a list of masterpieces, arranged according to period, country, and literary school, and then work through it in an orderly and systematic way. Lin Shu explained that as he knew no foreign language he was not in a position to draw up such a list, and that he saw no alternative to his present method. The books that his friends brought him were all well-known works, and there would be no point in translating them in a prearranged order.

If Tseng P'u had known anything about Lin Shu's temperament (and it does not appear that he had ever met him before) he would have known how inconceivable it was that Lin should ever work to schedule. Moreover, though Lin Shu translated chiefly because he liked translating and did not, so far as I know, ever aim consciously at 'influencing the future course of Chinese literature', the effect of his prodigious life-work was in fact to revolutionize Chinese fiction.

As to the desirability of programmes and schedules, the question is one which has again come conspicuously to the fore. As part of a new pre-occupation with cultural propaganda, various government-sponsored organizations are busy drawing up lists of works that ought to be translated. Young men with linguistic knowledge but often without any literary gifts are roped in to translate, without any particular enthusiasm, works whose only claim to attention is that they have got into an officially compiled list of 'masterpieces'. I have a feeling that this system is not going to work very well. What matters is that a translator should have been excited by the work he translates, should be haunted day and night by the feeling that he *must* put it into his own language, and should be in a state of restlessness and fret till he has done so. 'Masterpieces' were not always masterpieces and may at any minute cease to be so. Many of them owe their place on the list to all sorts of extrinsic and relatively ephemeral causes. Even so comparatively short a time ago as my own childhood a poem the title of which I pronounced 'Cassaby Anchor' was a 'masterpiece', and I had to learn it by heart. Perhaps one day it will come into its own again; but meanwhile let the translator read widely and choose the things that excite him and that be itches to put into English. If they are not scheduled as 'masterpieces' today, very likely they will be tomorrow. The Japanese pin their faith to translation by committee. Twenty people (with one exception all Japanese) seem to have taken part in the translation of the *Manyoshu* (the earliest Japanese anthology) published in 1940. The results were excellent, but this was due, I am sure, to the fact that the one Westerner concerned was Ralph Hodgson, and it seems clear that he was, in the final stage of the work, given a free hand. The next number in the series was *Japanese Noh Drama* (1954). Here eighteen people seem to have been involved; but it is clear that no Western poet took the bit between his teeth as I believe Ralph Hodgson to have done in the previous case. The result was that the lyric parts of the plays are simply prose, arbitrarily printed as though it were verse, as in the lines

> In recent years
> I have lived a country life.

The Japanese committee finds it 'regretable' that Japanese literature has hitherto been chiefly translated by Foreigners. I believe, on the contrary, that it is almost always better for the translator to be writing in his own language. It is in the highest degree improbable that a writer will command all the resources of a foreign language even as regards vocabulary, and when it comes to rhythm he is almost certain to be completely floored.

These scattered notes on translation deal principally with the Far East, because that is where my own experience lies. But almost all that I have said would apply equally to translation from European languages. I am afraid I may be felt to have taken rather an Only Tailor in the Street line. I have found fault with a good many other people's translations and in some cases have implied that I preferred my own. But I think it is natural that anyone should prefer his own translations. After all, he has made them to the measure of his own tastes and sensibilities, and it is as natural that he should prefer them to other people's as it is that he should prefer to walk in his own shoes.

(*Atlantic Monthly*, November 1948.)
Copyright 1958 by the Atlantic Monthly Company,
Boston 16, Mass.

# THE AINU EPIC

My foster-brother and foster-sister –
They it was who brought me up,
And so we lived.
In a castle magically built –
There I grew up.
There was a great pile of treasure
That rose like a cliff, and on top
Lay hand-guards in twos and threes,
Fit for the sword of a chieftain,
And when in twos and threes
Their tassels swayed,
There was a bright gleam on the wall,
So beautiful, so lovely!
In front of the treasure-stand,
On a seat of my own,
On my high seat I grew up.
And by it, to the left,
Was my white-wood bed, so marvellous
In the beauty of its shape.
Who was first reared in it
That it should have been made so lovely?
I did not know, but my thoughts

Were full of wonder.
And all this time
On my high seat I did nothing
But carve patterns upon treasures,
Figures upon sword-sheaths.
That was what I was bent on –
On that and nothing else.
Now it happened at this time
Some stray talk reached me
By roundabout ways
That at the mouth of the Ishkar
A golden sea-otter
Was diving for its food,
And that from the Man of Ishkar
To near villages
News came flying,
To far off villages
News had been brought,
And this was what it said:
'To whoever can dive into the sea
And bring back the Golden Otter
I will give my sister,
And all the treasure that is mine
Tied up in one bundle
Shall go with her as her dowry!'
And because it was so,
From near villages and far villages
The chieftains had come crowding
To the River-Mouth of lshkar,
And there they had set up
A great row of booths.
It was news of this,
Some stray talk of it,
That reached my ears

And one day I heard my sister's voice –
The lovely ring of her voice,
And this was what she was saying:
'Come now, you heroes that I tend,
Be sure that you pay no heed
To tales such as this.
It is a thing that happened long ago.
And now at the ebb of time
Has happened again;
No more and no less.'
And while my sister spoke
She fretted and fidgeted,
Moving her legs this way and that.
All this troubled me
When I turned it over in my mind.
But still, I carved my treasures,
Graved patterns on my sword
And so I passed my time.

## II

There came a night
When I could not get to sleep.
The god that lives under beds
Prodded me from below;
The god that lives in the beams
Stared at me from above,
Prodded and stared so hard
That as I lay on my bed
I tossed this way and that.
Why was I like this?
I could not make it out.
My brother and sister on their pillows
Were snoring loud,

Snoring both together
Suddenly, there on my bed,
I stretched myself, and at one bound
I was up on my feet.
I went to the treasure-pile,
I fumbled about in it
And pulled out a basket,
A basket finely lacquered,
The cords that bound it
One after another I untied;
I tilted off the cover.
I plunged my hand into the basket;
An embroidered coat,
A graven belt-sword,
A belt clasped with gold,
A little golden helmet –
All of them together
I tumbled out.
The embroidered coat
I thrust myself into,
The golden clasped belt
I wound about me.
The cords of the little helmet
I tied for myself,
So that it set firm on my head.
The graven sword
I thrust through my belt.
And though I tell it of myself,
I looked splendid as a god,
Splendid as a great god
Returning in glory.
And there upon the mat,
Though I had never seen them,
I copied deeds of battle, deeds of war,

Spreading my shoulders, whirling round and round.
Then I went out at the door,
And saw what in all my life
Never once yet I had seen –
What it was like outside my home,
Outside the house where I was reared.
So this was our Castle!
Never could I have guessed
How beautiful it was.
The fencing done long ago
Standing so crooked;
The new fencing
So high and straight.
The old fencing like a black cloud,
The new fencing like a white cloud.
They stretched around the castle
Like a great mass of cloud –
So pleasant, so lovely!
The crossbars laid on top
Zigzagged as the fence ran.
The stakes below –
Were swallowed deep in the earth.
In the tie-holes below
Rats had made their nest.
In the tie-holes above
Little birds had made their nest.
Here and there, with spaces between,
The holes were patches of black.
And when the wind blew into them
There was a lovely music
Like the voices of small birds.
Across the hillside, across the shore
Many zigzag paths
Elbowed their way.

The marks of digging-sticks far off
Showed faintly black;
The marks of sickles far off
Showed faintly white.
The ways went pleasantly;
They were beautiful, they were lovely.

The way down to the shore,
The hollow of the way,
I followed down when suddenly
Some god possessed me and from the ground I trod
A wind carried me high into the air;
High above the path to seaward.
And brought me to a harbour
Close to a harbour on the shore.
And coming from the sea
A pleasant breeze blew on me and the face of the sea
Was wrinkled like a reed-mat.
And on it the sea-birds
Tucking their heads under their tails,
Bobbing up their heads from under their tails
Called to one another
With sweet voices across the sea.
Over long stretches of sand
I strode, and as I went
The god that possessed me
Thundered in the sky above,
And swiftly along the shore-way
Hurried me to the village of Ishkar,
Near to Ishkar he carried me.
And the castle of Ishkar,
How beautifully it was built!
And under the white foam of the waves
(What they had said was true)

The golden sea-otter
Suddenly, like the glint of a sword,
Flashed above the breakers of the open sea.
And there in the shore-road,
In the middle of the wide road
Was a watch-tower marvellously built
With a ladder leading up to it.
Then in the castle
There was a noise and stir.
Suddenly as when the light comes at dawn
A woman came out from the castle.
I thought she would surely be beautiful –
The woman of the story I had heard.
But she had straight hair,
Reddish hair cut short
Half-way down her long chin.
With nothing beautiful about her
Save the jewels she wore.
It was a hideous woman that came out
And climbed up the ladder,
And sat down in the high tower.
I saw that at the mouth of the Ishkar
Were many booths in a row.
From the first of them came a sound
And an Ainu came out.;
But if indeed an Ainu,
More splendid than any I had known.
With a new moon and a full moon
His coat was blazoned,
And his hat with the same.
It was a fine man that came out of the booth.
He held his hands high
And towards the woman on the tower
Many times did homage.

The ugly woman
Laughed in scorn of him,
And thrust out her chin.
I had never seen him before,
But who else could he be
Than the Young Man of the East?

The golden sea-otter
Glinted like a sword;
Then the suck of the tide
Caught it and pulled it down.
Once to seaward
With outstretched hand
The young man pursued it;
Once to landward
With outstretched hand
The man made after it;
Then fell panting upon the rocks.
The Ugly Woman
Mocking at him
Wagged her long chin.
'How hateful she is!' I thought.
Then from a booth at the far end
A sound came
And one stepped out
Who, though I had never seen him,
I knew to be from Repunshir –
The Man of the Far Island.
He too raised his hands
Towards the woman on the tower
And did homage many times.
The Ugly Woman
Once more turned her face
Towards the harbour, towards the shore,

And saw the Man of Repunshir
Going after the golden otter.
Twice he chased it to seaward
With outstretched hand,
Twice to landward with outstretched hand;
Then fell panting upon the rocks.
'I was wrong about him,' I thought.
The Ugly Woman
Mocking at him
Wagged her long chin.
Then from the booth that was in the middle
Of that long row of booths
Again there came a noise
And a man came out,
If man not god one could call him,
For he was clothed from head to foot
In chain of gold,
In magic armour of gold
So cased and folded
That I wondered he could lift his sword.
But far more marvellous
Than all his trappings
Was that hero's face.
He raised his hands
And towards the tower
Did homage many times.
And now once again
The golden sea-otter
Sank with the suck of the tide.
Three times to seaward
With outstretched hand
He followed after it.
Three times to landward
With outstretched hand

The man, if man he was,
Chased it before him,
So that I was lost in wonder.
But just as dawn broke
He too, the Man of the Little Island,
Was cast upon the shore.
'I was wrong about him,' I thought.
The golden sea-otter
Under the foam of the waves
Was sucked in by the tide,
And I in my turn
Plunged into the surf.
Out to the breakers of the open sea.
It slipped from my hand,
But nothing daunted
I dived again like a sea-bird
And with one foot trod upon it.
It looked and saw what I was,
And so far from fearing me
It came up and floated between my arms
Like a water-bird floating.
Then seizing it by the throat
Up into the sky
Like a bird that had grown arms
Up into the sky I soared,
Straight back towards my castle
Swiftly I sped.
And soon, just as it had been,
I saw my home,
The castle of Shinutapka
Standing like a tall bowl,
With the ground-mist half-way up it,
Binding it round.
At the beauty of the castle

Great was my wonder.
I was near now; gently I pulled aside
The hanging door-flap.
My foster-brother,
My foster-sister
Were snoring loud and long.
All this had been in the night-time,
But now in the castle
Day had opened wide.
I threw down the golden otter
On top of the baskets and trays,
The vessels of sacrifice,
And on my high bed,
The bed made for me
I flung myself down.
I pretended to be asleep,
To be sound asleep on my bed,
As though I had never stirred.
And it seemed to me after a while
That I heard my sister rise from her bed;
There was a sound of fire crackling.
I peeped, and she was there by the stove.
Her head turned towards the things of sacrifice,
The baskets and trays.
She had seen the golden otter;
Her chin thrust towards it,
Thrust out to that side.
Then it seemed to me that I heard
My brother get up from his bed.
And my sister put her face near his
And whispered softly to him,
Glancing (my angry sister)
Towards the baskets and trays.
My brother turned that way

And anger blazed on his face;
He set his foot on the fire-rail
And wrenched it askew.
How could a face so beautiful
Be changed by anger,
Be twisted and hideous in its rage?
I was wondering at this
When from the white-wood bed to the left
A noise came,
And someone moved towards me.
And as I looked at him I thought,
'Once I believed that my foster-brother
Was in all the wide world
Matchless in beauty, but now
Here is a man that is like a god,
Splendid as a great god returning in glory.'
Hardly a shadow of beard
Yet showed on his face.
But his hair hung in tendrils,
Hung in eddies over his shoulders
And in his hair-tips
The light of day was entangled,
Gleaming and glinting
Over the hair of his head
Golden waters seemed to drip.
Who could he be, this Ainu so splendid?
As he came towards the stove
My foster-brother gave a glance
At the baskets and trays of sacrifice.
Then my true brother
(For this was my young brother
The god-like Otopush)
Caught sight of the golden otter,
And anger blazed in his face.

He sat down by the stove
And many rough words he spoke:
'Who else can it have been,
But he whom we have reared,
That brought the golden otter?
And now that this has been done
In the place where we live
There can be no more peace.
This is something that happened long ago
And now it has unburied itself
And come back afresh.
Because of what our little brother
Has seen fit to do for us,
War will come; nothing could be surer.'
But those three
Were afraid to speak their minds to me.
I laughed secretly;
I was very much amused.

There are one or two points that obviously need clearing up.
To begin with, you will naturally want to know how the poem
goes on; for what I have given is no more than a tenth part of
it. Naturally the people of Ishkar and their confederates try to
recover the golden otter. There are a number of battles, in
which the people of Ishkar are unsuccessful. There is a pause
in the fighting, and the hero and his allies decide to give a
great banquet, with dances and songs to amuse the gods, who
have been rather neglected during the fighting. Suddenly a
messenger arrives, asking for help for a lady whom I am going
to call Miss Malinger, which is what her name (Nishap-
tashum) literally means. She is the sister of a chieftain
belonging to the Ishkar confederacy. Having second sight she
knew that if her clan went with the other confederates to
recover the otter, the Hero, whom she admires, would be

killed; so she pretended to be ill, and her brother delayed the departure of his army till it was discovered that she was only shamming. Consequently he was late in coming to the aid of his allies, who were furious and decided to hang Miss Malinger. The messenger, who suddenly arrived at the banquet, had come to ask for the Hero's aid.

The Hero at once leaves the banquet and arrives just in time to cut Miss Malinger down. They fall in love and he carries her back as his bride. Soon however an enemy carries her off while the Hero is out hunting. There are more battles; Miss Malinger is recovered and the Hero leaves her at home while he goes out to make a final clearance of his enemies.

While he lies on the ground, exhausted by many battles, a beautiful girl appears and, bending over him, sings:

> If such a hero
> Fell to my hand
> What a boon to my village!

At this moment Miss Malinger, knowing by instinct that he is in danger, appears at the Hero's side and casts a spell upon the beautiful girl. The Hero steps up to the beautiful girl from behind, and undoes one by one the strings of her bodice. The passage that follows is strange and terrible:

> Her young breasts
> That were like two snowballs
> I fondled with my hand.
> She looked back over her shoulder
> And cried out, 'Is it you?
> I thought you were dead.'
> But while she was saying these words
> I hewed her limb from limb,
> And heard the swish of her soul,

Her evil soul as it rose.
Then Malinger came to me and said,
'Women should do battle with women
And this my evil sister
Should have fallen to my hand.
But now that before I could slay her
A godlike hero
Has meted punishment,
We have no more to fear;
Let us go back to our home.'
But I thought to myself,
'Where is this village of Peshutun
That the girl said she came from?
If without destroying it
I were now to go back home,
Would it not be said I was afraid?'
That was what I thought to myself.

That is the end of the poem. Apparently no version exists that carries the story any further. But the words with which it ends serve elsewhere as a stock introduction to fresh episodes, and the poem (at any rate as we possess it) must be said to break off rather than to end.

There are certain questions that I am sure you will want me to answer. It is not perhaps necessary to remind you that the Ainus were a primitive people living in the northern island of Japan, in the adjacent promontory of Sakhalin and in the Kurile Islands, a people that has now been almost entirely assimilated or died out. You probably know too that the Ainu language is apparently unrelated (apart from the borrowing of culture-words from Gilyak and Japanese) with any other speech. Two facts about the Ainus struck Japanese observers from the eighteenth century onwards – the richness of their oral literature and the length of their beards. This literature includes prose stories, songs, ballads and various kinds of long narrative poem. The long poem I have told you about is the most complete and most celebrated of these, and the one to which the term 'the Ainu epic' has generally been applied. It was intoned rather than sung. Each line has two stresses, which the reciter emphasized by tapping with a stick. Old women sometimes recited it, but more commonly the reciter was a man. Women had narrative songs of their own, which generally described how some man had fallen madly in love with them.

You will have noticed that the epic is told in the first person. This is true also of Ainu folk-tales and almost all their narrative literature. It has been suggested that this form is derived from that of shamanistic communications – the hero of the story speaks through the narrator's mouth just as the possessing deity speaks through the mouth of the shaman. But so far as I know this form of narration does not exist in other parts of the world where shamanism is even more extensively cultivated.

The epic was recited in connection with religious ceremonies, at sea when waiting for fish to bite, round the fire-side at home on long winter nights, and in fact whenever Ainus had time on their hands. The Ainus were not sure whether the hero would like strangers to know about his doings, and when asked by missionaries and others to recite were more apt to tell prose folk-stories. That was why Professor Basil Hall Chamberlain was able to write in 1886, 'the Ainus have apparently no popular tales of heroes', and he tells us that an Ainu chief whom he used as 'his informant' could scarcely recollect the name of any man of note, could not tell of one whom the nation had singled out as its favourite hero.

The epic as we possess it today was written down in European script by the Japanese professor Kindaichi during the 'twenties of the twentieth century, and published in 1932. Wakarpa, the old blind Ainu from whom he got the epic, died before the book came out. Was Wakarpa the Homer who put together a dozen or so hero-ballads and arranged them as a continuous narrative? Someone must, I think, have done this. But Wakarpa entirely disclaimed having done anything of the kind. He insisted that he had merely repeated the epic as he had learnt it. How old (if we accept that Wakarpa was not the author) is the epic likely to be? It is in an archaic form of Ainu; but this is the accepted language of all Ainu heroic songs and ballads, and proves nothing about the date of composition. If we say that it was composed between the ninth and the twentieth centuries, we shall not be far wrong; but I fear that you will not find so vague a dating very helpful or illuminating.

*(Botteghe Oscure, vii. 1951)*

# AINU SONG

I with my brother
In anger we left our home
And on the western borders
Of another land we lived.
But our village on the Sara,
Our old home, we could not forget;
Food would not pass our throats
And when we lay down to rest
All the time our tears flowed.
Over new-served food
The white mildew spread and spread;
Over old-served food
The black mildew spread and spread.
Then on a day
That in weeping, in weeping only,
We two had passed,
'Oh terrible, my sister,'
Said my brother to me,
'That you should have come to this.
See, of our old home an image,
A form have I carved.
Come here and look.'

So he said to me;
And when under my raised sleeve I looked,
Indeed it was so.
In the middle of the embers
Was the form, the image,
Of the home we had lived in,
And thus was it carved:
There, just as it had always been,
Was our village, and above it
Blue sky coming, blue sky going –
Oh the happiness, the joy!
And the long stretch
Of our village river,
No other can it be,
The river mouth high,
Looking high above;
The river source looking low,
Deep sunken and low.
As it goes by,
How even, how smooth!
The tips of the willow-trees
So thick on the shore,
The tips of the hazel-bushes
So thick on the bank,
The reed-clumps growing
So thick on the bank,
The rushes all growing
So thick on the shore.
And the men starting
For the morning-hunt, young men
Bow in hand, arrows in hand,
Some this way, some that,
Setting out along the mountain paths:
The young girls,

Sickle in hand,
Going out to cut the grass,
Following along the mountain paths…
To see it all before me,
Oh the happiness, the joy!
But in a little while,
For it was oniy embers,
It died away, and there was nothing left.
And since then, always,
No food have we eaten,
No morsel of food eaten,
But wept and wept only;
So has it been with us.

(*Listener*, October 1938.)

# THE OWL SPEAKS.
# AN AINU STORY

'In old days, when I spoke, it was like a voice echoing through a hollow bow-handle, a handle of rolled cherry-bark. But now I am feeble and old. Is there no one I can send, no bold and clever speaker, who will carry my complaints to the Country of Heaven?' So I said, tapping on the lid of my iron-wood locker; and suddenly a voice at my door said, 'Who bolder, who cleverer a speaker than I? You will not find a better messenger.' And when I looked, it was the young crow. I brought him into my house, and began at once, tapping all the while on the lid of my iron-wood locker, to instruct him about my complaints, so that he might go as my messenger to the Country of Heaven. For three days I instructed him about my complaints, dividing them into three headings; but while I was still speaking I suddenly noticed that the young crow, sitting behind the fire guard, had fallen asleep. At this I fell into a great rage, and setting upon the young crow I beat him to death with my wings. Then, while I tapped the iron-wood lid of my locker, I said again, 'Who will be my messenger and carry my complaints to the Country of Heaven?'

Suddenly a voice at my door said, 'I am a bold and clever speaker. What better messenger could you find?' And when I looked, I saw it was the mountain jay. I brought him in, and while I tapped upon the lid of my iron-wood locker I instructed him about my complaints, arranging them under four principal headings, and continuing for four days. But the jay fell fast asleep, sitting behind the fire guard. When I saw this I was in a great rage, and advancing upon him I beat the jay to death with my wings.

Then, tapping all the while on the iron-wood lid of my locker, 'I want a messenger,' I said, 'a bold and clever speaker to carry my complaints to the Country of Heaven.' Someone entered very quietly and politely, and when I looked, there I saw the young water-ousel in his god-like beauty, sitting on the seat at the left. Then tapping on the lid of my iron-wood locker, I began all night and all day to instruct him about the terms of my complaint. And when I looked at the ousel he showed no sign of wearying. Day and night he listened, for six whole nights and days. When at last I stopped speaking, he flew straight out of the window and up to the Country of Heaven. What I had told him to say was to this effect: There is a famine among the people of the world and they are at the point of death. And what is the reason? The gods in the Country of Heaven that have charge of deer, the gods that have charge of fish, have agreed together to send no more deer, to send no more fish. These gods no longer pay any heed at all to the prayers of the people, and when men go to the mountain they find no deer, and when men go fishing they get no fish. I am heart-rent to see this, and that is why I have sent a messenger to the god of deer and the god of fish.

Some days afterwards, I heard a faint noise in the sky, and when I looked, there was the ousel, more lovely than before, full of dignity and grace, returned from the Country of Heaven to tell me how he had delivered my complaint. 'The reason,' he said, 'why the god of deer and the god of fish in the Country of Heaven are sending no deer and no fish is that when men took deer they beat them over the head with a stick, flayed them, and without more ado threw the head away into the woods; and when they caught fish, they hit them over the head with a piece of rotten wood. The deer, weeping bitterly, went to the god of deer, and the fish with the rotten stick in their mouths went to the god of fish. These two gods, very angry, took counsel together and agreed to send no more deer and no more fish. But if men would promise to treat the deer they take with courtesy, and the fish they catch with courtesy, the gods will send them deer and fish.'

When I heard what the god of deer and the god of fish had said, I praised the young ousel and thanked him. 'It is true enough,' I said to myself. 'Men have treated the deer and the fish very scurvily.' So I visited men in their dreams when they were asleep, and taught them never again to do such things. Then they saw that it was bad to do as they had done, and ever afterwards they made all the gear with which they caught fish delicately. They decked out the heads of the deer daintily and made offerings before them. Henceforward the fish came happy and proud to the god of fish, with things lovely as prayer-sticks in their mouths; and the deer came happy, on the completing of their monthly shift, to make report to the god of deer. The gods of deer and fish were pleased, and sent plenty of fish, plenty of deer, so that now men had no more troubles, never felt the pinch of hunger, and I am happy about them in my mud. I am old and feeble, and for a long while I have been wanting to go away from here to the Country of Heaven. But I have always been afraid that there might be another famine among the people whom I protect, and so I stayed here. Yet now I feel that there is nothing to worry about; I am going to leave the bravest and strongest of men to take my place and protect the people, and am going away to the Country of Heaven.

So spoke the old god, the god that guarded the land, and flew away to the Country of Heaven.

(*New Statesman*, September 1948.)

# THE SECRET HISTORY
# OF THE MONGOLS

# CHAPTER ONE

# THE ANCESTORS

Dua the One-eyed was born with only a single eye in the middle of his forehead. But with it he could see what was going on three treks ahead. One day Dua the One-eyed and his brother Dobun the Clever set out to climb Mount Burkhan. Looking down from the top of it Dua saw that by the side of a river called Tunggelik a band of people was coming along down the stream. Dua said, 'In the midst of those people who are on the move there is a black cart, and in the front of it there is sitting a handsome woman. If she is not already married let us get her as wife for my younger brother Dobun.' So saying he told Dobun to go and have a look. When Dobun went among this band of people and looked at them he found that the woman was called Alan the Fair. She certainly was very handsome, and she was not married.

This band of people was the family of Khorilartai the Clever. Formerly the lord of the land of Kol-barkhujin, a man named Barkhudai the Clever, had a daughter called Barkhujin the Fair, who married a headman of the Khori-tumat clan named Khorilartai the Clever and at Arikh-usun she bore him a girl called Alan the Fair. The reason that Khorilartai was trekking was this: he was angry because in the Khoritumat territory there were some people who reserved to themselves the hunting of martens and squirrels and they prevented him from catching any. He heard that game was plentiful on Mount Burkhan, so he moved with his whole family and took refuge with one of the lords of Mount Burkhan, Shinchi the Rich. This was how the Khorilar clan-name came into being, and this was how Dobun the Clever got Alan the Fair as his wife.

After they became man and wife they had two sons, Belgunutei and Bugunutei. Dua the One-eyed, elder brother of Dobun the Clever, had four sons. When, after a while, Dua died the four sons did not treat Dobun as their uncle, but separated from him and went off on their own. Thus came into being the Dobun ('Four') clan. Afterwards Dobun the Clever went one day to a mountain called the Tokhochakh Heights to catch game. In the woods he met a man of the Uriangkha tribe who had taken and killed a three-year-old deer and was cooking its flanks and entrails. Dobun asked if he might have some of the meat. The Uriangkha man kept for himself the midriff along with the lungs and gave the rest of the meat to Dobun. When Dobun had got this venison and was carrying it home, on the way he met a poor man coming along, who had a boy with him. Dobun asked him 'What man are you?' The man said, 'I am of the Ma'alikh branch of the Baya'udai clan. At present I am in great straits. Give me some of that venison and you shall have this boy in exchange.' Dobun gave him one hind leg of the deer and in exchange took the boy to wait upon him at home.

After the death of Dobun, his wife Alan the Fair bore three sons called Bukhu-katagi, Bukhatu-salji and Bodonchar. Belgunutei and Bugunutei, the sons born while Dobun was alive, said to one another in secret, 'This mother of ours, though she has neither husband nor husband's brothers, has born three sons. The only man in the house is the servant from the Ma'alikh-baya'udai clan. Most likely they are his children.' However while they were saying this, their mother knew well enough what they were talking about.

One spring day their mother Alan the Fair was cooking some mutton that had been pickled in the winter. She called her five sons to her and making them sit in a row she gave each of them an arrow-shaft and told him to break it. When they had each done so she tied five arrow-shafts into a bundle and gave it to each in turn, telling them to break the bundle. None of them was able to do so. She then said, 'You two boys, Belgunutei and Bugunutei, are puzzled about who is the father of these other three sons of mine, and I do not wonder at it. You do not know that every night a pale-yellow man came in through the vent-hole of the roof or through the gap above the door and stroked my belly. When his light had gone deep into my belly he would slink away, following the rays of the sun or moon and looking like a yellow dog. Do not speak hastily. To one that knows of this it is clear that these three are children of Heaven and not at all to be compared to ordinary people. Only long hence when they become Emperors will they be seen for what they are.'

Alan the Fair then taught them a lesson, saying 'You five sons were all born from my one womb. You are like those five arrow-shafts just now, which taken one by one were so easy to break. If you brothers remain of one mind you will be like the arrow-shafts when they were tied together; no one will be able to break you.'

Not long afterwards their mother Alan the Fair died. When she was dead Belgunutei, Bugunutei, Bukhu-khatagi and Bukhatu-salji divided the property among themselves. To Bodonchar, whom they thought weak and silly, they gave no portion, treating him as though he were not their brother.

When Bodonchar saw that they did not treat him as brother he said, 'What is the use of my staying here? I had better go of my own accord. It is all one to me! If I die, I die; if I live, I live!' So he rode off on a white horse with dark markings, a horse that had a sore cutting deep into its back and a scanty tail. He went down the Onan river till he came to Baljun-aral, where he made himself a grass hut to live in. While he was living there he noticed a young yellow hawk that had caught a pheasant. A plan came into his head; he plucked some hairs from the tail of the horse, made a snare, caught the hawk and reared it. Once when he had nothing to eat he saw some wild game penned in against a cliff by a pack of wolves. He shot at the game and killed it. Sometimes he went and collected the scraps that the wolves had left, got a meal himself and was able to feed his hawk. He spent the whole winter living in this way. When spring came, the wild geese and ducks began to arrive, and Bodonchar after starving his hawk for a while released it, and it caught for him so many geese and ducks that he could not eat them all and hung some of them on a withered tree, where they stayed till they stank.

To the north of Duiren mountain there was a band of people who had come trekking along the course of the Tunggelik river. Bodonchar used every day to fly his hawk, and then go to these people, asking for mare's milk to drink. At dusk he went back to his grass hut and slept there. The people tried to make Bodonchar give them his hawk; but he would not. He never asked them who they were, nor did they ask him his name; they just went on as they were.

Afterwards Bodonchar's brother, Bukhu-khatagi, came along the Onan river to look for him. When be came to the shore of the Tunggelik he met the people who had camped there and asked them, 'Has a man of such and such an appearance, riding on such and such a horse been here?' 'Yes,' they said, 'there is indeed such a man with such a horse, just as you describe. He hunts with a yellow hawk and comes to us during the day to get a drink of milk. Where he spends the night we do not know. But when the wind is in the north-west a snow-storm of goose-feathers and duck-feathers comes whirling this way. We think he must certainly live over there. This is just about the time he usually comes. You had better wait here a bit.' Presently Bukhu-khatagi saw a man coming, and it was indeed Bodonchar. His brother claimed him and took him back with him. Bodonchar followed at a trot and as they went he said, 'A body fares badly without a head; a coat is no good without a collar'. His brother did not answer. Bodonchar said the same thing again. This time his brother answered him, saying 'You have said the same thing twice over. What do you mean by it?' 'Those people you saw just now beside the Tunggelik river,' said Bodonchar, 'have no chief to rule them; they make no difference between great and small. Such people would be easy to take. Let us go and make prisoners of them!' 'If that is how it is,' said his brother, 'let us go home now and when we brothers have talked things over we will go back and make prisoners of them.' When they got home, the brothers talked things over and it was decided that Bodonchar should go ahead and reconnoitre. While Bodonchar was reconnoitring he met a pregnant woman. He stopped her and asked 'What tribe do you belong to?' She said, 'I am a woman of the Adangkha-Uriangkha clan of the Jarchi'ut tribe. That is who and what I am.'

All the rest of those people the five brothers captured and brought home with them, and as a consequence of this raid they had abundance of beasts, food and servants.

The Khabul Khan ruled over all the Mongols. But though he had seven sons he did not choose one of them to succeed him, but instead made his cousin Sengum-bilge's son Ambakhai ruler of the Mongols. Along the river Urshi'un that joins the two lakes Buyur and Kolen there was a tribe of

Tartars to whom Ambakhai gave his daughter in marriage, bringing her to them in person. When doing so he was captured by some of the Tartars and sent by them to the Golden Khan. (He was known to the Chinese as the Emperor Shih Tsung. He reigned from 1161 to 1190 over the foreign Chin [in Mongol, Altan] kingdom which at that time held North China. It was the duty of vassals to hand over important prisoners to their overlord and though there were frequent wars between the Altan Khan and the Tartars they must when they captured Ambakhai have for the moment been acknowledging him as their overlord.) When Ambakhai was leaving, Balakhachi of the Besut clan took back a message. The message ran: 'To Khutula, that is one of the seven sons of the late Khabul Khan and to Prince Khada'an that is one of my ten sons: I, the ruler of all the peoples, because I went in person with my daughter to give her to her husband, was taken captive. In future take warning by what has happened to me! And one thing more: do not fail to punish my enemies, even if in the doing of it you grind away the nails of five fingers, destroy the tips of ten fingers.'

At that time Yesugei, the father of Chingis Khan, was hunting with his hawks by the Onan river when he met a Merkit called Yeke-chiledu who was bringing back a wife he had married from among the Olkhun'ut people. Yesugei saw that she was very handsome and at once hurried home to fetch his elder brother Prince Nekun and his younger brother Daritai the Hearth-ward (i.e. the youngest son). When the three of them appeared, Yeke-chiledu was afraid. He whipped up his horse, galloped across a ridge, rounded a jutting hill and so came back to his wife's cart. 'I do not like the look of those three men at all,' she said, 'I am sure they mean harm to you. Make off as fast as you can. If you escape alive, you will be sure to find some other woman like me, and if you miss me, call that other woman by my name.' So saying she took off her shirt and gave it to him as a keepsake. Yeke-chiledu had barely time to stretch across and take the shirt from her without dismounting when he saw Yesugei and his two brothers coming. He whipped up his horse and fled upstream along the Onan. The three brothers went in pursuit, crossing seven hillocks during the chase. But they could not catch up with Yeke-chiledu. In the end they turned back and bundled off the bride, Yesugei leading her cart, Prince Nekun showing the way and Daritai, the youngest, walking beside the shaft. The bride's name was Ho'elun. She said wailing, 'Never once was my husband's hair blown by the wind; never once has he had to bear hunger in his belly. Now, galloping off by himself, what hardship will be his!' The sound of her sobbing was so loud that it shook the waters of the Onan and the forests of the valley. Daritai said to her, 'Your husband by now has crossed many ridges and forded many streams. No wailing of yours can make him turn his head. If you were to look for his tracks you would never find them, Be quiet and wail no more!' Whereupon they took her back with them and gave her to Yesugei as his wife.

As Ambakhai Khan when taken prisoner had spoken of the Khabul Khan's son Khutula and his own son Khada'an, the Mongol Taichi'ut people all gathered together in the Khorkhonakh valley and made Khutula their ruler. Then they feasted under the Great Tree. They were all feeling very happy and danced round the tree till their feet wore a deep trough in the ground.

After Khutula became ruler he and Prince Khada'an went against the Tartars to take vengeance on them. They fought thirteen battles with Kodon-barakha and Jali-bukha, but failed to get their revenge. During these battles with the Tartars Yesugei took prisoner from among them two Tartars called Temujin-uge and Khori-bukha. At that time Yesugei's wife Ho'elun was with child and beside the Onan river under the

Deli'un-boldakh mountain she bore Temujin (i.e. the future Chingis Khan). When he was born, he was grasping in his right hand a clot of blood in the shape of a knuckle-bone playing piece. It was because he was born at the time his father captured Temujin-uge that he was given the name Temujin. Ho'elun bore four sons, Temujin, Khasar, Khachi'un and Temuge, and one daughter called Temulun. When Temujin was eight Khasar was six, Khachi'un was four and Temuge was two. The girl Temulun was still in the cradle.

# CHAPTER TWO

# EARLY LIFE OF CHINGIS KHAN

When Temujin was eight his father took him to his mother's people, the Olkhunu'ut, to find him a future wife. Between the two mountains Chekcher and Chikhurkhu they met a man of the Onggirats called Dei-sechen. He said, 'Friend Yesugei, where are you off to?' Yesugei said, 'I am taking this child to his mother's people, the Olkhunu'ut, to find him a wife.' Dei-sechen said, 'This son of yours has bright eyes and a light in his face. Last night I dreamt that a falcon with the sun and moon in its two claws flew to me and perched on my hand. I said to someone, "Simply to dream of seeing the sun and moon is no unusual thing. But this falcon with the sun and moon in its claws perching on my hand must be an omen." Friend Yesugei, it is clear that your coming today with this child is the answer to my dream. There can be no doubt that it is a good omen for you Kiyan people. From old times till now we Onggirats have never fought to win fresh lands or peoples; but whenever there was a handsome girl among us we have always given her in marriage to your Khans, to set on the seat that belongs to a queen. When a marriage is to be made one judges the man by whether good order is kept in his camp. But with a girl what matters is her looks. Friend Yesugei, I have got at home a girl who is very young. Come with me and have a look at her.' And he took Yesugei home with him. When he got there and saw the girl she was indeed beautiful, and Yesugei was very pleased. She was nine – a year older than Temujin. Her name was Borte. He spent the night there and on the second day he asked if he might have her. Dei-sechen said, 'I wonder why people say "What has to be asked for time and again is highly prized, what is quickly given is scorned". Such a thing as a girl growing old in the family where she was born cannot be so I will give this girl to your son. You can leave him here with me, to become my son-in-law.' So the two parties came to an agreement and Yesugei said, 'My son is scared of dogs. Do not let the dog give him a fright!' Then he went off, leaving his spare horse as a betrothal present.

On his way back, when he reached Chekcher, Yesugei met some Tartars who were having a feast. The journey had made him hungry and thirsty, so he dismounted and stayed with them, thinking they did not know who he was. But they recognized him and said, 'Yesugei the Kiyan has come.' They remembered that in old days he had taken them prisoner and they still felt a grudge against him. So they secretly mixed poison and gave it him to drink. Yesugei mounted his horse and was on his way back when he felt there was something amiss with him. After riding for three days he reached his home; but by now he was much worse.

Yesugei said, 'I am very ill. Who is at hand?' Old Charakha's son Monglik was there. Yesugei sent for him and said, 'My sons are still young. I took Temujin to he a son-in-law and on the way back I was secretly poisoned by the Tartars. I am very ill indeed. I want you to see to it that your "brothers" and "sister-in-law" (Yesugei's sons and his wife Ho'elun) are properly looked after, and I also want you to go and fetch back

Temujin as quickly as you can.' No sooner had he said this than he died.

Monglik obeyed, and when he came to Dei-sechen he said, 'Yesugei is missing Temujin sadly and sent me to fetch him.' 'Well, if he is missing him,' said Dei-sechen, 'I do not mind his going to visit his father, so long as he comes back at once.' So Monglik took Temujin back with him.

In the spring of that year the two widowed queens of Ambakhai Khan, Orbei and Sokhatai, were making offerings to the ancestors. Ho'elun was late in starting and was not given her share of the sacrificial food. Ho'elun said, 'Is it because you say to yourselves that Yesugei is dead or perhaps that my sons are still young or why is it that you do not give me my share of the sacrificial meat of the Great Ones? Already I see with my own eyes that you do not give me food and drink; and it looks as though when you move camp you will go off without telling me.' Orbei and Sokhatai, the two widows, said, 'In a case like yours custom does not demand that you should be invited at all, and only that if food happens to come your way you should eat it. Ho'elun thinks,' they said, 'that because our husband Ambakhai Khan is dead she can safely speak to us like this. All things considered it might not be such a bad plan to leave this mother and her children in the camp and not take them with us when we move.' On the second day after that they did indeed move camp and the leaders Tarkhutai-kiriltukh, Todo'en-girte and others actually did leave the mother and her children behind. When old Charakha protested, Todo'en-girte said, 'The deep waters are dry, the shining stone is shattered', and heedless of the old man's protest they started off. More than that, Todo'en-girte ran a spear into the old man Charakha's back.

When the old man Charakha was lying wounded in his tent Temujin came to see him. The old man said, 'He has taken away with him the people your father brought together as well as all my people. When I protested, he stabbed me.' Temujin wailed, and left him. But Ho'elun mounted her horse and having got someone to bring her the battle-standard she put herself at the head of the people and succeeded in bringing half of them back. But in the end even these did not stay with her. All followed the Taichi'uts.

When the Taichi'ut brothers abandoned Ho'elun and her children she, being a clever woman, knew how by gathering fruits and digging up roots to feed her children. At this time of her great distress she managed to bring them all through childhood to full growth, showing promise already of one day becoming Khans.

These children of hers, though brought up on green-stuffs, flourished remarkably and were a match for any one. To provide food for their mother they made hooks by bending needles and fished in the Onan river or made nets to catch fish and feed her.

One day the four brothers, Temujin, Khasar, Bekter and Belgutei were sitting together hooking fish when Temujin caught a gold-coloured fish. His step-brothers Bekter and Belgutei snatched it away from him. Temujin and Khasar went home and said to their mother, 'We caught a gold-coloured fish, but Bekter and Belgutei snatched it away.' 'Why do you brothers behave like that?' she said. 'You have not, as the saying goes, "any friend save your own shadow or any whip but your own tail". We have been wronged by the Taichi'uts and are unable to take vengeance upon them, and yet you choose this time to behave just like Alan the Fair's five sons in ancient times, falling out with one another. You must not do that!'

Then Temujin and Khasar, cross at what their mother said, went on, 'Some time ago he took away a sparrow we shot and now he has taken away a fish we caught. If that sort of thing is to happen we cannot stay here.' So saying Temujin and Khasar tore aside the door-curtain and went out.

Meanwhile Bekter was sitting on a hillock minding some horses. Temujin hid behind the hillock and Khasar in front of it. They drew arrows from their quivers and were about to shoot, when Bekter saw them and said, 'The Taichi'uts have done us a wrong that we cannot put up with. You ought to be thinking, "How can we take vengeance on them?" Instead you suffer me no better than if I were a hair that had got into your eye or a splinter stuck in your mouth. If I must die, then let me die. But do not discard my Belgutei.' So saying he sat cross-legged, waiting for their arrows. Temujin and Khasar, from in front and behind, shot Bekter dead.

From the look on their faces when they got home Ho'elun knew what had happened. 'The one of you,' she said, 'was born clasping a black blood-clot in his hand. The other was like the wild dog (*khasar*) that devours its own afterbirth. You are like the panther that dashes itself against the cliff-side, like the lion that cannot quell its wrath, like the boa-constrictor that swallows its prey alive, like the falcon that flings itself at its own shadow, like the pike that gulps silently, like the randy he-camel that bites the heels of its own young, like the wolf that works havoc under cover of the snow-storm, like the mandarin-duck that eats the ducklings that cannot keep pace with her, like the jackal guarding its lair, like the tiger that with no second thought pounces on its prey, like the wild *barus* (unidentified) that dashes into things at random! With no friend but your own shadow, no whip but your own tail, having suffered at the hands of the Taichi'uts such wrongs as cannot be endured, how are you going to take vengeance? I was just wondering how you would get through, and now you must needs do a thing like this!'

So she rebuked her sons, quoting the sayings of the men of old.

Some time afterwards the Taichiu'ut Tarkhutai-kiriltukh said, 'What about Temujin, his mother and her other children whom we have left behind? No doubt by now, quick as the chicks of flying birds, they have grown their wings, quick as the young of running beasts they have filled out.' He went with his friends to look at them, and when Temujin and his mother and brothers saw them coming, they were afraid. Belgutei broke branches from the tree of a thick wood and dragging them with his bill-hook made a palisade. He also took the three little ones, Kachi'un, Temuge and Temulun and hid them in a cleft of the rock. Khasar and the Taichi'uts were shooting arrows at one another when the Taichi'uts shouted, 'Bring your elder brother Temujin. We do not want any one else'. This frightened Temujin. He got on to his horse and galloped off into the mountain woods. The Taichi'uts saw him go and caught up with him at the mountain called Tergune. Temujin bored his way into a thicket. The Taichi'uts could not get in, so they surrounded the wood and mounted guard. He spent three nights in the thicket and then, while he was dragging his horse out of it, his saddle fell to the ground straps and all. When he went back and looked at it both the breast-strap and the girdle-strap were still fastened. He said, 'It is possible for a saddle to come off even if the girdle-strap is still fastened. But how can a saddle fall off if the breast-strap is fastened? Surely this must mean that Heaven does not want me to go on?' So he went back into the wood and stayed another three days. When he once more came out he found that a huge white boulder as big as a tent had toppled down and was blocking the way out of the thicket. 'Surely this must mean that Heaven does not want me to go on,' he said, and he went back and stayed another three days. Altogether he stayed there nine days with nothing to eat. He said, 'How can I bear to die ingloriously like this? I had far better leave the wood.' With the knife he used for sharpening arrows he cut a way through the trees at the side of the rock that blocked the entry into the wood and led his horse down the hill. The Taichi'uts who were mounting guard at once seized him.

When Tarkhutai-kiriltukh took Temujin prisoner he gave orders to his people that he was to pass one night in each group of tents. While he was being passed round in this way the sixteenth day of the fourth month came, when the Taichi'uts hold their feast on the banks of the Onan river, not returning to their tents till sunset. At this time Temujin's gaoler was a young weak man. When Temujin saw that the Taichi'uts had scattered, he knocked down the young weak man, hitting him on the head with the cangue he was wearing, and escaped. When he reached the woods on the bank of the Onan he lay down. But he was afraid some one might see him, so he went and lay on his back in the shallows of the river, with his body in the water and only his face showing.

The young man who had let him get away shouted, 'The prisoner has escaped!' and at once all the Taichi'uts who had gone back to their tents arrived in a throng. The moonlight was so strong that one could see just as in the day-time, and helped by it they searched in one place after another in the woods by the Onan river. While Temujin was still lying in the water, Sorkhanshira of the Suldus clan who was one of the search-party passed close by and saw him. 'It is because you think of such clever ruses that the Taichi'ut brothers are envious of you. Do not do anything rash. Just lie where you are. I will not give you away.' So saying he went on his way.

When the Taichi'uts talked of going back and making a fresh search, Sorkhanshira said, 'As you could not find him when it was daylight what chance have you now that it is dark? Let us go back the way we came and make a thorough search in the places we did not look at before. Then if we are not successful we can separate and meet again tomorrow to go on with the search. A man with a cangue on his back cannot have got very far.' So he said and when the searchers were on their way back Sorkhanshira again passed by where Temujin was and said, 'Our search is over for the moment. We shall be coming back to renew it tomorrow. After our party scatters go and find your mother and brothers. If you meet any one, do not tell him I saw you.' So saying, he went on.

After the searchers had scattered, Temujin thought to himself, 'Recently when I was being passed round to be guarded in one group of tents after another, the night I was in Sorkhanshira's tent his sons Chimbai and Chila'un took pity on me and during the night took off my cangue so that I might sleep in comfort. And now when Sorkhanshira saw me he told no one at all and once again just went on his way. If I were now to go to his tent he would certainly help me.' So he went down the Onan river to took for Sorkhanshira.

He knew how to find the tent, for from nightfall to dawn mare's milk was beaten there. He listened for this sound as he went and when he heard it, he went into the tent from which the sound of mare's milk being beaten was coming.

Sorkhanshira said, 'I told you to go and look for your mother and brothers. Why have you come back here?' But his sons Chimbai and Chila'un said, 'When a sparrow is chased by a sparrow-hawk into a thicket, the thicket saves the sparrow's life. If even a thicket can do so and we fail to save a man that comes to us we are not so good as a thicket.' So they took off Temujin's cangue and burnt it. Then they hid him in a cart the back part of which was loaded with wool. They told their younger sister Khada'an to look after him, saying 'On no account tell anyone, whoever he may be.'

On the third day the Taichi'ut brothers said, 'It looks as though someone were hiding him. We had better do a bit of searching among our own people.' The search brought them to Sorkhanshira's tent. They looked everywhere they could think of, in the tent itself, in the other carts, under the bed. Last of all they searched the cart loaded with wool, raking out the wool that was at the door of the cart and finally getting to the wool that was in the back part of it. At this point Sorkhanshira said, 'In such hot weather as this, if there was any one in the wool, how could he endure it?' Whereupon the people who were searching came down from the cart and went away.

After they had gone Sorkhanshira said to Temujin, 'You very nearly brought me to my end, "smoke scattered, fire put out." Now go and find your mother and brothers.' He gave him a liquorice-coloured mare with a white mouth, that had never borne a foal, but gave him no saddle. He cooked for him a lamb that had been fattened by the milk of two ewes, he gave him mare's milk in a leather pail, one bow and two arrows, but no fire-making gear, and so set him off on his way.

Temujin started on his way and reached a place where there had formerly been a stockade. From there he followed some old tracks up the Onan river till he came to a river called Kimurkha which flows into the Onan from the west. Along the side of that small river there were tracks where some one had passed; so he went and searched upstream along that small river. At the side of it was a mountain called Beder, at the foot of which there was a hill standing by itself called Khorchukhui, and here he met his mother and brothers. After meeting them he took them on to some hills called Gurelgu which lie south of Mount Burkhan. Among those hills is the Senggur river and at the side of it is a small hill called Khara-jirugen and a blue lake. Here they pitched camp and stayed, supporting themselves by catching marmots and gerbils to eat.

One day Temujin's eight broken-white geldings were stolen from the encampment. Apart from these there was a liquorice-coloured brown horse that his brother Belgutei had taken marmot-hunting. In the evening Belgutei came back with a load of marinots. Temujin said to him, 'Our horses have been stolen.' 'I'll go off in pursuit,' said Belgutei. Khasar said, 'You can't; I will.' 'Neither of you can,' said Temujin. 'I'll go.' So he mounted the liquorice-coloured brown horse and following the tracks left in the grass by the eight horses he started off in pursuit. After he had gone for three days and nights on the fourth day early in the morning he saw as he went on his way a brisk boy surrounded by a herd of horses, milking a mare. He asked him, 'Did you see eight broken-white geldings come?' The boy said, 'Before sunrise I saw eight such horses being driven past here, and I can show you which way their tracks go.' So saying he put the horse Temujin was riding to graze and gave him a white horse with a black spine. The boy did not go back to his home, but covered his leather pail and leather dipper with grass and said, 'It is you this time who are in great trouble; but this kind of trouble might happen to any one. I'll go with you to get back your horses. My father's name is Nakhu the Rich. I am his only son, and my name is Bo'orchu.' When he had said this, they followed up the tracks for three days and nights and on the evening of the third day they came to a group of tents, outside which the eight horses were standing. Temujin said, 'Friend, you stay here. I'll go and drive away those horses.' Bo'orchu said, 'I said I'd come with you as your companion. How can I stay here?' They both charged straight in among the horses and drove them away.

One after another the thieves joined in the pursuit. One of them who was riding on a white horse and held a lasso-pole in his hand had almost drawn level with them when Bo'orchu said, 'Give me your bow and arrows, and I will fight with him.' Temujin said, 'I don't want you to come to harm for my sake. I will fight with him.' So saying he turned and shot an arrow. The man on the white horse pointed his lasso-pole at Temujin and said, 'Look, he has halted.' At this the robber's companions in the rear all pressed forward. But the sun had set and dusk had turned into black night. Seeing this those who were coming up in the rear lost heart, halted, and were soon left behind. Temujin and Bo'orchu rode all that night and for three days and nights, till they came to where Nakhu the Rich was. Temujin said to Bo'orchu, 'But for you I would never have got back these horses. Let us go shares in them. How many do you think you ought to get?' Bo'orchu said, 'I saw you were in trouble, so I gave you a helping hand. I had no intention of making anything out of it. I am my father's only son, my family is well able to supply all my needs. I have no desire for anything of yours; if I had, it would be no credit to me to have acted as a friend.'

When they went into Nakhu's tent they found him weeping and wailing; for he thought that his son Bo'orchu was lost. When he suddenly saw the two of them arrive, and saw that one of them was his son, on the one hand he wailed and on the other he scolded. Bo'orchu said, 'What have I done wrong? I saw this good companion was in trouble and went off with him as a friend should. Now I have come back again'. So saying, he took his horse and galloped off to fetch the leather pail and leather dipper that he had covered with grass after milking. He killed a lamb that had been fattened on the milk of two ewes and making them into a tidy pack to carry with him on his horse he furnished Temujin with supplies for his journey. Nakhu the Rich said, 'You two young people must always look after one another and never desert one another!' Temujin after he left, travelled three days and nights, and came at last to his home beside the Senggur river. His mother Ho'elun and his brothers, Khasar and the rest, were in low spirits about him and were now delighted to see him come back.

Long ago when Temujin was eight he parted with Lady Borte, the daughter of Dei-sechen, and now taking his brother Belgutei with him he went down-stream along the Kerulen river to fetch her. When they reached a point between the two mountains Chekcher and Chikhurkhu they found Dei-sechen's home. He was very glad indeed to see Temujin, and said, 'I had heard that the Taichi'ut brothers were envious of you and I was very sorry about it, and was indeed in despair. But here you are at last!' So saying he gave his daughter Borte to Temujin to be his wife. Both Dei-sechen and his wife Chotan saw Temujin and his bride on their way. At the curve of the Kerulen river at the place called Urakhjol, Dei-sechen turned back, and his wife Chotan escorted her daughter the rest of the way to Temujin's home.

After Chotan had escorted her daughter to Temujin's home and had left her there and gone back, Temujin felt that he wanted the company of Bo'orchu. So he sent Belgutei to summon him. When Bo'orchu saw Belgutei, without telling his father, he mounted a brown horse with an arched back and putting in his saddle-pack his blue woollen overcoat, he went with Belgutei. After that he and Temujin were comrades and were always together.

Leaving the bank of the Senggur river they trekked to a cliff called Burgi at the source of the Kerulen river, and under it they made their camp. Lady Borte, the daughter of Chotan, in order to perform the rite of giving a ceremonial present to the parents-in-law on first seeing them, had brought with her a black sable overcoat. Temujin said, 'In old days my father Yesugei Khan became the bond-brother (*anda*) of the Ong Khan, ruler of the Kereits, and consequently he counts as my father. He is now living beside the Tula river, in the black forest. I shall take this overcoat and give it to him.' Upon this Temujin and his three brothers took the overcoat with them and came into the presence of the Ong Khan. Temujin said, 'In old days you and my father became bond-brothers; so you count as my father. I have now brought to you the present that my wife brought as the ceremonial gift given to parents-in-law on first seeing them.' So saying, he handed over the black sable overcoat. The Ong Khan was delighted to get the sable overcoat and said, 'I will bring together again your people who have deserted you; your people who have scattered in all directions to the last man I will unite. That promise shall remain inscribed under my heart.' When he had said this, Temujin went home.

There came to him from Mount Burkhan an old man called Jarchi'udai, carrying on his back a blacksmith's bellows and leading his son called Jelme. He said, 'When you were born on Deli'un-boldakh I gave you black-sable swaddling clothes. At the same time I gave you my son Jelme, but as he was still very young, I took him away to bring up. Now, however, I want you to take this boy to saddle your horse and open the door for you.' So saying, he gave him his son.

After a time, early one day when the morning twilight was on the point of turning into dawn, an old woman who waited upon Ho'elun said, 'Mother, mother! Get up at once! I hear a sound that shakes heaven and earth. What if it should be those terrible Taichi'ut brothers, who once did us such injury, coming back again?' Mother Ho'elun said, 'Wake my children at once!' Ho'elun herself got up at once, as did also Temujin and his brothers. Ho'elun, Temujin, Khasar, Khachi'un, Temuge the Hearth-ward, Belgutei, Bo'orchu and Jelme each mounted a horse of his own. Ho'elun took the girl Temulun in her arms. Only Temujin was provided with a lead-horse. Lady Borte had no horse to ride. Temujin and his brothers mounted at once and climbed towards Mount Burkhan. The old serving-woman, whose name was Kho'akhchin, intending to hide Borte, made her sit in a black cart and harnessed to it a speckled bull. They went upstream along the brook Tenggeli, dusk coming upon them as they went. Just before dawn they met a band of soldiers coming towards them. 'Whose people are you?' the soldiers asked. The old woman said, 'I belong to the household of Temujin. I went to the big tent to shear sheep and now I am going home.' The soldiers said, 'Was Temujin in his tent or not? How far is it from here?' The old woman said, 'For that matter, it is no great distance. But I came out by the door at the back of the women's quarters, and I do not know whether Temujin was at home or not.' So she said.

After the soldiers went away the old woman Kho'akhchin whipped the speckled bull that was yoked to the cart to make it go faster, and the result was that the axle of the cart broke. She was about to leave the cart and hurry on foot into the mountain woods, when at that very moment the soldiers came back, bringing Belgutei's mother whom they had captured and were carrying pick-a-back. 'Is there any one in the cart?' they asked. 'No,' she said, 'it is loaded with wool.' 'Dismount!' said the soldier to his comrades. At this, the soldiers dismounted and pulled open the door of the cart. When they looked, what should they see inside but a young married woman sitting there? They dragged her down from the cart and, along with the old woman, they took her up with them on horseback. Then following the tracks that Temujin had made in brushing through the grass they rode up Mount Burkhan.

Pursuing Temujin the soldiers went round the Burkhan brae three times, without being able to catch him. At one place after another, when they tried to intercept him by taking a short cut, they met with such boggy ground or thick woods that they could not get through. The only thing they could do was to follow him along the same track that he had taken, and consequently they were quite unable to catch him.

The soldiers in question were the chiefs of three Merkit clans: Tokhto'a of the Uduyit Merkits, Dayir-usun of the U'uas Merkits, and Kha'atai-darmala of the Kha'at Merkits.

These three had come to avenge the wrong that had been done when Ho'elun was taken from Yeke-chiledu by Yesugei. They said now, 'We have had our revenge for the seizing of Ho'elun by capturing his son Temujin's wife. The vendetta is over.' So saying they went down from Mount Burkhan and returned to their homes.

Temujin was not sure whether the Merkits had really gone home. or were lurking in ambush. So he sent Belgutei, Bo'orchu and Jelme to spy on them from behind. Only when they had been away for three nights and he saw that the Merkits were really no longer in the neighbourhood, did Temujin come down from Mount Burkhan. Then beating his breast, he spoke to Heaven: 'Because old mother Kho'akhchin has ears as keen as those of a weasel and eyes as sharp as an ermine's, I was able to escape, and my little life was sheltered and preserved. To this mountain for ever afterwards I will make offerings, and my sons and grandson too will make offerings as I did.' Having spoken like this, turning towards the sun he hung his belt over his neck and, his hat on his hand, beating his breast, he knelt nine times and made a libation of mare's milk.

Having done this Temujin, with Khasar and Belgutei, went to see To'oril the Ong Khan, ruler of the Kereits, who was living in the black forest beside the Tula river. Temujin said, 'Taking me by surprise the chiefs of the three Merkit tribes have captured and carried off my wife. How, I wonder, will the Khan my "father" rescue and restore to me my wife?' So he said and the Ong Khan answered, 'Last year when you gave me the sable overcoat, I said I would gather together for you your people who were scattered, and that promise has remained always inscribed in my heart. Now I will carry out my words by destroying the Merkits and by rescuing your wife Borte and restoring her to you. You can tell my "brother" Jamukha so. He is now at the Khorkhonakh valley. I here will raise twenty thousand horsemen, to be the right wing; Jamukha will raise twenty thousand more, to be the left wing. It will be for Jamukha to fix the day on which the two armies are to meet.' So saying, he went away.

After Temujin and his brothers got home, Temujin sent Khasar and Belgutei to Jamukha with the message: 'My wife has been captured by the Merkits. You and I share a common ancestor. How is this wrong to be avenged?' They were also to tell Jamukha what the Ong Khan had said. Khasar repeated all this to Jamukha, and Jamukha said, 'I did indeed hear that my bond-brother Temujin's wife had been captured, and was deeply grieved. Of those three Merkits, Tokhto'a is on the Bu'ura steppe, Dayir-usun is at Talkhun Island, between the Orkhon and Selenge rivers, Kha'atai-darmala is on the Kharaji steppe. We can make rafts, binding logs with twitch-grass, go straight across the river Kilkho to Tokhto'a's territory and then, as suddenly as though we had jumped down through the sky-hole of his tent, take him and his people prisoner down to the last man.' Jamukha went on: 'Tell Temujin and the Ong Khan that I have already marshalled my armies. When my "elder brother" the Ong Khan starts on the expedition, let him pass under Mount Burkhan and joining forces with Temujin come on and meet me at Botokhan-bo'orji.' When he had said this, Khasar and Belgutei went away. On their return they told Temujin what Jamukha had said and then went off to give the message to the Ong Khan. When the Ong Khan heard what Jamukha had said, he ordered twenty thousand men to get on horseback and starting from beneath Mount Burkhan make for the cliff called Burgi, on the Kerulen river. It was here that Temujin now was, as he had heard that the great army of the Ong Khan was to pass that way and had consequently moved his camp and going upstream along the Tunggelik he had camped under Mount Burkhan at the side of the brook Tana. Temujin advanced with his army from there and met the Ong Khan with his own ten thousand men, the Khan's brother Jakhagambu with another ten thousand, twenty thousand in all, were encamped at Ayil-kharakhana on the river Kimurkha.

Temujin, the Ong Khan and Jakhagambu having thus joined forces went on to Botokhan-bo'orji at the source of the Onan, the place originally fixed for their meeting with Jamukha. Jamukha had already arrived there three days before. When he saw the armies of the Ong Khan and the rest, he placed his twenty thousand men in order of battle and the Ong Khan and the rest did the same. It was not till they arrived face to face that they recognized one another. Jamukha said, 'We agreed to be here on the appointed day even if a storm was raging. We Mongols regard a simple word of assent as though it were an oath and are agreed that any one who is not true to his word can no longer he counted as an ally.' The Ong Khan said, 'I arrived three days late at the appointed place. Jamukha my "brother", it is for you to decide what scolding or punishment I deserve.' That was what he said.

Starting from Botokhan-bo'orji they came to the side of the river Kilkho, bound together logs to make rafts and crossed the river. On coming to the Bu'ura steppe they took prisoner Tokhto'a's wife and all his people down to the last man. They might have caught Tokhto'a himself still asleep; but when they were crossing the Kilkho there were on the bank of the river some fishermen and hunters of Tokhto'a's who, travelling all through the night, went on ahead and warned him. Accordingly Tokhto'a, Dayir-usun and a few others, taking nothing with them, went downstream along the Selenge river and fled to the region of Barkhujin. All night long the Merkit people fled in panic down the Selenge closely pursued by our soldiers who were managing to do a lot of pillaging, though it was still night. As he went Temujin, in the midst of these fleeing people, kept calling out the name of his wife Borte. Borte, who was indeed among those people, heard him and recognized the voice as that of Temujin. She jumped down from her cart and along with the old woman Kho'akhchin ran up to Temujin's horse and seized the bridle. There was bright moonlight at the time and each was now sure that it was the other.

While it was still night Temujin at once sent a messenger to say to the Ong Khan and Jamukha, 'I have found the person I was looking for. Let us stop journeying through the night and pitch camp here on the spot.' That was the message he sent, and there and then they pitched camp. The Merkit people, who had been fleeing in disorder, also pitched camp and slept there. Such is the story of how Lady Borte was recovered.

When, earlier on, Tokhto'a of the Uduyit, Dayir-usun of the U'uas and Kha'atai-darmala, those three Merkit chiefs, had come at the head of 300 men, because in the past Ho'elun, who was the wife of Tokhto'a's brother Chiledu, had been seized by Yesugei, they came to take vengeance. When, having spiralled round Mount Burkhan three times, they failed to catch Temujin and only succeeded in taking his wife Borte, they made over Borte to Chiledu's younger brother Chilger the Wrestler, to be his wife. Now, when the armies of the Ong Khan and the rest arrived Chilger got into a panic and took to his heels, saying, 'I am like the jackdaw whose proper fare would be scraps of skin, but yet aspires to eat the flesh of the wildgoose and cormorant. Because, in the same way, I tampered with Lady Borte I have now brought disaster to all the Merkit people – disaster that will soon be upon my own head. Even were I to cast away my own life and bore into some dark and narrow place, what shelter could it give me!' So saying he fled.

Among the captives Kha'atai-darmala was singled out to wear a cangue and show Temujin and the rest the most direct way to Mount Burkhan. Belgutei's mother, someone told him, was 'in that camp over there'. When he went to take her away, he entered the tent by the right-hand side of the door at the same moment as his mother, dressed in a tattered sheepskin coat, went out by the left-hand side of the door. Outside the tent she said to someone, 'I hear that my sons have become princes. Here the people have mated me to a man of low birth. How can I look a son of mine in the face?' Having said this she ran off into the thick woods and could not be found.

Because of this, Belgutei ordered that every single Merkit who came into sight was to be shot at with a bone-headed arrow and told 'Bring back our mother!' The 300 Merkits who had circled three times round Mount Burkhan were utterly exterminated. As for the wives they left behind, those that would be any good as wives were taken as wives and those that would be better as slaves were made into slaves.

Temujin thanked the Ong Khan and Jamukha, saying, 'Ong Khan my "father", Jamukha my "brother", because you two were my comrades Heaven and Earth gave me new strength and I was able to take revenge on stalwart foes. Hence I brought destruction to the Merkit people and took captive their wives. Let us now go back.' This he said to them.

At the time when the Udu'it Merkits were fleeing in panic, they left behind in their camp a boy of four called Kuchu. He was a pretty boy with bright eyes. He wore a dress of water-sable skins cropped and sewn together, a sable cap and boots made from the skin of the fore-legs of a deer. The soldiers picked him up when they passed and as a present they gave him to Mother Ho'elun.

After Temujin, the Ong Khan and Jamukha had together overthrown the domed tents of the Merkits and captured their high-born women, they retired from the Talkhun Island tract that lies between the two rivers Orkhon and Selenge. Temujin and Jamukha retired towards the Khorkhonakh valley; the Ong Khan went behind Mount Burkhan and passed through the Hokortu valley, Khacha'uratu-subchit, and Huliyatu-subchit, hunting wild game as he went. Then he retired towards the black forests by the Tula river.

When Temujin and Jamukha reached the Khorkhonakh valley they both pitched camp there, and remembering how when in the old days they became bond-brothers, they had exchanged presents, they now said, 'Let us renew our friendship!' When they first became bond-brothers Temujin was ten years old. They were playing 'knuckle-bones' on the ice of the Onan river, and Jamukha gave Temujin a playing-piece made of roebuck-bone. In return Temujin gave him a 'knuckle-bone' piece with molten bronze poured into it, and they became bond-brothers. Afterwards, when spring came and when they were both shooting with their little wooden bows, Jamukha gave Temujin a bone arrow-head with perforated calf's-horns stuck on to it, that whistled as it went through the air, and Temujin in return gave him an arrow-head with a top of cypress wood. That is the story of how they twice became bond-brothers.

Temujin and Jamukha said, 'I have heard that among the sayings of old men in bygone days there is one that tells us: "When two men become bond-brothers it is as though they had but one life between them. Never do they desert one another, but are the defenders of one another's lives." Such is the manner of their love. Let us now renew our bond and be dear to one another.' So they spoke, and Temujin put round Jamukha's waist a golden belt that he had taken from the Merkits, and at the same time gave him from the spoil he had taken a mare that had not foaled for several years. Jamukha in return gave Temujin a golden belt that he had taken from the Merkit chief Dayir-usun, as well as a horse with a corn on its forehead. Then under a bushy tree in front of the cliffs of Mount Khuldakhar in the Khorkhonakh valley they feasted together. When night came they slept together under one blanket.

The love that Temujin and Jamukha bore one another continued for a year and a half. One day when they moved camp, it being the sixteenth day of the fourth month, they went on ahead together in front of the carts. Jamukha said, 'Let us now pitch camp along a hill-side, so that our grooms may lodge comfortably in their tents. Let us rather pitch camp along a gully, so that our shepherds and lamb-herds may have something to put into their throats.'

(Jamukha names two incompatible alternatives as a hint – at any rate in Borte's opinion – that his interests are incompatible with Temujin's and that they must part. The constantly repeated theory that Jamukha is expressing sympathy with the lower classes, i.e. the shepherds, is based on a mistranslation of the Chinese version. For a similar cryptic saying compare Bodonchar's 'A body fares badly without a head' on page 239. I may however easily have failed to understand Jamukha's saying. If so I am in good company, for even his boon-companion Temujin did not know what it meant.)

Temujin heard this in silence. He dropped behind and when his mother's cart caught up he repeated to her what Jamukha had just said. 'I do not know what he meant,' said Temujin, 'so I did not reply, and have come to you, mother, to find out.' Before Ho'elun could say anything, Temujin's wife Borte said, 'I have heard it said about your bond-brother Jamukha that he readily takes to new friends and grows tired of old ones. He is now tired of us and I rather think that what he said just now means that he is planning some move against us. Let's not pitch camp here. It would be far better to keep on the march all night and get clear away from him.'

Temujin said, 'Borte is quite right', and as she had recommended he did not pitch camp, but kept on the march throughout the night. On the way they passed the place where the Taichi'uts were. The Taichi'uts took fright and that same night withdrew to Jamukha's camp, leaving behind them a small boy called Kokochu. Our soldiers picked him up and gave him to Mother Ho'elun to look after.

Khorchi, of the Ba'arin, said when he came, 'Both Jamukha's ancestor and mine were born from the womb of one and the same woman who was captured by our august ancestor Bodonchar, so that I ought not to part from him. I did so because of a divine revelation that made me see with my own eyes a broken-white cow which came and walked round Jamukha. It butted his tent-cart and in doing so broke one of its horns. Then that cow, pawing up the dust, bellowed towards Jamukha saying, "Jamukha, give me back my horn". There came too a hornless ox dragging one of the piles of a big (i.e. a Khan's) tent. It followed the tracks that Temujin's cart had made, bellowing: "Heaven and Earth have decided between them that Temujin is to be ruler of the land. I have come laden with the land, that I may present it to him." Such was the revelation that I was made to see with my own eyes. Temujin, in return for my having repeated these words to you, when you become ruler of the land, what will you do to make me happy?' Temujin said, 'If I do indeed become ruler, I will make you leader of ten thousand.' Khorchi said, 'If after my acquainting you with portents so significant you only gave me leadership of ten thousand, how can I be content? Give me that leadership, but in addition from among the most beautiful women of the land let me choose thirty to be my wives. And again, to whatever I say to you you must promise always to pay heed.'

# CHAPTER THREE

## CHINGIS BECOMES
## KHAN OF THE MONGOLS

ltan, Khuchar, Sacha-beki and all of them, after consulting together, said to Temujin, 'We appoint you as our Khan. If you will be our Khan, we will go as vanguard against the multitude of your enemies. All the beautiful girls and married women that we capture and all the fine horses, we will give to you. When hunting is afoot, we will be the first to go to the battue and will give you the wild beasts that we surround and catch. If in time of battle we disobey your orders or in time of peace we act contrary to your interests, part us from our wives and possessions and cast us out into the wilderness.' Such was the oath they made to serve him. They made him Great Khan, with the name Chingis.

Chingis said to Bo'orchu and Jelme: 'When I had no companions you were the first to become my comrades; I have not forgotten it. You are to be at the head of all these followers of mine.' And to his other followers he said: 'All of you left Jamukha, thinking to come to me. If Heaven and Earth give their protection, you elders will now and long afterwards be my blessed comrades.' Speaking thus, he gave charges to all of them. After Chingis became Khan he sent Dakhi and Sugegei to the Ong Khan To'oril, ruler of the Kereits. The Ong Khan said, 'You were quite right to make Temujin your Khan. What would become of you Mongols without a Khan? Don't go back on what you agreed upon at the start.' Such was his discourse.

Chingis also sent Arkhai-khasar and Charkhan as messengers to Jamukha. Jamukha said to them, 'Give the following message to Altan and Khuchar. Tell them that it was through them that a rift was made between my comrade Temujin and me, with the result that we parted. Ask them, "Why did you not take Temujin as your Khan while he and I were still together? What was your object in waiting till now to make him Khan?" Tell them, "Do not do anything to disturb my comrade Temujin's peace of mind. Be perfect companions to him".'

After this, when Jamukha's younger brother Taichar lived at the water-spring Olegei, at the foot of Mount Jalama and Chingis' comrade Jochi-darmala was living on the Sa'ari Steppe, Taichar stole Jochi-darmala's herd of horses. His comrades did not dare go in pursuit, and Jochi-darmala went off all alone to recover them. It was night when he got alongside of his horses, and crouching low down over the mane of the horse he was riding, he shot an arrow which severed Taichar's spine, and came home with the horses that had been stolen from him.

Because his brother had been shot and killed, Jamukha led his whole tribe, along with thirteen other groups, thirty thousand men in all, across the Ala'ut and Turkha'ut ranges to fight with Chingis, who was then at Jurelgu. Two men of the Ikires clan, Mutke-totakh and Boroldai, came and gave Chingis warning. From among the thirteen rings of tents that formed his camp he raised an army of thirty thousand and went to meet Jamukha. A battle took place at Dalanbaljut, in which Chingis was repulsed. He retreated, not halting till he came to the defile of Jerene, on the Onan river.

Then, after Jamukha had gone back to his camp, Jurchedei of the Uru'ut clan, and Khuyilder of the Mangkhut, each bringing all the men of his family, left Jamukha and came to Chingis. Monglik of the Khongkhotan also came, bringing his seven sons. Chingis, in high spirit because these people had come, held a feast in the woods beside the Onan river. First a jug of mare's milk was served to Ho'elun, Khasar, Sacha-beki and the rest. Next a jug was served to Sacha-beki's father's concubine Ebegei. Seeing this, Sacha-beki's mother Khorijin and his father's other wife Khu'urchin, those two great ladies, said, 'We ought to have been served first!' and they flogged the steward Shiki'ur. Shiki'ur said, 'If Yesugei and Prince Nekun were still alive, people wouldn't be flogging me like this,' and he sobbed loudly.

At the time of the feast, Chingis told Belgutei to hold his horse outside the feasting place and act as Keeper of Order. Among the Jurkin, Buri the Wrestler kept order. A man of the Khadagins came and stole a bridle-rope, and was arrested by Belgutei. Buri the Wrestler came to the man's rescue and Belgutei, in the course of the struggle, received a gash between the shoulder-blades. He made light of it and walked off streaming with blood. Chingis, who was sitting in the shade of a tree, caught sight of him and asked, 'Why did he do that to you?' Belgutei said, 'I did get a wound, but it is not very bad, and I don't want "brothers" to be on bad terms on my account.' Chingis did not listen to his appeal, and a fight took place, those on each side arming themselves with branches cut from trees or wooden pounders for making koumys. The Jurkins got the worst of it, and Chingis' party followed up their success by carrying off the two Jurkin ladies, Khorijin and Khu'urchin. The Jurkins then came and negotiated, and the ladies were given back. Soon afterwards, but while messengers were still coming and going, Chingis received information that the Tartars ruled by Megujin-se'ultu and others had cast off their allegiance to the Golden Khan and that the Khan had ordered his Chief Minister Prince Ching to lead an army against them and destroy them, driving back Megujin upstream along the Ulja river.

Chingis said, 'Remembering that since in past times the Tartars destroyed my ancestors and my father I am at enmity with them, and I should do well to take this opportunity of attacking them.' So he sent a messenger to the Ong Khan of the Kereits, saying, 'The Golden Khan has sent Prince Ching to drive back Megujin and his Tartars upstream along the Ulja. It is they who are the enemies who destroyed my ancestors and father. You, my "father", must help me to attack them from this side while Prince Ching attacks them from the other.' The Ong Khan agreed, and having spent three days in marshalling his army he came leading it in person. Chingis also sent a messenger to the Jurkin leaders Sacha-beki and Taichu, telling them of his plan to take vengeance, and asking them to come and help. He waited for them six days, but they did not come.

Chingis and the Ong Khan then led their armies down the Ulja river and attacked the Tartars from one side, while Prince Ching attacked them from the other. The Tartars had set up a stockade at Khusutu-shituyen. It was stormed by Chingis and the Ong Khan, and the Tartar Megujin-se'ultu was killed.

(The account of the battle in the Chinese *History of the Chin dynasty*, chapter 94, is as follows:

'There was a great battle in which the enemy's tents, cattle and sheep were all taken. Most of them fled to the Olja river. Prince An-kuo was sent in pursuit, and they scattered and fled at top speed. Heavy rain was falling and it was very cold. Eight or nine out of every ten of the enemy died.'

The expedition was led by the Chief Minister, Prince An, later known as Prince Hsiang. Why the *Secret History* calls him Prince Ching, nobody has been able to explain. The battle took place in 1196.)

When Prince Ching of the Golden Country heard that Chingis and the Ong Khan had stormed the stockade of the Tartars and had killed Megujin and the rest, he was delighted. He gave Chingis the title of Ja'ut-khuri ('Leader of hundreds'?) and gave the title of 'Prince' to the Ong Khan. He said to Chingis, 'By killing Megujin and the others, you have been exceedingly helpful. When I get back to the Golden Country I shall inform the Emperor of this, with a view to his giving you an even higher title, that of Commissioner for Quelling Risings.' Having said this, he returned. Chingis and the Ong Khan joined in pillaging the Tartars and then went back, each to his camp.

The soldiers of Chingis, when they were in the camp of the Tartars, picked up a little boy who was wearing a hoop of gold above his nose. Round his waist he had a sash made of thread of gold and lined with sable-fur. They gave him to Mother Ho'elun. She said, 'This is certainly a child of noble birth.' She called him Shikiken-khutukhu and brought him up as her sixth child.

The camp where Chingis had left the old people and children was beside Lake Hariltu. Some people of the Jurkin clan came and stripped off the clothes of fifty people in this camp, and killed ten. Chingis was furious when news of this reached him. He said, 'Why are we treated by the Jurkin like this? Once before, when we were feasting in the woods beside the Onan river, people of theirs flogged my steward. It was they too who made a gash between Belgutei's shoulder-blades. Now when I asked them to join me in avenging the wrongs done by the Tartars to my ancestors, they did not come, but instead sided with the enemy and so became my enemies.' So saying he led an army to destroy the Jurkin. When he had reached the Seven Hills, near the Kerulen river, he made prisoners of the Jurkin people. Only Sacha-beki and Taichu succeeded in fleeing empty-handed to the Teletu Pass, where they were caught by Chingis. He said to them, 'What was it you said to me a while ago?' The two of them said, 'We have not kept to what we said.' Then they stretched out their necks, that they might receive their punishment, and he slew them.

After he had slain the Jurkins Sacha-beki and Taichu he went back to the camp of the Jurkins and removed the Jurkin people. At that time Telegetu the Rich, of the Jalayir clan, made his eldest son Gu'un-u'a take his (i.e. Gu'un-u'a's) two sons, Mukhali and Bukha, to Chingis, and do homage to him saying, 'Let them be your slaves for ever and if they ever desert your gate ham-string them and gouge out their hearts and livers!' Telegetu also made his second son Chila'un-khaiyichi take his two sons Tongge and Khashi to Chingis and to do homage to him, himself saying, 'Let them be the guardians of your golden gate, and if they ever leave it, cut off their lives then and there!' He also gave his third son Jebke to Chingis' younger brother Khasar. This Jebke had found in the camp of the Jurkins a small boy named Borokhul, whom he gave to Mother Ho'elun.

First and last Ho'elun was given four small boys, Kuchu, Kokochu, Shikiken-khutukhu and Borokhul. For those boys each day she became an eye with which to see and each night an ear with which to hear, and so she reared them.

One day Chingis told Buri the Wrestler to wrestle with Belgutei. Before that, when these two wrestled, Buri had never needed more than one hand and one foot in order to throw Belgutei and keep him on the ground. This time Buri pretended to be weaker than Belgutei and to have been thrown by him. Belgutei, pressing down upon him, looked back at Chingis. Chingis bit his lower lip. Belgutei knew what he meant. He put his knee against Buri's back and holding him round the neck with both his hands and forcibly dragging back Buri's head towards him, he broke his spine. Buri said, 'I was not really beaten. It was because I feared Chingis that I pretended to be the weaker and so gave my life.'

Of the seven sons of the Khabul Khan the eldest was called Okin-barkhakh, the second was called Bartan the Valiant. Bartan's son was Yesugei, and Yesugei's son was Chingis. The Khabul Khan's third son was Mongler, and Mongler's son was Buri the wrestler. But Buri, in choosing his comrades, skipped the descendants of Bartan and consorted with the fierce descendants of Okin-barkhakh. Hence it came about that though he was the strongest man in the land, in the end it fell to his lot to have his back broken and so to die.

(Chingis was of course punishing Buri for his attack on Belgutei. What was meant by 'skipping' the descendants of Bartan will easily be seen from the following scheme:

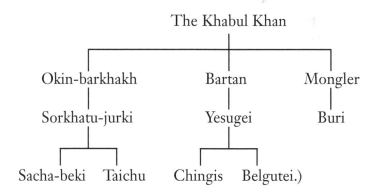

The Khabul Khan

Okin-barkhakh     Bartan     Mongler

Sorkhatu-jurki     Yesugei     Buri

Sacha-beki   Taichu     Chingis   Belgutei.)

Afterwards, in the year of the Cock (AD 1201) the Khadagin and ten other clans met at the Alkhui Spring and consulted together, intending to make Jamukha their lord. When they had sacrificed a horse and sworn oaths they went down along the Ergune river and when the reached the river-island at the Ken river they set up Jamukha as their Khan. They meant to attack Chingis and the Ong Khan. But news of their intention was brought to Ching is at Gurelgu by Khoridai of the Khorilas. Chingis informed the Ong Khan and the Ong Khan collected his forces and joined Chingis. When the Ong Khan and Chingis had met they went down the Kerulen river to face Jamukha. Chingis sent out Altan and two others as scouts; the Ong Khan sent his son Sengum and two others as scouts. From among these scouts some were sent on to Enegen-guiletu, Chekcher and Chikhurkhu to prospect. When Altan and the others got to Utkiya, the man who had been scouting at Chikhurkhu came and announced that the enemy was about to arrive. Altan and the others then went towards them to get news. On the way they met Jamukha's scout A'uchu the Valiant and three others and spoke to them. But they saw that night was coming on and went back to spend the night in the camp of their main forces.

Next day the armies of Chingis and Jamukha got into contact at Koyiten and drew up in battle-order, facing one another. While they were marshalling their forces two members of Jamukha's army, called Buyirukh-khan and Khudukha, who possessed the art of raising storms, wanted to attack Chingis' army down the storm. But unfortunately for them the storm ricochetted, utter darkness filled Heaven and Earth, and Jamukha's army was unable to advance. They all fell into gulleys, and Jamukha and the others said to one another, 'This can only mean that Heaven is not supporting us!' His army broke up in complete confusion.

After Jamukha's army broke up, the Naiman and the other ten peoples who had supported him all returned to their own settlements. Jamukha seized the people who had raised him to be their Khan and took them back with him down the Ergune river. Upon this, the Ong Khan set out in pursuit of Jamukha, while Chingis pursued the Taichi'ut leader A'uchu. When A'uchu got back to his own settlement he moved his people across the Onan river, marshalled his armies and waited for Chingis to come and do battle with him. When Chingis arrived they fought several bouts, and then when night came the two armies bivouacked facing one another where they had fought.

When Chingis was fighting with the Taichi'ut he got a wound in the neck which bled to a frightening extent. It fell to his retainer Jelme to suck out the obstructed blood. At midnight Chingis came to himself and said, 'My blood has dried up of itself. I am very thirsty.' Jelme took off all his clothes, went straight into the enemy's camp and looked in the lockers of their carts for fresh mare's milk, but could find none. There was only a pail of sour milk, so he brought this back. No one had seen him come or go. Then he went to get water to mix with the sour milk and gave the mixture to Chingis to drink. The more he drank the thirstier he became. He had drunk three times before he stopped. Then he said, 'Now I can see clearly with my eyes and understand with my mind.' He sat up and while he was sitting there, dawn came. He then saw that round where he was sitting the ground was flowing with a regular slush of blood. He said, 'Why did you deal with it like that? Surely it would have been better to dispose of it a bit further off?' Jelme said, 'I was far too busy to go to a distance. Moreover I was frightened of leaving you. I swallowed as much of the blood as I could and only spat out the rest. Still, I did manage to swallow quite a lot!' Chingis again said, 'With me wounded like this, how came you to go naked into the enemy's camp? If they had caught you, I suppose you would have had to tell them I was wounded.' Jelme said, 'If I had been captured I would have said to them, "I was intending to desert your side, but having found out I meant to desert they took away my clothes and were about to kill me when I managed to break away." They would certainly have believed that all this was true and would have given me clothes and taken me into their service. And just as certainly – I would have jumped on to one of their horses and escaped.' Chingis said, 'Once before, when the Merkits were harrying me at Mount Burkhan, you saved my life; and now you sucked out the blood from my neck. When I was thirsty, you risked your life to get me sour milk to drink and so brought me back to my senses. These three good deeds that you have done to me will remain for ever in my heart.'

Next day, when Chingis looked at the enemy, he saw that they had drifted away during the night. Most of the people they had left behind in the camp did not think they had any chance of getting clear away and had stayed where they were. Chingis mounted his horse and was driving back some of the people who had got away, when up on a mountain-ridge he saw a woman who called out to him 'Temujin!' He sent some one to ask who she was, and she said, 'I am Sorkhanshira's daughter Khada'an. The soldiers are just going to kill my husband. That is why I called to Temujin to come to the rescue.' As soon as he heard this Chingis did indeed go to the rescue; but by the time he arrived the husband had already been killed. Chingis made his camp in the place where this had happened, and bringing Khada'an to him he made her sit at his side. Next day Sorkhanshira, her father, came to see him, accompanied by Jebe. These two had both originally been retainers of the Taichi'ut Todoge. Chingis said to Sorkhanshira, 'In old days when I had a cangue upon me, you and your sons showed kindness to me. Why have you been so slow in coming?' Sorkhanshira said, 'My own wish was to come to you. But I feared that if I did so the Taichi'uts would destroy all my family. That is why I didn't come till now.'

Chingis then asked Jebe, 'During the battle of Koyiten who was it that, shooting from the top of the ridge, broke the neck-bone of my horse?' Jebe said, 'It was I that shot. And now, my Khan, if you have me killed, all I shall do will be to defile a patch of ground no bigger than the palm of a man's hand; but if you spare me, I vow to put forth such strength that the deepest waters will rend before me, the hardest rock be dashed to pieces!' Chingis said, 'As a rule enemies want to hush up the damage they have done and do not speak of it. You, on the contrary, have not tried to hush it up. That means I can take you as a comrade.'

The Taichi'ut leader Tarkhutai-kiriltukh, remembering that he had wronged Chingis in the past, hid in the woods. He had an old retainer named Shirgu'etu who, along with his two sons, now planned to take their master Tarkhutai-kiriltukh and hand him over to Chingis. Tarkhutai-kiriltukh was so fat that he could not ride on horseback. So the old retainer and his sons put their master Tarkhutai-kiriltukh into a cart. Tarkhutai-kiriltukh's younger brother and son heard what was happening and went off in pursuit. When he saw them coming the old retainer Shirgu'etu took fright. He held down his master Tarkhutai-kiriltukh, drew his sword and said, 'If I kill you, I shall pay for it with my life, and if I don't kill you, I shall still be put to death. If I am going to die anyhow, I would rather you die first.' At this Tarkhutai-kiriltukh called out to his younger brother and son, who had come to rescue him, 'He is going to kill me. He will have done so by the time you arrive, and what use will my corpse be to you? You had better turn back. If you do so he won't kill me, but will take me to Temujin, as he planned. I am certain that Temujin will not actually kill me as, apart from the wrongs I did to him, I did also at one time show kindness to him.' His brother and son then turned back, and Shirgu'etu and his sons drove on, with Kiriltukh in the cart, till they reached Khutukhul. At this point the old retainer's son Naya'a said, 'If we take him to Temujin, Temujin will say that we have laid hands on our rightful master and that he therefore cannot take us as comrades. In fact, he will certainly put us to death. We had far better let Kiriltukh go free and then say, when we get to Temujin, "We did at first lay hands on Kiriltukh, meaning to bring him to you. But then we remembered that after all he was our rightful master, so we let him go." If we say that, Chingis will certainly accept us as comrades.' So they let their master Kiriltukh go. When they got to Temujin they said everything that Naya'a had suggested. Chingis said, 'If you had brought him here, I should have killed you. But as you could not bear to behave so to your master and let him go, all is well.' With that, he gave a special reward to Naya'a.

(I have slightly expanded the above section which is laconic to the verge of unintelligibility. The Mongol text is much fuller, but in places confused and defective.)

Afterwards, when Chingis was at Tersut, Jakha-gambu, the younger brother of the Ong Khan, came and surrendered. It happened just when the Merkits were about to attack Chingis, and now he and Jakha-gambu fought with the Merkits and drove them back. Again some peoples who had been routed and dispersed – members of the Kereit tribe and also of clans subject to the Kereits, such as the Tubegen and Dongkhayit – also came and surrendered.

The way in which long ago the Ong Khan, ruler of the Kereits, and Chingis' father Yesugei had become bond-brothers was this: the Ong Khan had killed several of his father Khurchakus-buyirukh's sons, and his father's younger brother Gurkhan determined to kill the Ong Khan. (Khurchakus stands for Cyriacus. He was a Nestorian Christian and had a Greek baptismal name.) Gurkhan pursued the Ong Khan into the Khara'un mountains, and the Ong Khan eventually arrived at Yesugei's camp with only a hundred followers. Yesugei drove away Gurkhan and pursued him into the land of the Tanguts. He then gathered together the Ong Khan's former subjects and restored them to him. That was the reason why the Ong Khan and Yesugei became bond-brothers.

After that the Ong Khan tried to kill a remaining younger brother of his called Erke-khara. The brother fled to Inancha, the Khan of the Naiman. Inancha raised an army against the Ong Khan and drove him away into the land of the Emperor of the Black Cathayans.

(The Cathayans [Kitai] had ruled over part of north China. When their dynasty was brought to an end by the Golden Khan [Chin dynasty], a Cathayan prince (in 1123) fled with his followers to Central Asia and founded a vast empire, with its northern capital at Balasagun in Northern Turkestan.)

But before long the Ong Khan turned his back on the Emperor and set off across the lands of the Uighurs and Tanguts. He and his followers lived by milking five goats and by pricking blood from their camels and drinking it. When the Ong Khan got to Lake Guse'ur, Chingis remembering the old ties that united him with the Ong Khan, sent the valiant Sugegei to meet him. Later he came himself to the source of the Kerulen and escorted the Ong Khan to his own camp, where he made his people provide for the Ong Khan and his followers.

The Ong Khan's younger brother Erke-khara and many of his officers and others denounced him saying, 'The Ong Khan has a wicked nature. He killed his brothers and has done great harm to his people. How are we to pay him out? But to go back for a moment – when he was six he was carried off by the Merkits and made to pound at a treadmill. When he was twelve he was captured by the Tartars, along with his mother, and made to watch their herds. Afterwards, afraid that the Naimans would kill him, he fled to the Chu river in the land of the Moslems, where he put himself at the disposal of the Black Cathayan Emperor. But in less than a year he turned his back on the Emperor and left him. He passed through the lands of the Uighurs and Tanguts and was in great straits, when Temujin came to the rescue and provided for him. Now he has forgotten all that Temujin did for him and is intending evil against him. What ought we to do?'

After they had said this a certain Altun-ashuk went to the Ong Khan and repeated everything that had been said. Whereupon the Ong Khan seized all those who had taken part in the discussion – El-khutur, Khulbari, Prince Alin and the rest. Only the Ong Khan's younger brother Jakha-gambu escaped by taking flight to the Naimans. El-khutur and the rest were put in bonds and imprisoned in a tent. The Ong Khan said to them, 'Have you forgotten what you promised when we were passing through the lands of the Uighurs and Tanguts? That is the kind of people you are; but I am not going to behave to you as you would behave to me.' So saying he made all those who were present spit in their faces, and then set them free.

Afterwards, in the autumn of the Dog year (1202) Chingis faced in battle, at Dalan-nemurges, the White Tartars and three other Tartar tribes. Before the battle he gave these orders to his troops, 'If we are victorious, there must be no private looting. There will be an equal distribution of the booty when the campaign is over. If our army is driven back to where we first drew up in battle array, all troops on reaching this point must turn round and give fight again. Anyone not turning round and facing the enemy when he reaches this point, will be beheaded.'

They did however defeat the Tartars, and then on reaching the Ulkhui-Shilugeljit river they completely pillaged the homecamps (*a'uru'ut*) of the four Tartar tribes. At the beginning of the battle Altan and others disobeyed the order and took private loot. Chingis ordered Jebe and Khubilai to confiscate everything they had taken.

When he had pillaged the four Tartar tribes, Temujin held a secret council with his kinsmen and proposed as follows: 'As revenge for the slaying of our father by the Tartars it is now proper that we should put to death all their males who stand as high as the linch-pin of a cart. The rest, male and female, are to be used as slaves.'

After this had been agreed to, when Belgutei was leaving the council, he met the Tartar Yeke-cheren who asked 'What were you discussing today?' Belgutei said, 'We are going to put to death any of you Tartars who stands as high as the linch-pin of a cart.' Yeke-cheren passed this on to the other Tartars, who at once went and occupied a stockade on the hill-side. Chingis gave order that the stockade should be stormed, but his men suffered heavily in taking it. After the stockade had been stormed all male Tartars who stood as high as the linch-pin of a cart were duly put to death.

When he learnt what had been decided at the council, Yeke-cheren said to the Tartars, 'When they put us to death, let us each hide a knife in his sleeve and at least kill one of them, so that we may have something to pillow us when we die!' This was put into effect, with the result that many of the troops carrying out the execution were killed or wounded. When it was all over Chingis said, 'An important decision reached by the members of his own clan leaked out owing to Belgutei, with the result that many of our soldiers were wounded or killed. From now onwards, when matters of importance are discussed, Belgutei is not to be present. His duty will be to deal with brawls, thefts or the like that take place outside. Only when the council is over and one cup of drink has been ceremonially offered are Belgutei and Daritai to be admitted.'

Chingis took the Tartar Yeke-cheren's daughter Yesugen to be one of his wives. Finding herself in favour with him she took occasion to say, 'I have an elder sister called Yesui who is more beautiful than I and would be a fit wife for a Khan. She married recently, but I don't know where she is now.' Chingis said, 'If she is really so beautiful, let me look for her. If I find her, would you be willing to resign your place to her?' Yesugen said, 'If only I could see her, I would gladly let her take my place.' Upon this Chingis sent someone to look for her, and she was found in the woods, taking refuge along with her husband. When he saw people coming the husband fled, and Yesui was brought back. When Yesugen saw her she gave up her place to Yesui and made her sit in her stead.

One day when Chingis was drinking outside his tent, with Lady Yesui and Lady Yesugen sitting with him, Yesui sighed deeply. This aroused Chingis' suspicion and he made Mukhali and some others tell those who were present at the gathering each go and stand with his own camping-group. When they had done so there was one young man left over, with no kin to go to. Chingis asked 'Who are you?' The young man answered, 'I am Yesui's husband. When she was first captured, she escaped and we went into hiding. But now that things have settled down I thought I might venture to come out of hiding. I did not think I should be recognized among so many people.' Chingis said, 'He is a descendant of my enemies. He can only have come here now to spy upon us. All the rest of his kind have been slaughtered. Why should I hesitate in his case?' and he had him beheaded at once.

That Dog year (1202) when Chingis was destroying or imprisoning the Tartars, the Ong Khan went off to do the same to the Merkits. He pursued their leader Tokhto'a into the Barkhujin lowlands, killed his eldest son Togus-beki and seized his two daughters and his wife as well as the two other sons and all his people. Of all the booty he took he did not give one thing to Chingis.

After that Chingis and the Ong Khan attacked the Naiman Buyirukh of the Guchugut clan who was at the Ulukh-takh by the Sokhokh river when Chingis and the Ong Khan arrived.

He had not time to draw up in fighting formation, and retreated across the Altai mountains. They pursued him as far as Khumshinggir on the Urunggu river, where they met an officer of Buyirukh's who had come to reconnoitre. This man, whose name was Yedi-tublukh, was driven up into the mountains by a reconnaissance-party of Chingis', where he was seized owing to his saddle-strap breaking. They then continued the pursuit as far as Lake Kishil-bash, where Buyirukh was soon reduced to great straits.

When Chingis and the Ong Khan were on their way back they met a warlike Naiman, Kokse'u-sabrakh, who had drawn up an army in the Bayidarakh valley-mouth, meaning to do battle with them. Chingis and the Ong Khan also drew up their army in battle-array; but as it was late in the day they spent the night where they were. During the night the Ong Khan lit false fires where his camp had been and went off up the Khara-se'ul river.

Jamukha was with the Ong Khan when he made off. He said to him, 'My comrade Temujin has been sending messengers back and forth to the Naimans, and this time, when we moved camp, he stayed behind and does not seem to be following us. This can only mean that he has surrendered to the Naimans.' And Jamukha cried out to the Ong Khan, 'My Khan my Khan! I am the crested-lark that stays put; Temujin is the sky-lark that breaks off and goes home.' At this Gurin the Valiant nicknamed Rouge-faced, who happened to be present, said, 'How can you slander your "brother" in this way, merely in order to curry favour?'

(The Mongolian crested-lark does not migrate in the winter, whereas the sky-lark migrates to the south. Cheeks pink as though rouged were a sign of courage.)

Chingis spent the night where he was and when he looked about at daybreak he saw that where the Ong Khan had been stationed there was now rio one at all. He said, 'He has discarded me as one parts with the food offered as a burnt offering!' He then crossed the Altal by way of the Eter valley and made straight for the Safari steppe, where he encamped. Even adding up the whole total of those belonging to the Nalman faction he found the Naimarts were no longer a force that need be reckoned with.

Meanwhile however the warlike Naiman Kokse'u-sabrakh attacked the Ong Khan from behind and captured his son Sengum's wife and people. He also carried off another portion of the Ong Khan's people and cattle that were on the pass of Telegetu.

Some time before, Khudu arid Chila'un, two sons of Tokhto'a, Khan of the Merkits, had joined the Ong Khan. They now availed themselves of this opportunity to leave him and along with their people went down the Sd erige river to join their father.

When the Ong Khan's wife and people were captured by Kokse'u-sabrakh the Ong Khan sent a messenger to Chingis saying, 'You must send your Four Heroes to save us.' Chingis accordingly sent Bo'orchu and the three other heroes to marshal an army and go to the Ong Khan s assistance. Before the four heroes arrived Sengum had already ranged his forces in battle against the Naimans at Hula'an-khut. His horse was hit in the leg by an arrow and Sengum himself was on the point of being captured. But meanwhile the heroes arrived and rescued him. They also rescued the Ong Khan's wife and people, and restored them to him. The Ong Khan said, 'In old days his good father Yesugei rescued my defeated people and restored them to me. Now Yesugei's son Temujin has sent his four heroes to rescue my defeated people and restore them to me. So help me Heaven and Earth to do as I desire, I swear to repay his kindness.'

The Ong Khan also said, 'Yesugei my comrade once rescued my defeated people and restored them to me. Now his son

Temujin has done the same. For whose benefit did father and son put themselves to such trouble? I am an old man. Whom am I to put as ruler over these my people? None of my younger brothers have any ability, and I have only one son, Sengum; and that is as bad as having no son at all! I must get Temujin to be Sengum's "elder brother". Then I shall have two sons, and my mind will be at rest.' Accordingly he met Chingis in the black woods beside the Tula river and they went through the ceremony of becoming father and son. To start with, the Ong Khan had become the bond-brother of Chingis' father, Yesugei; that was why Chingis called the Ong Khan his 'father'. On this occasion they renewed the bond that made them father and son, saying, 'When we attack our many foes, we will attack them both of us together; when we hunt wild beasts, we will hunt them both of us together. If any one tries to make trouble between us, we will take no notice of what he says, but only believe such stories as each tells to the other face to face.' When this was settled between them, they continued for a time to have great affection for one another.

Chingis wanted this affection to be even greater and therefore sought the hand of Sengum's elder sister Cha'ur-beki for his son Jochi and as exchange offered his daughter Khojin as wife to Sengum's son Tusakha. Sengum, exaggerating his own importance, said, 'If a girl of ours went to his family, she would have to stand all the time behind the door, with her face to the north; but if a girl of his came to us, she would be seated with her face to the south.' He scorned the idea and would not consent to the marriage. This was a setback to Chingis' feelings towards the Ong Khan and Sengum.

Jamukha noticed that Chingis no longer felt towards them as before and in the year of the Boar (1203), in the spring, after discussing the matter with Altan and others he set out with them to Berke-elet, which is to the north of the Jeje'er heights, and coming to Sengum slandered Chingis, saying, 'Temujin through his messengers is in continual communication with Tayang, the Khan of the Naimans. The words "father" and 'son" are still on his lips; but when it comes to deeds, it is a different matter. Can you really still have confidence in him? If you do not get rid of him before he can carry out his plans, you will find yourselves in an awkward position. But if you decide to get rid of Temujin, I'll help you by joining in on the flank.' At this Altan and Khuchar said, 'I'll kill for you all the sons of Mother Ho'elun.' Ebugejin and Khardakidai said, 'We will seize their hands and feet (helpers) for you.' To'oril said, 'It would be far better to go and make prisoners of Temujin's people. If his people are made prisoners, what can he do?' Khachi'un-beki said, 'Sengum, whatever you decide to do, I'll go with you – to the topmost bough or the bottom-most abyss!'

When Sengum heard what Jamukha and all the others said, he sent Sayikhan-tode'en to repeat it all to his father the Ong Khan. The Ong Khan said, 'Why do you think such things of my "son" Temujin? At present we enjoy his support, and if we now have such evil thoughts about him, Heaven will certainly not love and protect us. What Jamukha has been saying is a wild exaggeration.' When the Ong Khan would not consent, Sengum sent another messenger to say, 'Every man that has mouth and lips says the same. It is impossible not to believe it.' When Sengum had sent message after message and still the Ong Khan could not be convinced, he finally went in person and said, 'Even now when you are still there Temujin does not regard us as of any account. When you, my father, are "old" (i.e. dead), he certainly won't bring himself to let us remain in control of the people that our ancestors have been at such pains to bring together.' The Ong Khan said, 'I can't reject you, who are my own son. But we enjoy Temujin's support, and it is wrong to think evil of him. If we do that, Heaven will certainly not love and protect us.' Seeing that his father would not agree, he went away in a huff. But the Ong Khan called him back, saying, 'Apart from whether Heaven withdraws its love and protection or not, how can I reject either of you, who are my sons? Go and do as you like. As to whether you people are able to conquer Temujin, that is for you to decide!'

Upon this Sengum held a council with the others at which they decided as follows:

'Temujin once asked for our girl Cha'ur-beki. We will now fix a time for the Day of Betrothal and invite him to come and eat at the Betrothal Banquet. When he arrives we will seize him then and there.'

When this had been agreed upon they sent someone to invite Chingis, who set out with ten followers. On the way he spent a night with old Monglik. Monglik said, 'When we asked for that girl of his, he gave himself airs, looked down upon us and would not give her. Why has he now gone out of his way to invite you to come and eat the Feast of Betrothal? Temujin my boy, you're being unwise. You had far better excuse yourself, saying, "It is spring and my horses are lean; at the moment I am feeding up my horses and cannot go".' Chingis agreed, and sent Bukhatai and Kiratai to the Betrothal Feast; himself he turned back and went home. When Sengum saw Bukhatai and Kiratai come, he said, 'They have seen through our plot. Now the only thing for us to do is to go off at once, surround them and capture them.'

When Altan's younger brother Yeke-cheren came home from the council at which this had been agreed, he said, 'It was decided at the council today that tomorrow we are to go and seize Temujin. If some one were to go and warn him of this, I wonder what he could claim as reward.' His wife Alakhchit said, 'Mind what you're saying! One of the servants might overhear you and think you meant it seriously.' And as a matter of fact, just at the time when this conversation was going on, one of the grooms, a man called Badai, arrived bringing some mare's milk. He heard what was said and repeated it to another groom, Kishilikh. Kishilikh said, 'I'll go too and see if I can pick up anything more.' When he got there, he was just in time to hear Yeke-cheren's son Narin-ke'en, who was sharpening an arrow, say to the others, 'What we said just now is a thing for which our tongues ought to be taken out! What's to stop the servants from passing it on?' Then he turned to the groom Kishilikh and said, 'Go and catch the white horse and the chestnut and tether them. I shall be starting off early tomorrow.' When Kishilikh heard all this he went off and repeated it to Badai, saying, 'I've just got confirmation of what you said. Let's go and warn Temujin.' So they went and caught the horses and tethered them in readiness, slaughtered a lamb at their own quarters and cooked it with wood from their benches as fuel. Then each of them mounted one of the two horses that they had already tethered and that same night they arrived at the back of Temujin's tent and repeated all that Yeke-cheren and his son Narin had said, adding 'Beyond any doubt it really is a fact that they are going to come and seize you.'

When Chingis heard what Badai and Kishilikh told him, that very night he passed on the news to any trusted comrades that were at hand and leaving behind all his household properties he went and took refuge on the north side of the Mao Heights. On the way, he ordered Jelme to stay behind and keep a look-out on the rear. On the afternoon of the next day he rested at the Khalakhaljit sands. Meanwhile Chigidai and another, who were grooms of Alchidai, arrived announcing that from the south of the Mao Heights, looking into the distance, they had seen dust rising at Hula'an-burukhat, which meant that the enemy were coming. Chingis at once rode off. While coming in company with Jamukha the Ong Khan asked him, 'What fighters has Temujin with him?' Jamukha said, 'He has the peoples of the Uru'ut and the

Mangkhut who are good fighters. Even in a mêlée they never break rank, and from the time they are children they are used to lances and swords. Their banners are either many-coloured or black. When you see them, be on your guard.' The Ong Khan said, 'In that case, the Jirgin hero Khadakh had better lead the attack upon them, supported in the rear by Achikh-shirun of the Tumen-tubegen and the heroes of the Olon-dongkhayit clan. Prince Khori-shilemun shall be next in support, leading a thousand of the Bodyguard. Behind the Bodyguard my own main army will attack.' And he added, 'Jamukha my "younger brother", I place you in command of my army.' At this Jamukha left the Ong Khan and went off alone. To some of his comrades he said, 'I have never once yet been able to bring myself to fight against Temujin. Now the Ong Khan tells me to command his army! Judging by that, he is not so good a friend as I. I ought to report this to my comrade Temujin.' Whereupon he sent a messenger to Temujin to repeat what the Ong Khan had said. He added, 'Such men as he will certainly never conquer you. Don't be afraid, but be on your guard!'

When Chingis was told of Jamukha's words, he said, ' "Uncle" Jurchedei, I should like you to lead the vanguard. What do you think of that?' Just as Jurchedei was beginning to answer Khuyildar said, 'I will lead the vanguard; but if anything happens to me, you must bring up my orphans.' Jurchedei said, 'My Uru'uts and Khuyildar's Mangkhuts will fight as vanguard in front of the Khan.' That having been said, the people of those two clans lined up in front of Chingis. They had scarcely taken up position when the Ong Khan's vanguard, the Jirgins, attacked. The Uru'uts and Mangkhuts advanced to meet them and routed them. While they were pursuing the defeated Jirgins, Achikh-shirun of the Tumen-tubegen clan, who were part of the Ong Khan's rearguard, attacked, and pierced our Khuyildar, who fell from his horse.

The Mangkhuts turned back and stood where Khuyildar had fallen.

Jurchedei then led the Uru'uts against the Tumen-tubegen and routed them. While he was pursuing them, there was an attack by the Olon-dongkhayit, but Jurchedei defeated them. The same thing happened when Prince Khori-shilemun attacked with his guardsmen. At this point the Ong Khan's son Sengum, without telling his father that he meant to do so, also attacked. Jurchedei shot him in the cheek, and he fell. When they saw that Sengum had been hit by an arrow and had fallen all the Kereit warriors withdrew and stood where Sengum lay.

Chingis, having defeated the Ong Khan and seeing that it was late, withdrew his troops and took the wounded Khuyildar back with him. That night he moved camp to a place some way off from where the battle was fought.

At dawn next day a roll-call was held and it was found that Ogodei, Borokhul and Bo'orchu were missing. Chingis said, 'Ogodei and his trusted friends Borokhul and Bo'orchu dead or alive would certainly never leave one another.' That night Chingis, fearing that the enemy might come in pursuit, drew up his troops in readiness for battle. When it was light, he saw some one coming from the rear who on arriving turned out to be Bo'orchu. When Chingis beating his breast had addressed Heaven, Bo'orchu said, 'My horse was shot down by the enemy and I was running on foot when I saw the Kereits turn back and stand where Sengum lay. Very opportunely I saw that the pack of one of their pack-horses had slipped. I cut away the pack, mounted the horse, galloped off and picking up your tracks came to you here.'

Not long after, a second man arrived. When they looked more closely it seemed as though two legs were dangling under him. It turned out to be Ogodei and Borokhul riding one on top of the other, on the same horse. Borokhul had blood on his mouth, for Ogodei had received an arrow-wound in the neck and Borokhul had sucked away the clotted blood. When Chingis saw him he wept and his heart was very sore. He at once cauterized the arrow-wound and gave him something to ease his thirst. Borokhul said, 'Judging by where they are raising dust, it seems that the enemy have gone towards Hula'an-burukhat, in front of the Mao Heights.' On hearing this, Chingis marshalled his army and went up the Ulkhui-shilugeljit river till he had entered the district of Dalan-nemurges.

Later, Khada'an-daldurkhan left his wife and came to Chingis saying, 'When the Ong Khan's son Sengum was hit by an arrow, the Ong Khan said, "He challenged to the fray one whom he ought not to have challenged! And so, alas, it came about that a 'nail' was driven into my son's cheek. As soon as my son comes to himself, let us order a fresh attack." Whereupon Achikh-shirum said, "No, no, Khan! Before you had a son, you entreated and prayed for a son to succeed you. Having in answer to your prayers got this son Sengum, let us take care of him. More than half of the Mongol people are with us here. As for the people who haved joined with Temujin in his desertion of us, where can they go now? Each man only has his one horse; they have nowhere to spend the night save under a tree. If they don't come to us, we can go and take them as easily as one picks up horse-dung." The Ong Khan agreed, saying, "Leave my son in quiet and take good care of him", and he went home.'

Chingis left Dalan-nemurges and moved his men down the Khalkha river. A count was held, which showed that his army numbered 2,600. He himself with 1,300 men kept to the west side of the river, while 1,300 Uru'uts and Mangkhuts moved along the east side. While they were hunting in order to obtain provisions, Khuyildar, whose wound was not yet properly healed, despite the protests of Chingis galloped after the prey.

His wound reopened and he died. They buried him half-way up the side of Mount Ornu'u, above the Khalkha.

Chingis now moved and encamped on the east side of the brook Tunggelik. He sent Arkhai-khasar and Sugegei to give this message to the Ong Khan:

'I have now encamped on the east side of the brook Tunggelik, The grass is good and my horses are fat. "Father," what have I done that you should be angry with me and try to scare me? If you are cross with me, why don't you give me a quiet talking-to instead of ruining my home and all my belongings? I can't help thinking someone must have made mischief between us. Didn't we once at the Hula'a-nu'ut hills of the Jorkhalkhun range agree that if anyone tried to make trouble between us we would not listen, but would only believe in what was said face to face? Now, "Father", have we ever had it out face to face? I and my followers may be few; but it is as though we are many. We may be bad; but it is as though we were good. Moreover, you and I are like the two shafts of a cart; if one of them is broken, the ox cannot pull it. We are like the two wheels of a cart; if one is destroyed, the cart cannot move. Am I not now like a single shaft, a single wheel? If you now have some complaint to make against me, send a messenger to tell me about it.'

When the Ong Khan heard this he sighed and said, 'I was under obligations that made it wrong for me to part from my "son" Temujin, but I parted from him.' He was very unhappy and taking a knife he stabbed his little finger till it bled. Then he poured the blood into a small birch-bark pail and said, 'If seeing my "son" Temujin I would do him any hurt, may I be stabbed till blood like this flows.'

Chingis sent to Jamukha the following message:

'It was because you were jealous that you put a distance between me and the Khan, my "father". Formerly every day the one that was up earliest used to take the Khan my "father's" mare's milk and drink it out of his blue Chinese cup, and because I was always the first to rise, you were jealous of me. Now you can take a long drink from the Khan my "father's" blue Chinese cup, without a thought about how much you are consuming.'

To Altan and Khuchar he sent the message:

'I don't know what you had in your mind when you left me. You, Khuchar, are the son of Prince Nekun. To start with we asked you to be Khan among us, but you refused. Altan! Your father Khutula Khan once ruled over the Mongol people and consequently you were asked to become Khan; but you too refused. Among the descendants of Khutula's eldest son there were Bartan's sons Sacha-beki and Taichu; but they too were unwilling. In the end you all of you asked me to be Khan and I very reluctantly accepted. Despite this you have now left me. As things are, be good comrades to the Ong Khan! You must not "have a beginning but no end", or people will criticize you saying, "They depended entirely on Temujin; without him they are no good at all." What you must do is to guard the sources of the three rivers and make sure that no outsiders camp there.'

Chingis sent another message, this time to Sengum, saying:

'I was born to your father as a child with clothes on, whereas you were born to him naked (i.e. natural, not adopted), but he brought us both up without making any distinction. You got it into your head that there was a danger of my thrusting myself ahead of you, and in your jealousy you drove me away. It is for you now to stop causing distress to your father. Early and late, going in and going out, you should be doing all you can to distract him from his sorrows. If you can't overcome this old jealousy, it can only be that, wanting to become Khan in his stead while he is still alive, you purposely torment him. If you send me a reply, send two messengers.'

Chingis entrusted this message to Arkhai-khasar and Sugegei, who brought it to Sengum. Sengum said, 'I am sure that in giving the message he never once referred to the Ong Khan as "the Khan my father", but instead called him the "old assassin". And in my case he certainly never spoke of me as "comrade"; instead he called me "the shaman Tokhto'a" who tagged along close behind the tail of the Turkestan sheep.'

(We do not know this story, but the implication is perhaps that Sengum was eagerly awaiting the Ong Khan's death.)

'I know well enough what his message means; the next thing to happen will be that he marches against us in battle. Bilge-beki and Todo'en! Raise the battle-standard and put our horses to graze so that they may be in good fettle. There is no doubt about what's coming.'

At that Chingis' messenger Arkhai-khasar left the Ong Khan's camp and came home. Sugegei however stayed, because his wife and children were with the Ong Khan. Arkhai-khasar repeated to Chingis what Sengum had said.

Chingis at once moved camp and settled at Lake Baljuna. Here he met Cho'os-chakhan and others of the Khorulas clan, who surrendered without fighting. There was also a Moslem called Asam who bad come from the quarters of Alakhush the Digit-khuri, of the Onggut tribe. He had a thousand wethers and a white camel and was about to go down the Ergune river to buy sables and squirrel skins. He was watering his wethers at the Baljuna lake when he met Chingis.

While Chingis was living at Lake Baljuna, his younger brother Khasar, leaving behind his wife and his three sons Yegu, Yesungge and Tukhu in the hands of the Ong Khan, fled empty-handed at the head of a few companions and came to look for Chingis. When he reached Mount Khara'un he went along the ridge, but could not find him. He fell short of provisions and was reduced to eating the raw hide and tendons of an ox. When at last he found his elder brother Chingis at Lake Baljuna, Chingis was delighted to see him. It was agreed that they should send Khali'udar of the Je'uriyedei and Chakhurkhan of the Uriangkhadai as messengers from Khasar. They were to say to the Ong Khan, 'My elder brother Temujin has disappeared altogether, leaving no trace. I have trodden his path, but could not find him. I called to him, but he could not hear. At night I gaze at the stars, with the earth for my pillow. My wife and children, O Khan my father, are with you. If you will send some one trustworthy to me, I will come back to you.' Before despatching them Chingis said to the messengers, 'When you go, I shall move from here at once. When you come back from the Ong Khan you will find me at Arkhal-ge'ugi on the Kerulen.' Having fixed the place of meeting he sent on Jurchedei and Arkhai-khasar as scouts and himself camped at Arkhal-ge'ugi on the Kerulen.

When Khali'udar and Chakhurkhan got to the Ong Khan they repeated what had been said. The Ong Khan had just set up his gold-dusted tent and was feasting. When he had heard what Khali'udar told him he said, 'If that is how it is, tell Khasar to come.' He then sent Iturgen, who was suited to serve as a man of trust, along with Khali'udar and the other. When they were coming near to the place agreed upon, Iturgen saw a vast encampment looming up and at once turned and fled. Khali'udar had a fast horse and caught up with him, but not daring to lay hands on him only got in front of him and barred his path. Chakhurkhan's horse was slow, but from the farthest point that an arrow would carry he shot Iturgen's horse on the point of its buttocks, so that it collapsed upon its haunches. He then took Iturgen into arrest and brought him to Chingis, who handed him over to Khasar to execute.

Khali'udar and Chakhurkhan said to Chingis, 'The Ong Khan is taking no steps to defend himself. At present he has put up his golden pavilion and is feasting. We should do well to march day and night, and fall upon him unawares.' Chingis said, 'Yes,' and told Jurchedei and Arkhai-khasar to go on ahead as scouts, pressing on day and night. When they reached the defile of Jerene in the Jeje'er heights they surrounded the Ong Khan and began a slaughter that lasted three days and three nights. On the third day the Ong Khan's people could resist no longer and surrendered. Meanwhile the Ong Khan and his son Sengum had somehow or other managed to break through the encirclement and escape. Taking part in this battle there was a man called Khadakh the Valiant. He said, 'I could not bear to let you seize and slay my rightful lord. That is why I fought for three days, so that he might have time to get clear away. If you are going to put me to death, I am ready to die; but if you do me the favour of letting me live, I will strive for you with might and main.' Chingis said, 'One who could not bring himself to desert his lord, but fought on against us alone that his lord might have time to get clear away, is surely a fine man! Of such a one as he one may make a comrade.' So he did not kill him, but ordered him to bring a hundred of his people to Khuyildar's widow, to be her slaves and attendants for ever. And because in the beginning Khuyildar had been the first to say that he would fight, Chingis ordered that his sons and grandsons should always receive the bounty that is accorded to orphans.

The Ong Khan and Sengum fled empty-handed to the camp of Didik-sakhal near the waters of the Nekun. The Ong Khan was thirsty after this long journey and was going down to the stream to drink when a Naiman scout called Khori-subechi seized him. He said, 'I am the Ong Khan,' but the scout did not believe it, and killed him.

Sengum had not gone down to the stream, and when this happened to the Ong Khan he made for the Gobi desert. Here Sengum, along with his comrade Kokochu and Kokochu's wife, looked for water to drink. Seeing some wild-asses that were being bitten by flies, Sengum dismounted and giving his horse to Kokochu to hold he was creeping up stealthily towards the wild-asses intending to shoot at them. Meanwhile Kokochu fled, taking Sengum's horse on the lead. Kokochu's wife said, 'In former times he gave you fine clothes to wear and good food to eat. How can you desert him like this, your rightful master and lord?' Saying this she stayed where she was and would not go with him. Kokochu said, 'You think perhaps that if you stay here Sengum will marry you?' She said, 'I know people say that women have dog's (i.e. unblushing) faces. All the same, you might at least give him this golden cup of his, so that he may be able to get himself a drink.' Kokochu took the golden cup and dashed it to the ground. Then, along with his wife, he went to Chingis and told him the whole story of how he had abandoned Sengum. Chingis said, 'I can't take such a man as this for comrade.' He rewarded the wife, but killed Kokochu.

Tayang, the Khan of the Naimans, was the son of a lady called Gurbesu. She now said, 'The Ong Khan was an old khan who had ruled from long ago. Bring me his head to look at. If I recognize it as really his, I will make an offering to it.' She then sent a messenger to Khori-subechi telling him to cut off the head and bring it to her. She recognized it as the Ong Khan's and to the accompaniment of musical instruments she made an offering to it. While she was doing so, the head laughed. Seeing this, Tayang thought it an evil omen, threw the head on to the ground and trod it to pieces. Kokse'u-sabrakh was there and said, 'You have cut off a dead man's head and then stamped it to pieces. Now the dogs are barking and there is an ill-omened sound in their bark. In old days your father Inancha-bilge Khan once said, "I am old and my wife here is young. My son Tayang is soft and weak, born as the result of my prayers to the gods. I fear that when I am dead he will not be able to keep my numerous people." That was what he said, and now sure enough in the barking of the dogs there is a sound that foretells defeat. The rule of queen Gurbesu is harsh and at the same time our Tayang Khan is soft and weak. Apart from hawking and hunting he has no skill or bent.'

Some time later Tayang Khan said, 'To the east there are some Mongols at the sight of whose quivers the former Khan of the Kereits, old Ong Khan, fled in panic and died. It looks as though they mean to set up their ruler as grand Khan. But just as in heaven there can only be one sun and one moon, on earth there cannot be two masters. Let us now go and take those Mongols.' His mother Gurbesu said, 'Those Mongol people stink and they wear dark (grimy?) clothes. What could we do with them if we *did* take them? We should have to keep them at a distance. However, if we found any good-looking women among them, we could make them wash their hands and milk the cows and goats for us. They would be all right for that.' Tayang said, 'That being so, where's the difficulty? Let us go and snatch their bows and arrows.'

When Kokse'u-sabrakh heard these words of Tayang Khan's he sighed and said, 'You ought not to brag like that. Never let me hear you say such words again!' But Tayang did not pay any attention. He at once sent Torbi-tash as messenger to Alakhush the Digit-khuri, Khan of the Ongguts, to say to him, 'To the east of here there are some Mongols. You shall be my right hand and I will set out from here. Then together we will seize their bows and arrows.' Alakhush replied, 'I have no intention of being your right hand,' and so far from agreeing, he sent a messenger to Chingis saying,

'Tayang of the Naimans is going to come and snatch your bows and arrows, and he asked me to be his right hand. I refused, and wish now to inform you of this. If you don't take measures to prevent it, I fear he may succeed in seizing your bows and arrows.' At this time Chingis was hunting at Teme'en Steppe. When he received this message, there and then, at the hunt, he held a council. Many of those present said, 'Our horses are lean, it is a bad moment for us.' But Chingis' youngest brother Temuge said, 'How can you make the excuse that your horses are lean? *My* horses are fat, and after hearing such news as this, how can I sit still and do nothing?' Belgutei too said, 'What is the use of being alive, if one's bows and arrows have been snatched from one? Surely the thing for a man to do is to die where his bows and arrows are! The Naimans think that because their country is large and their people many, they have the right to brag. Here is *our* opportunity to seize their bows and arrows. If we go and do it, we shall certainly find that they have fled, leaving their great herds of horses quietly grazing, their homes empty; their people will all have taken refuge among the hills and woods, Let us ride off at once!'

On the sixteenth day of the fourth month of the Rat year (AD 1204) Chingis sacrificed to his battle-standards and went off to fight against the Naimans, going up stream along the Kerulen. He sent Jebe and Khubilai ahead as scouts and when they got to the Sa'ari Steppe they met some Naimans scouting on the Khangkha-khan heights. While the scouts of both sides were chasing one another this way and that, the Naimans captured one of our people, who was riding a white horse with a broken saddle. They said to one another, 'True enough, the horses of the Mongols are lean.' Afterwards Chingis with his main army reached the Sa'ari Steppe and camped there. Dodai-cherbi said to Chingis, 'We are few in number and have travelled a long way. We had better turn out our horses to graze and establish decoy troops in large numbers all over the Sa'ari Steppe. (That is, people of all kinds, other than combatants, were to be disguised as soldiers). At night every one should light five fires. The Naimans are in great force, but their ruler is timid and weak. He has never been far from home and will certainly be bewildered and deceived. Then when our horses have had their fill we will press back their scouts, make straight for their main camp and fall upon them before they have time to draw up in battle-order. In this way we should be sure to win.' Chingis took his advice.

The Naiman scouts did indeed look down from the hill-top and say, 'If the Mongols are really so few as we thought, how is it that the fires they have lit are numerous as the stars?' When sending the man and horse they had previously caught to Tayang Khan they said, 'The Mongol armies fill the whole of the Sa'ari Steppe. They seem to be increasing every day. One can judge this by the fact that the fires they light at night are numerous as the stars.'

When his scouts went out, Tayang Khan was on the bank of the Khachir stream at Khangkhai. When he heard what the scouts reported he sent a messenger to his son Guchuluk saying, 'The horses of the Mongols may be lean, but the fires they light are numerous as the stars, and they must certainly have a very large army. I have been told that the Mongols are very tough; you may prick them in the eye and they do not blench, you may prick them on the cheek and they do not wince. If we became too closely involved now, it would afterwards certainly be difficult to disengage. I am told that the horses of the Mongols are lean. The thing for us to do is to move our people across the Altai Mountains, then marshal our armies and lure the Mongols on. By the time they reach the Altai their lean horses will be exhausted, whereas our fat horses will just be at the top of their form. Then we can turn round and fight with them successfully.'

When Tayang's son Guchuluk heard these words, he said, 'There's that old woman Tayang, frightened again! If the Mongols are really so numerous, where can they all have come from? A good half of them have ranged themselves with Jamukha and are with us here. My father Tayang has never in his life been farther away from home than the place where the pregnant women urinate or the calves eat their fodder. No wonder he is now afraid!' Having said this he sent a messenger to repeat it to his father. When Tayang heard that his son had called him 'an old woman', he said, 'Let us hope that when it comes to the actual fighting Guchuluk "the strong and brave" won't let down his reputation!' His officer Khori-subechi said, 'Your father Inancha-bilge in old days when fighting with an enemy that was his match never let them see "the back of a man or the hindquarters of a horse". How comes it that you are already in a state of panic? If only we had known sooner that you were going to behave like this, we should have done better to put your mother Gurbesu in command of the army, woman though she is! Kokse'u-sabrakh, alas, is old and the discipline in our army is very lax. It looks as though the fortunes of the Mongols were on the upward turn.' So he said with a sigh and after giving his horse a tap with his quiver he went off elsewhere. (Presumably he joined the Mongols.)

When Tayang heard Khori-subechi's words he said angrily, 'To have a life that must end and a body that must meet hardship is the common lot of man. If that is what you all say, let us face them and fight it out!' He went down the Tamir river and crossed the Orkhon and went on till he reached Chakir-ma'ut, on the east side of the cliffs of Mount Nakhu. When his scouts saw the Naiman army, Chingis drew up his own forces in battle-order and with them formed the vanguard. He put the central army under the leadership of his younger brother Khasar and put Temuge in charge of the reserve horses. Upon this, the Naimans retired to a point in front of the cliffs of Mount Nakhu and halted along the fringe of the mountain. The scouts of Chingis then threw back those of the Naimans and pursued them to the foot of the mountain.

At that time Jamukha was with the Naimans and Tayang asked him, 'Who are those that chase all before them, like a wolf that pursues a flock of sheep right into the fold?' Jamukha said, 'Those are my comrade Chingis' "four dogs", fed on human flesh and kept till now bound in leash on a rope of iron. Those "dogs" have foreheads of bronze and fangs like chisels. Their tongues are awls and their hearts are of iron. They use their ring-swords as horse-whips. They drink the dew and ride on the wind, but in time of battle they eat human flesh. Now they have been loosed from their leashes of iron and come dribbling in their zest! Those "four dogs" are Jebe, Khubilai, Jelme and Sube'etei.' Tayang said, 'That being so, let us get a bit further away from those evil men!' and he retreated till he was standing astride the mountain. (That is, with one foot in the plain and one on the mountain-side.)

He asked again, 'Who are those warriors that come joyous as colts that crowd round their mother when they have had their fill of milk?' Jamukha said, 'Those are they who having slain a brave man armed with lance and sword, strip the clothes from his back. They are the Uru'uts and the Mangkhuts.' Tayang said, 'If that is how it is, let us get a bit further away from these evil men,' and he led his people to a place higher up the mountain. He asked again, 'And behind them, that one there who is pressing forward like a falcon ravenous for food, who is he?' Jamukha said, 'That is my comrade Temujin. His whole frame is clad in armour of iron. True enough he comes like a falcon ravenous for food. Do you see them? You people once said, "If we met the Mongols we would gobble them down as one might the kid of a goat, not leaving so much as the skin of a hoof unswallowed." Well, now have a look!' Tayang said, 'One can't help being frightened of them,' and he led his people to a place higher up the mountain. He asked again, 'Who is it that comes next, with a great throng of warriors?' Jamukha said, 'It is one of mother Ho'elun's sons whom she fed on human flesh so that he grew to be three spans tall and can eat a full-grown cow at one sitting. He is covered up with three layers of iron armour, so that it takes three strong bulls to drag him along. He can swallow a man complete with bow and arrows without choking, and even when he has gulped down a whole man, he is still hungry. When he is angry he can shoot across a mountain with his *angkhu'a* (?) arrow and pierce ten men, even twenty men right through. When any one attacks him, with a wide space of steppe between them, shooting with his *keyibur* (?) arrow he can pierce him and and his armour right through. When he stretches his bow to the full he can shoot nine hundred yards, when he stretches it only a little, he can shoot five hundred yards. He has never been like other men, but more like some huge boa-constricter. His name is Khasar.'

Tayang said, 'That being so, let us press on together to a place higher up the mountain.' Again he asked, 'Who is that coming up behind?' Jamukha said, 'That is Ho'elun's youngest son Temuge, called the Hearth-ward. He is lazy and likes to go to sleep early and rise late. But among the many warriors he was never once the last to take the field.' Upon this, Tayang climbed again and did not stop till he came to the very top of the mountain.

Jamukha then left the Naimans and told Chingis what he had said to Tayang, adding 'When Tayang heard what I told him, he became dazed with fear and his one idea was to get to the top of the mountain; he did not look at all like meaning to do any fighting. I have abandoned him. Comrade, act with care!'

Chingis saw that it was getting late, so he surrounded Mount Nakhu and prepared to spend the night thus. During the night the Naimans tried to escape. Many of the horses and their riders fell over precipices in the darkness, and the dead lay heaped upon one another. Next day Tayang was captured. His son Guchuluk was not at hand and managed to escape. He had a few followers with him and when he saw that his pursuers were catching up with him, he tried to fortify and hold a position on the Tamir river. But he did not succeed and continued his flight. At the foot of the Altai mountains, his situation became more and more desperate and all his people were captured.

At this time, too, the Mongols who had sided with Jamukha, such as the Jadaran and the Khatagin, all surrendered to Chingis. When Tayang's mother Gurbesu came to him Chingis said, 'Wasn't it you who said that we Mongols smell bad? I am surprised you should come.' He then admitted her to his household.

In the autumn of the Rat year (AD 1204) Chingis fought with Tokhto'a the Khan of the Merkits at the Kharadal spring, forced him back and pursuing him to the Sa'ari Steppe took prisoner all his people. Tokhto'a himself, with his two sons Khudu and Chila'un and a few comrades, managed to escape. When the Merkits were captured, Dayir-usun of the U'uas branch of the Merkits offered his daughter Khulan to Chingis. On their way Dayir-usun and his daughter were held up by troops who were out of control. Presently they met Naya'a an officer of the Ba'arin clan. Dayir-usun said to him, 'I am taking this girl to offer her to Chingis.' Naya'a said, 'Let us go together and take your daughter to Chingis. If you go ahead by yourself, these unruly troops will kill you and rape the girl.' Naya'a then kept the girl for three days before bringing her to Chingis. Chingis was very angry and said, 'Put him on trial and interrogate him down to the minutest detail!' While the interrogation was in process, Khulan said, 'Naya'a said, "I am a great officer of the Khan. Let us go together and present this girl to Chingis." It was only because there were disorderly troops on the road that he delayed. If he had not done so, I don't know in what condition I should be now. Do not question him any further at present, but if you will be so good – for my virginity is still just as when by Heaven's command my father and mother gave me birth – examine me in this respect, and that will make an end of the matter.' Naya'a also said, 'I was only serving my master's interests as best I could. All beautiful girls and good horses got from other tribes must be handed over to one's lord. If any other thought than this was in my mind, then let me die!' Chingis said, 'What Khulan suggested is quite right.' So that very day they tested her and it was found that she had indeed not been ravaged. Because of this Chingis took her into great favour and let Naya'a go, saying 'This is a very faithful man and may well in future be entrusted with affairs of great importance.'

When the Merkit people were captured, Chingis gave the wife of Tokhto'a's son Khudu to Ogodei. But a portion of the surrendered Merkits revolted and fortified a position on Mount Taikhal. Chingis ordered Sorkhanshira's son Chimbai to take the right hand army and attack them. Himself he went off in pursuit of Tokhto'a, but when he reached the Altai mountains he stopped and wintered there. Next year (AD 1205) in the spring he crossed the Arai ridge. Meanwhile Tokhto'a of the Merkits and Guchuluk of the Naimans had met and marshalled their forces at the Bukhdurma headwaters of the Erdis river. Chingis arrived there and fought with them. Tokhto'a was hit by a stray arrow and died. They were unable to take his body with them, so they cut off his head and took that. Men and horses fled routed. More than half of them were drowned when trying to cross the Erdis, and the rest scattered and disappeared. Guchuluk of the Naimans fled through the land of the Uighurs and Kharlukhs to the Chu river, which is in Moslem territory, where he joined the ruler of the Black

Cathayans. The Merkits Khudu, Khal (?) and Chila'un retreated through the lands of the Khangli and the Kimcha'ut. Chingis returned to his home camp.

Meanwhile Chimbai captured the position at Taikhal where the revolted Merkits were trying to make a stand, and killed or captured them all. There was a further revolt of Merkits in Chingis' home camp, but it was put down by his servants in the camp. Chingis said, 'If we leave them all together in one place, they will rebel again', and he had them distributed one here and one there.

In that year of the Ox (AD 1205) Chingis made and gave to Sube'etei an iron cart, and bade him attack Tokhto'a's sons, Khudu and the rest. He said to him, 'When we defeated Tokhto'a his sons fled and escaped, like a wild horse that bolts dragging the lasso-pole with it or a deer that when it has been shot runs off with the arrow still sticking into it. But even if they fly up into the sky, you like a falcon will pursue them and bring them down; even if like marmots they burrow into the ground, you shall be the spade that will dig them out. If like fish they plunge down into the sea, you shall be the net that will drag them out.' And he added, 'You will be crossing high mountains and great rivers. You must not begin to spare the soldier's horses only when they are already lean, or begin to husband your food-supplies only when they are running out. On the way you must not lightly go off hunting; if you are obliged to hunt in order to restock your provisions, you should do so only in accordance with your requirements. You are not to allow the horsemen to pass the crupper or connect the bridle. In that way the soldiers will not dare to gallop. Anyone disobeying this command, if he is someone known personally to me he is to be sent to me to deal with, if not known to me, he is to be penalized on the spot. This order is to be taken very seriously. If by Heaven's aid you capture Tokhto'a's sons, you are to execute them on the spot.' He went on, 'When I was young the three Merkit leaders captured me, after having chased me three times round Mount Burkhan. A people from whom I have suffered such wrongs once again I curse! It is because I wish you to pursue them to the utmost end that I have made for you an iron cart. Even when you are far away from me, it must be as though I were at hand. Go, and Heaven will certainly help you!'

After Chingis had made captive the Naimans and Merkits, Jamukha's people fell into his hands along with the Naimans and he was left with only five comrades, with whom he lived the life of a vagabond. Once when they had climbed up on to the Tanglu mountains they killed a wild Argali sheep, cooked it and ate it. While they were eating it Jamukha said, 'It is not everyone's son who today has killed an Argali sheep, cooked it and ate it!' When he said this his five comrades seized him and brought him to Chingis' camp. Jamukha told someone to say to Chingis, 'To think that the black crow should seize the wild duck, that slaves could seize their master! The Khan my comrade will certainly not be mistaken.' Chingis said, 'Men who have dared to seize their true lord, how can I keep by me? Such men and their sons and grandsons must all suffer the penalty of the law!' So saying he had them all executed in Jamukha's presence, whereas to Jamukha he sent the message, 'I once let you be one shaft when I was the other, but you separated yourself from me. Now we have come together again and could be comrades, each reminding the other when he forgot anything, waking the other if he dozed off. Though you did once go your own way, yet you behaved as a comrade that brought me blessing and good fortune, and when it became a question of actual warfare between us, you were greatly distressed. When I first fought with the Ong Khan, you reported his intentions to me; that was the first time you did me a good turn. When it came to fighting with the Naimans, you pitched a tale that frightened them; that was your second good turn.' 'Go to Jamukha,' he said, 'and tell him what I have just said.'

On getting this message Jamukha said, 'When we were young and became sworn-comrades, we drank the drink that cannot be digested (each other's blood), spoke the words that cannot be forgotten (oath of friendship). But others came between us and we separated. When I think of the words that were spoken then, I am shamefaced and dare not meet my comrade. Now you want me to be your comrade again. But when I was your comrade, I was never a true comrade. Now you have gathered together all the peoples and established yourself in the great seat of honour, and it is impossible for me to be your comrade. If you do not kill me, I shall be like a louse on your collar, like a thorn inside the lower border of your coat. I shall make you uneasy in your mind by day and prevent you from sleeping soundly at night.

'Your mother is wise and you yourself are a valiant hero, your brothers are skilful, your comrades brave. You have seventy-three geldings. I lost my father and mother when I was small and have no brothers. My wife is a shrew, my comrades untrustworthy. Because of all this I am no match for you, my comrade, who enjoy the ordinance of Heaven. If you now grant me the favour of letting me die at once, your mind will be at rest. And if as well you let me die without shedding blood, after my death I will protect and aid your descendants forever.'

When Chingis heard of these words of Jamukha, he said, 'My comrade Jamukha, although he went his own way, never once really plotted harm against me. He is one who is capable of learning better ways. However, he cannot bring himself to go on living and I was going to give orders for his execution. But when I took the omens, they were not favourable. Moreover he is a notable man and could not be harmed without due reason. But there is such a reason. Say to him from me, 'Once, because Jochi-darmala and Taichar had been stealing each other's horses, you for no other reason plotted to revolt against me and we fought at Dalan-baljut. You drove me into the defile of Jerene and very much frightened me. Now I invite you to be my comrade, but you refuse, I should like to spare your life, but that is impossible. However you shall die without your blood being shed, as you said that you desired.'

He ordered Jamukha to be killed at once, without shedding his blood; and he was buried with great pomp.

# CHAPTER FOUR

## CHINGIS BECOMES GREAT KHAN OF ALL THE TRIBES IN MONGOLIA

After Chingis had made subject to him all the many tribes he set up at the source of the Onan river a white banner with nine pendants and became Great Khan. This was in the year of the Tiger (1206).

Chingis said: 'I have now assigned their tasks to my sons-in-law and to the ninety-five commanders of a thousand. Among them there are officers who have rendered particularly great service to me and I am going to reward them further.' He then told Shigi-khutukhu to summon Bo'orchu and Mukhali. Shigi-khutukhu said, 'To whose services are those of Bo'orchu and Mukhali superior, that they should be further rewarded? I have been in your family since I was a child, all the time till I became a grown man, and never once left you. To whose services are mine inferior? What reward are you now going to give me?' Chingis said, 'You became my sixth brother and have had your share, just like my other brothers, enjoying the privilege of being allowed to sin a hundred times without punishment. Now that I have subdued all the peoples, I want you to listen and look for me. No one shall be allowed to act contrary to what you say. If there are cases of robbery or fraud, it will be for you to mete out punishment, slaying those who ought to die and punishing those who ought to be punished. You are to decide all disputes arising out of division of family property, and are to write your decisions on the Blue Register, in which no one is to be allowed ever to make alterations.' Shigi-khutukhu said, 'I am the youngest brother. How can I dare receive the same portion as all my other brothers? But if you intend to bestow a favour, give me the peoples who live within earthen walls.' Chingis said, 'You shall have what you ask for, having no doubt thought the matter out'. Shigi-khutukhu, having received his reward, went and summoned Bo'orchu, Mukhali and others to receive theirs. Chingis said to Bo'orchu... 'When I was passing the night at Dalan-nemurges, ready to fight with the Tartars, heavy rain fell. You wanted me to get a good rest, and spreading out a felt shirt you stood over me and kept me from getting wet. Only once, all the time till dawn, did you shift your feet – a proof of great heroism!'

Chingis said to Borokhul, '...when the whole tribe of the Tartars was destroyed, a certain Khargil-shira fled, but having nothing to eat he came back again to my mother Ho'elun's tent and said he had come to get clothes and food. My mother said, "If you have come for clothes (his clothes had been stripped from him as booty) and food, sit down there." So he sat down on the right-hand side, behind the door. Meanwhile Tolui (son of Chingis), who was then four, came in at the door. As he was going out again, Khargil-shira picked him up and put him under his arm. Then he drew a knife. My mother screamed, "He has murdered the child!" Borokhul's wife Altani was sitting, as it happened, on the left side of the tent. She rushed out, stopped the man by seizing his hair, caught hold of the hand in which he held the knife he had drawn and dragged it back with such force that the knife fell to the ground. At the time Jetei and Jelme were behind the tent slaughtering an ox. They heard Altani scream and coming armed with knife and axe they killed the man. Afterwards Altani, Jetei and Jelme quarrelled about to which of them the chief credit belonged. Jetei and Jelme said, "If we had not come so quickly, how could you, a single woman alone and unaided, have dealt with him? Tolui would have been killed." Altani said, "If I had not screamed, you would never have come. And if I had not caught him by the hair and jerked the knife out of his hand, by the time you came he would already have been dead." As the result of this argument the chief credit was given to your wife Altani.'

Again, Chingis ordered Borokhul to lead an expedition against the Khori-tumats. Their leader Daidukhul had died and his wife Botokhui-tarkhun was ruling the people. When he drew near, Borokhul sent three men ahead of the main army. But when he was going late in the evening along a path through deep woods he suddenly found himself cut off by enemy scouts who without his knowing it had worked round to his rear, and Borokhul was killed. Chingis was very angry when he heard of this, and wanted to lead a fresh attack upon the Tumats in person. However, Bo'orchu and Mukhali dissuaded him. Finally Dorbei-dokhshin was sent. He maintained very strict discipline, and as a ruse sent a party of men to make a lot of noise at the place where Borokhul had been cut off, while with his main army he advanced by a small track made by a red bull (animal unidentified). Fearing that his men might loose courage and hang back he made each of them carry ten rods on his back, with which anyone who halted was to be punished. Each man also carried a hand-blade, an axe, a saw and a chisel with which to clear a path through the trees. They arrived in this way at a hill-top from which they looked down at the Tumat people below them just as though they had been looking down through the roof-hole of a tent. They then went straight ahead, caught the enemy unawares, while they were seated at a banquet, and took them prisoner.

Before this Khorchi and Khudukha were both taken by the Tumats and held by their queen Botokhui-tarkhun. The way it happened was as follows: Chingis had promised Khorchi thirty wives. Khorchi knew that the Tumat women were particularly handsome, and went to fetch thirty of them, but this led to a revolt of the Tumat, and they took him prisoner. When Chingis heard of this, as Khudukha knew the habits of the forest peoples, he sent him to rescue Khorchi. This only resulted in Khudukha also being captured. When the Tumats were finally subdued (AD 1217) a hundred of the Tumat people were given to Borokhul's heirs. To Khorchi were given thirty Tumat girls; to Khudukha was allotted queen Botokhui-tarkhun.

# Chapter Five

## Struggle with the Shaman Teb-tenggeri

*M*onglik, of the Khongkhotan clan, had seven sons. The fourth was called Kokochu. The name under which he acted as a *shaman* was Teb-tenggeri. The seven brothers ganged up and beat Chingis' younger brother Khasar. Khasar went and complained to Chingis who, happening at the time to be angry about something else said, 'You always claimed to be a match for anyone. How came you to let them beat you?' At this Khasar wept and went away. For three days he stayed away from Chingis. Meanwhile Teb-tenggeri came to Chingis and said, 'The Spirit who carries messages for Eternal Heaven came to me and said, "For a time Temujin is to rule over the people, but he is to be succeeded by Khasar". You had better get rid of Khasar, or one does not know what will happen!' When Chingis heard this, that very night he went and put Khasar under arrest. Kuchu and others told Chingis' mother Ho'elun what had happened. She got into a cart drawn by white camels and travelling all night she came to where Khasar was just as the sun was rising. There before her she saw Chingis holding Khasar by the sleeves of his coat, having stripped him of both hat and belt, and now engaged in cross-questioning him. When Chingis saw his mother coming he was very much startled and afraid. Ho'elun got down from the cart in a rage, freed Khasar and gave back to him his hat and belt. Then she sat cross-legged and baring her breasts laid them on his knees, asking, 'Do you see these? They are the breasts from which you drank. What crime has Khasar committed that you should destroy your own kin? When you were small you drank up all the milk of one breast, Khachi'un and Temuge could not even drink up the milk of one breast. Only Khasar drank up the milk of both my breasts and brought comfort to me. Because of that you, Temujin, have talent, but Khasar has vigour and can draw the bow. Whenever the peoples have revolted, with his bow and arrows he overcame them. But now that all our enemies are destroyed, you have no use for him.' Chingis waited till he saw that his mother's anger had abated and then said, 'Great is my fear, great is my shame!' and so saying he withdrew. Afterwards, however, without letting his mother know, he took most of Khasar's people away from him, only leaving him with 1400. But she found out and was very much distressed, so that she aged rapidly. Jebke, who had formerly been consigned to Khasar, fled to the Barkhujin country.

Afterwards many of the people of sundry dialects gathered round Teb-tenggeri, so that they were more than those who were with Chingis. Among those that did so were Temuge's people. He sent his man Sokhor to fetch them back, but Teb-tenggeri flogged him and sent him home to Temuge with a saddle harnessed to his back. Next day Temuge went in person, but the seven brothers gathered round him saying, 'How dared you send someone to fetch back your people?' They were on the point of flogging him when Temuge said in terror, 'I ought not to have sent him'. They said, 'As you admit that you have done wrong, you must do penance', and they made him kneel in the rear. Next day very early, before Chingis was up, Temuge went to his tent and kneeling down told him what had happened. When he had finished speaking, he sobbed. Before Chingis could say anything Lady Borte, yawning and stretching, covered her breasts with her blanket and said weeping, 'What is all this? First these men of the Khongkhotan clan flogged Khasar, and now they have forced Temuge to kneel. What can it mean? If while you are still here they dare to misuse your younger brothers, that have shot up like cypresses, afterwards when you are old (i.e. when you die) what chance is there that the peoples, so like tangled hemp or a flight of birds, will bring themselves to be ruled by your small, bad sons?' Having said this, she sobbed. Chingis said to Temuge, 'When Teb-tenggeri comes, it is up to you!' At this Temuge got up, left the tent and gave instructions to three wrestlers.

After a while Monglik arrived, followed by his seven sons. Teb-tenggeri had just reached the right-hand side of the drinking-vessels and sat down there when Temuge grabbed him by the coat-collar, saying, 'Yesterday you made me do penance. Now let us see which is the better man!' Temuge then dragged him out of the tent, and while this was happening, Teb-tenggeri's hat fell at the side of the brazier. His father Monglik picked it up and having held it to his face and smelt it, be put it in the folds of his dress. Chingis said, 'That's right! You two go off and wrestle.' When they were outside the three wrestlers, who had been posted at the threshold, came forward, seized Teb-tenggeri, broke his spine and threw down his body at the end of the row of carts on the left. Temuge went back into the tent and said, 'Yesterday Teb-tenggeri forced me to do penance. But today I had hardly begun to put matters to the trial with him when he lay down, pretending that he was not able to get up. A poor sort of opponent he turned out to be!' Teb-tenggeri's father Monglik

315

well knew what had happened and said weeping, 'I have been your faithful comrade since the days before you became sovereign, down till now...' But before he had finished speaking the six surviving sons of Monglik, taking their stand so as to block up the door and completely surrounding the brazier, bared their fists. Chingis rose to his feet in dismay, crying, 'Stand aside I am going out'. So saying he left the tent and stood outside, surrounded by guardsmen armed with bow and arrow. When he saw that Teb-tenggeri was dead, he had the body covered with a work-tent, and moved camp.

The door and roof-hole of the tent that had been used to cover Teb-tenggeri's body had been blocked up and guards set to watch it. But just before dawn on the third day, the roof-hole opened and the body went out by it, of its own accord. The tent was thoroughly examined, and it was clear that this was what had happened. Chingis said, 'Teb-tenggeri flogged my younger brothers and slandered them without cause. That is why Heaven did not love him, but took him away body and all.' Then he scolded Monglik, saying, 'You failed to give proper teaching to your son. He tried to put himself on a level with me, and this brought him to his end. If I had known that that was the sort of people you are, I should long ago have had nothing for it but to put you to death as I did Jamukha, Altan and Khuchar.' Further he said, 'However, one who changes in the evening what he has said in the morning or changes at dawn what he said the night before, is bound to be ashamed of what people say of him. So I will stick to what I have said about you in former days and not condemn you to death,' and he stopped being angry.

After Teb-tenggeri's death Monglik and his sons were completely discredited.

# LA VIE DE PIERRE RUFFIN. A REVIEW

a vie de Pierre Ruffin. Orientaliste et Diplomate 1742–1824. Tome premier. Par Henri Dehérain. (Paris: Geuthner. 250f.) So characteristic of time, place and function is everything which happens in this book that dates, titles, geography might (one feels) almost as well have been omitted. One could have supplied them all. Thus when we find Ruffin setting out to stir up trouble between two heavily armed countries we know at once that he was, by calling, a diplomat; when we find his employer, the Baron de Tott, conducting electrical experiments in the intervals of diplomacy we know we are in the eighteenth century. A mysterious present arrives in Ruffin's tent. He opens the parcel and finds it is a human head; instantly we realize that we are among the nomads of Tartary. We read of 'un vénérable vieillard, d'une noble et belle figure pleine de dignité et de douceur' and we guess at once that this aged man carries a bundle of huge keys at his waist. He is the gaoler of Ruffin's prison, the Castle of the Seven Towers. For by an irony of Fate Ruffin, sent to the Orient to stir up one war, and successful in doing so, found himself in the end deprived of liberty (though not of Savoy wine, goose, chicken, duck, lobster, melons, grapes, figs) by another war – Napoleon's Egyptian campaign – for which he was in no way responsible.

This was not Ruffin's first prison. He had been detained at St Petersburg for many months by an action of the Russian Government which M. Dehérain finds 'difficilement excusable'. One might, however, find an excuse in the fact that Ruffin's business in life at the moment was to stir up ill-feeling against the Russians. Later he was entrusted with a milder task. It fell to him to 'show round' the *envoyés barbaresques* who were just then arriving in shoals at Versailles.

Madame Vigée Lebrun saw him at the theatre one day with the envoys of Tipu Sahib; she found the group 'si extra-ordinairement pittoresque' that she wanted to paint them, But 'la conduite des Barbaresques est un genre de commission épineux' notes Ruffin in his journal. They were subject to outbursts of inexplicable passion. Suleiman Aga, from Tunis, threw his food out of window. This volume closes in 1804. Twenty exotic years remain to be recorded.

(1931.)

# THE COAL-SCUTTLE

*(from the German of Franz Kafka)*

*C*oal? None. Empty the scuttle, senseless the shovel, icy
the breath of the stove, the room glazed white; stiff with
frost the trees at the window. Heaven a silver shield
blocking the path of prayer.

Coal. I must have coal. Am I to freeze to death? Behind me
the pitiless stove, in front of me a heaven as pitiless. What can
I do but take the middle way? To the coal-merchant's; and as
fast as I can. This time I must prove to him, so that he cannot
put me off as he has done many times before, prove to him
that there is not a splinter of coal left in my scuttle – that in all
the firmament no sun can warm me but he. I will come like the
beggar who staggers to the back-door and sinks with so death-
like a weariness on the doorstep that the cook feels herself
forced despite the careful habits in which she has been
brought up, to part with the grounds of this morning's coffee.
Yes, I will go to the merchant, and little as he likes it the mere
dread of that anathema 'Thou shalt not kill' will force him to
fling a few lumps into my scuttle.

And look at my scuttle. How light, how airy it is! So empty
that it can scarcely hold to the floor. Surely that will impress
him! Steady now. As a scuttle-rider I come. All goes well. I

have a firm hold on the handle. There are some awkward turns on the staircase. What does it matter? I have my scuttle under perfect control. And once we are in the open, how gracefully the scuttle rises! Just a touch of the long goad and my patient camel shakes the desert dust from its quivering knees. Down the fast-frozen lane we speed, sometimes higher than the first-storey windows; never as low as the front doors. But not in all our flight have we risen so high as now when, hovering above the merchant's house, we look down into the arched cavern where he cowers at a little table making up his accounts. He is wiping his forehead. The heat in there is too much for him. That is why he has opened the door.

'Coal-seller!' I call with a voice weak as dying embers, a voice muffled by the white clouds of my own frozen breath, 'Let me have some coal. Look, my scuttle is so empty that I can ride upon it. I will pay you when I can.' He put his hand to his ears. 'What's that he's saying?' he asked, calling over his shoulder to his wife who was sitting at her crochet work by the stove. 'Is he a customer?' 'No,' she said in a comfortable voice, breathing gently to the rhythm of her crochet needles, while delightful sensations of warmth and comfort poured in upon her from the purring stove. 'No,' she said, 'I don't hear anyone.'

'Yes, yes,' I called. 'Surely you know me? This isn't the first time I have been to you. I have always dealt with you and always mean to. But unfortunately at the moment I am in difficulties.'

'My dear,' the coal-seller said. 'I rather believe there is someone asking for me. Hadn't we better do something? It must be an old customer, too, judging from the familiar way he is calling out to us.'

'What has come over you?' she said; and resting for a moment from her crochet work she pressed it to her bosom while she stared at her husband. 'There's no one there at all,

The street is empty. All our customers have been served. No one will be coming for days. We might quite well put up the shutters and have a holiday.'

'But please!' I called out to them. 'Here am I sitting on my scuttle,' and tears that were too cold for my cheeks to feel trickled on to my coat. 'You must surely see me. Look up here. A shovel-full. That is all I ask. Two shovel-fulls would be more happiness than I could bear. You won't miss the stuff. All your customers have been served. Heavens, what joy it would be to hear it rattling into the scuttle.'

'I suppose I'd better go,' said the coal-merchant at last, and was just waddling up the cellar stairs when his wife came up after him and took him by the arm. 'You stay where you are,' she said. 'If anyone goes up it had better be me. Just think how you were coughing this afternoon! But that's what you are; if it's business (not that there's any real business this time) you forget all about your wife and children, and go ruining your lungs. Come on now, let me go instead.' 'All right then,' the coal-merchant said. 'But I'll call up to you the different sorts we could let him have, and the prices.' She came up the stairs to the street-door. 'Good morning,' I said. 'Could you oblige me with a shovelfull of coal? You won't have to send it round. I have come with my scuttle and can take the coal back with me. It needn't be good quality.' Any sort will do. I shall be able to pay you presently.' This word 'presently' chimed on her ears with a sudden fatal discordance, breaking into the peace that tolled from the neighbouring church-tower. 'What sort does he want?' shouted up the merchant, 'Nothing,' the woman called down. 'It's nothing. I can't see anything or hear anything. There's no one here. But that's six striking. It's time to close. The weather looks like turning even colder and we shall be busy tomorrow.'

She sees nothing, hears nothing. Yet she undoes her apron, and flapping it at me, tries to shoo me away. And not in vain.

My scuttle is a good steed, but lacks resistance – is indeed too light, too empty to withstand the slightest pressure. One touch of a woman's apron is enough to take it off its feet. 'You wretch!' I call after her, as she makes her way back to the shop with an air half of contempt, half of satisfaction at having so well dispatched the business. 'You wretch! I asked you for a shovel-full of the poorest coal, and you gave me nothing!'

And so saying, I mounted into the region of unending icebergs and have never been seen again.

(Not hitherto printed; included here by permission of Messrs Seeker and Warburg, publishers of the authorized translation.)

# THE HYMN OF THE SOUL

From the apocryphal *Acts of St Thomas*

When I was a little child
Living in my kingdom, in my father's house,
Happy in the wealth and rank
Of those that reared me –
From the East, our home,
My parents sent me out.
The treasures of our store-room
They tied for me in a bundle;
Large, yet so light
That I could carry it in my hands:
Gold of Beth-Ellaye,
Silver of Gazzak the Great,
Rubies of Hind,
Agates of Beth Kashan;
And at my belt was tied *adamas*,
That can crush iron.
And they took off the glittering robe
That in their love they had made for me,
And my purple cloak
That was measured and woven to my stature,
And they made a pact with me,

And lest I should forget
They wrote it on my heart:
'If you go down into Egypt
And bring that only pearl
That is in the midst of the sea,
Guarded by the snorting dragon,
Then you shall put on again your glittering robe
And the cloak that you delight in,
And with your brother, next in rank,
Be heir to our kingdom.'
I left the East, and went down,
And there were two couriers with me,
For the way was dangerous and hard to find,
And I was young to take it.
I passed the borders of Maishan, the meeting place
Of the merchants of the East.
I came to the land of Babel,
I entered the walls of Sarbug.
I went down into Egypt,
And my companions left me.
I went to the place of the dragon;
I lived close to his lair,
Waiting till he should be asleep,
So that I might take the pearl from him.
I was quite alone,
A stranger to those with whom I lived.
Then one of my own race, a freeman,
A man of the East I saw,
A youth fresh and comely,
A son of chieftains.
He came to me and was my friend;
I made him partner in my quest,
Warning him against the Egyptians,
Against consorting with the unclean.

But I wore a dress like theirs
Lest they should scorn me as a stranger,
Lest when I went to take the pearl
They should rouse up the dragon against me.
But whether by this means or that
They saw I was not their countryman.
They dealt with me cunningly,
They gave me their food to eat.
Then I forgot I was a son of kings,
And served their king.
I forgot the pearl
For which my parents had sent me.
The burden of their food lay heavy on me,
And I fell into a deep sleep.
But all that had happened to me
My parents knew, and were very sad.
There was made a proclamation in our Kingdom
That all should hasten to our gate,
Kings and princes of Parthia –
All the nobles of the East.
They made a plan to save me,
That I might not be left in Egypt.
They wrote a letter to me
And every noble put his name to it:
'From your father, king of kings,
And your mother, mistress of the East,
From your brother next in rank,
To our son in Egypt, greeting!
Rise from your sleep and listen
To the words of our letter.
Remember that you are a son of kings;
See to what slavery you stoop!
Remember the pearl
For which you hurried to Egypt,

Think of the glittering robe,
Recall your glorious cloak
That you shall wear again as your finery
When in the list of the valiant
Your name is cited.
With your brother, our next of rank,
You shall be heir in our kingdom.'
My letter! A letter from the king
Sealed with his own right hand
That it might be safe from the wicked,
The children of Babel and the cruel demons of Sarbug.
It flew in the likeness of an eagle,
King of all birds;
It flew and lighted beside me
And became all speech.
At its voice and the sound of its rustling
I started and rose from my sleep.
I took it up and kissed it
And loosened the seal and read;
And according to what was traced on my heart
Were the words of the letter written.
I remembered I was the son of kings;
I missed my free estate,
I remembered the pearl
For which I had been sent into Egypt,
And I laid a charm on the terrible one,
The snorting dragon;
I hushed him to sleep, lulled him to slumber,
For my father's name I named over him
And the name of our next-in-rank,
And of my mother, queen of the East.
I snatched away the pearl
And turned to go back to my father's house.
Their filthy and unclean dress

I stripped off and left in their country;
I took my way straight back
To the light of our home, the East.
And my letter, my awakener,
I found before me on the road;
And as with its voice it had aroused me
So with its light it led me on.
Dweller in silk,
It shone before me with its form;
With its voice and guidance
It quickened me on my path,
With its love it drew me on.
I went forth and passed by Sarbug,
I left Babel on my left hand
And reached Maishan the great,
The harbour of the merchants,
That sits upon the shore of the sea.
And my bright robe that I had stripped off
And the cloak it was wrapped in
From Ramtha-Reken my parents sent me to
By the hand of treasurers
Whose faithfulness they trusted.
I had forgotten how it was fashioned,
For I was a child when I left it
At my father's house.
And now as I came towards it
The dress seemed to me
Like a mirror of myself.
I saw in it all my whole self;
I went to myself in going to it.
We were two in distinction,
Yet one in likeness.
And the treasurers, too, who brought it
I saw in like manner

That they were two, yet one in likeness;
For one kingly sign was graven on them,
As on the hands of him that had restored it to me.
Here was my treasure, my wealth,
My bright embroidered robe,
Gay with many colours.
With gold, beryls, rubies and agates
And sardonyx of every hue,
Skilfully worked in its high home.
With stones of *adamas*
All its seams were fastened,
And the picture of the king of kings
Was embroidered all over it.
And like the sapphire stone
Were its many hues.
And again I saw that all over it
The motions of knowledge were quivering.
And I saw it making ready
As though it would speak to me.
I heard the sound of its voice
As it spoke to those that brought it down:
'I am the active in deeds
(Whom they reared for him before my father;) [1]
I perceived in myself that my nature
Grew according to his labours.'
And in its kingly movements
It poured itself out over me,
And on the hand of the givers
It hastened, that I might take it.
And love urged me on,
That I should run to meet it and receive it.

[1] Unintelligible both in Greek and the Syriac.

I stretched out my hand and took it,
With the beauty of its colours I clothed myself.
My cloak of bright colours
I cast round me in its whole breadth.
I dressed in it, I went up
To the gate of greeting and homage,
To the Majesty [1] of my father who sent it to me;
For I had done his commandment
And he too had done what he promised.
And at the gate of his princes
I mingled with his nobles,
For be rejoiced in me and welcomed me,
And I was back with him in his kingdom;
For with the voice of praise
All his servants glorify him.
And now they promised that to the door
Of the king of kings I should be brought;
That bringing my gift and my pearl
I should come before the king.

(*Encounter*, December 1953.)

---

1 *Ziwa*, the sign of kingship.

ORIGINAL PIECES

# THE PRESENTATION

The boys at a school decided to give a present to a master who was leaving. Apart from one or two of his favourites they all hated him, for he was mean, ill-tempered and tyrannical. But now, partly because they felt that half a crown was not much to give to someone who had been used to exact far greater tolls – of leisure, health and comfort, for he constantly detained them on holidays, gave double evening-tasks, or made them (not to speak of canings and ear-twistings) stand for hours in a draughty passage outside his class-room door – and partly from a lingering fear of displeasing him, for they could not believe in the sudden removal from their lives of someone who had done them so much harm, they were easily persuaded to subscribe.

All but one. This one was not less frightened of the master than were the rest. He had indeed suffered more than any, since he possessed a certain spirit of independence; and this made it difficult for him to humour the stupid whim by which the master delighted to assert the arbitrary nature of his authority.

To these whims the other boys, to whom so much that happened at school seemed merely senseless and capricious, had in some measure grown accustomed. Thus they consented to number the pages of their exercise-book alternately in Roman and Arabic figures, to write their Christian names in book-type and their surnames in capitals, to stand at attention in front of the master's desk till he sent them to their seats, and this every time they entered the room; to write English on alternate lines but French on every line. These things and the master's sneers and punishments seemed to them at last no more arbitrary than the genitive of *domina*, and no more useless. But to this one boy the trivial and purposeless discipline which the rest, in the hope of currying favour, were ready enough to submit, seemed despicable and humiliating, and through constantly disregarding it he became the special target of the master's sarcasm and abuse.

He had no experience of subscriptions. He had been told that the head boy would give the present (it was to be a clock with glass sides) and imagined him taking it quietly to the master's room on the last day of term. The other boys, no doubt, would know that he had refused; but this did not trouble him. It was in fact more out of contempt for their servility than with any desire to revenge himself on the master that he now stood aside. Indeed he did not suppose that the master himself would know what he had done, and had such an idea occurred to him he would not have dared to refuse, for though the master's reign was over the mere thought of his rage was still terrible.

On the final day early in the morning all the boys were summoned to the largest class-room. They arrived in high spirits; at last they were beginning to realize that this great burden of fear and oppression had been removed forever from their lives.

The headmaster was standing on the dais with the retiring master by his side. He scanned the benches row after row, looking eagerly into each face. Then he shut his eyes. 'What happy faces,' he murmured to himself. 'What wonderfully happy faces!' After standing for awhile in silence he asked them if they knew why they were so happy, so much happier than other boys? No one dared reply. 'Then yours,' he continued, thus placing them in a dilemma, 'like that of fishes or birds is a shallow soulless joy.'

They smiled uneasily. But to their great relief (for they thus unexpectedly escaped the inconvenience of having to invent their own reply), he proceeded to explain the reason of their happiness. It was due, he declared, entirely to a system which he himself had invented. Everyone was agreed, he said, that without order and obedience no school could exist. Now at other places, he was sorry to say, order was maintained by severity and enforced by fear. 'What I have invented,' he claimed, 'and some think that I have reason to be proud of my discovery, is a system in which discipline no longer figures but is replaced, boys, my dear boys, by imagination and love.' He told them, again looking from face to face, that they were very ordinary boys, more fortunate than most in that they were here, but in no other way either better or worse. Certainly it was not the boys but the masters, the devoted staff who have made the place so different from all other schools. And there was one, the headmaster said, who would surely stand out in their memory forever as the noblest product of his system, the most perfect embodiment of his ideal – discipline through imagination and love.

All this seemed to have no connection whatever with the school as they knew it and least of all with the master in relation to whom it was spoken. But as they listened it seemed to the boys that what the headmaster was saying could not be merely untrue. Somewhere all this sympathy, kindness and patience had certainly existed, and if it had not existed for them the fault was theirs. Though the retiring master stood before them and though his name (not the one by which they themselves generally called him) had frequently been mentioned, they had the feeling that not he but a quite different person, some such paragon of goodness as the headmaster had described in his speech, were now being taken from them, and they were deeply moved.

At last the headmaster sat down and the retiring master rose. He said that much though it had gratified him to hear the Headmaster's words he could not in reality claim praise for having put into practice, possibly with even greater thoroughness than any of his colleagues, the high ideals of the school. Strictness, discipline, rules and regulations of all kinds were things that had never come natural to him, and if there was one thing with which after all these years he must reproach himself it was that he had perhaps made work too much like play and had thus unfitted his pupils for the arduous realities of life.

Then the head boy stepped forward with the clock and laid it on the desk, making as he did so a short speech that he had learnt by heart. He spoke so low that no one heard what he said. The retiring master took his hand and shook it warmly. The head boy said something to him which must have been to remind him that the present was from all the boys and at the same time he produced what was evidently a list. The master glanced at it quickly, nodded and began to pass along the benches, shaking each boy by the hand and saying 'I thank you.'

The boy who had not subscribed was trembling. His heart beat quicker and quicker as the master passed from row to row. He could not be thanked for what he had not done. He began to frame words. His heart beat so loud that he did not know if they were audible. 'I did not subscribe.' 'But you will give me your hand.' He felt it taken and as the master grasped it the boy began to weep. To weep with pride that his hand had been grasped by the noble and patient man whom the headmaster had described in his speech. For the real master, the one who had bullied and raved and played the tyrant for so many years, had ceased to exist; a little grave-side eloquence had eclipsed a hundred thrashings, ear-pullings, calumnies and impositions.

(*Nation*, May 1924.)

# IN THE GALLERY

*B*ehind iron railings, across a huge cobbled space, umbrellas laboured unevenly, seeming at moments to press so close into the welter of the stone that the eye lost them as it loses a boat at sea. At last, as though struggling shoreward across the long ladder of the surf, they swayed slowly up the dripping steps and at the top suddenly rippled and collapsed, disclosing between the pillars a herd of baffled pilgrims, who before pressing through the narrow doors, now turned for an instant towards the courtyard and the town, as though to drink in a last breath of reality before plunging into an abstract, inanimate world.

It seemed that beyond the massive portico must open out some vast luminous space; but behind the glazed swing-doors the pilgrims came suddenly upon a dark shallow lobby, where a woman in a shawl held her knitting very close to her eyes, while through the thick air, from a doorway at her side, came a smell of cooking and the sound of birds moving in a cage. Now one by one the pilgrims began to filter through a turnstile into the main hall. Some – for the most part the rougher and stronger of them – through sheer timidity did not press hard enough, and, when they faltered, the woman with the shawl pushed them through like clothes through a creaking mangle.

Two curving staircases with marble balustrades met on a wide empty landing where darkly, with its back to a high window, stood the life-size statue of a man in evening dress, with drooping moustaches and long hair parted at the side. There were medals and orders on his coat, the ribbon and pins that held them were all shown, as were too the watchchain, the heavy signet and the rings on his right hand. But though these were metal rendered in metal, they were not more real than the undulating silk necktie and the elastic sides of his shoes. His left hand was slipped rather furtively into the trouser pocket, as though he were feeling for a tip.

The long room, from doorway to doorway, was full of travel. Weaving itself into the sound of their own hushed footfall the pilgrims still heard the uneasy rattle of the night train, and into the dark pools on the wall there crept the image of a breakfast-tray, lying on an unmade bed.

And just as their own thought-pictures, now cavernously framed in gold, took on a mirrored gravity and distinctness unknown in the common world, so too during the journey of which this pilgrimage through the gallery was part, their own image of themselves had gradually cleared and crystalized. They saw themselves no longer as dim lay-figures, called to life only by a series of costumes and occupations – not as a succession of personalities – but as one thing always, that travelled and visited and travelled, perpetually filling and unfilling the same bag, perpetually feeling in the same pocket for change and keys.

And yet the pilgrim's personality, now so strangely sharpened and clarified, was largely an affair of chance. A book, a pair of gloves snatched up at the last moment had fixed his picture of himself and coloured the whole journey.

The air was close and difficult to breathe. It was indeed not so much air as a tight, sweet vapour that rose from the thickly waxed floor. In such an atmosphere any movement would have been tiring, and that of walking was doubly so, for the floor was highly polished, slippery as ice, and the pilgrims, not daring to raise their feet, shuffled down the long gallery like flies clawing the glass walls of an air-tight trap. Their movements, in this lethal cage, became dreamier and dreamier, and but for the sounds of the night-journey, a lock that continually strained and rattled, water that sighed in a pipe, a childish ding-dong bell, the last despairing whistle of a distant engine – echoes that like the remnants of a tempest still snapped and fluttered in the ravaged corridors of the brain – they must have fallen asleep.

But suddenly into this inert and desiccated world there burst a sweep of cumbrous activity. Under the high square door and straight down the long room was pushed a lady in an invalid chair. She did not look to right or left but, propped stiffly on a pile of cushions, between which a picture-paper was thrust, her hands folded over the knob of the steering-bar, she gazed intently at the lines on the glassy floor as though all her strength were concentrated on reaching the end of the long gallery.

The two men who pushed the chair bent so low that their faces could not be seen. This attitude gave them an air of extreme solicitude; they seemed to be anxious that the invalid should be spared the effort of raising her voice, should be able at any moment to convey the most faintly whispered complaint or request. The lady's lips, however, though always slightly parted, never moved, and at times it seemed as though the attention of the two men were fixed not so much on the furtherance of her small passing wishes as on the fulfilment of her main desire: to keep a straight and continual course towards the door at the end of the long room; and for this

341

purpose it was necessary that they should attend not so much to her as to their own feet, planting them in an intricate angular pattern, to obtain a steady purchase on the slippery floor.

The travellers had pushed on into the second room, which appeared to be in all respects identical with the first. But one of them after a while stumbled against something that proved to be a long low seat and, to save himself from falling, suddenly sat down. The others quietly ranged themselves by his side. Here for a time, as previously in the dining-car with its access of space and light, stretching their legs and safely testing the glassy composition of the floor, they enjoyed, on this soft yet solid couch, an extraordinary sense of respite and relief. But with a great gold-framed space on the wall in front of them, they could feel themselves, like birds assembled on a telegraph wire, still to be at work, still to be passively obeying the mysterious impulse of their migration.

It had been growing steadily lighter, and now the sun came out, making all at once a complete and convenient looking-glass of the dark rectangle in front of which they sat. One of the pilgrims stepped forward to arrange his tie; but immediately there was a cranking and jarring in a far corner of the room and a slight flapping sound overhead. With one accord a whole series of yellow blinds spread across the glass roof. By the time the pilgrim had raised his hands to his neck the mirror had ceased to exist. The others looked at him apologetically as, still fingering his bow, he gazed with a certain resentment at the scene which, abolishing his own image, had slanted into the golden frame!

Two naked men in plumed helmets were rescuing an empty bird-cage from a ruined church. Towards the flat blue distance a camel, led by chanting angels, carried lashed to its back a marble fountain and a trumpet draped in cloth of gold.

342

There was a long silence, broken by the sudden wailing of a child. They gave him a disc to pay with, a white, numbered disc, such as each of them had exchanged for his dripping encumbrances, while they themselves continued to gaze spellbound by the inexplicable revelation that confronted them. Often on their journey things no less astonishing – cities of shapeless slag or rivers of fire plucked from a tangle of trucks, wires and magic lights – had flashed on to the screen of their senses in the hurry of the dark; or at dawn, having steamed quietly into a huge station they had jolted out of it again, finally coming to an unexpected standstill close beside an isolated row of shallow houses on the outskirts of the town.

Then their minds, leaving the steamy carriage, had been projected through the sharp stillness of the morning air, under half-pulled blinds, into a dingy bedroom where a headless figure lay across a wooden chair, or a broken saucer moved as though drawn by wire over the space between the stair-rail and the door. But even these dim vistas and hasty prefigurements, compared with what was now before them, had seemed to the pilgrims to be full of scenic purpose. The fountain? The angels? A sort of bewildered discomfort held the travellers rooted to the spot, waiting for the word, the syllable that should release them.

Slowly, as though drawn by the unspoken question, a white-haired pensioner in a peaked cap, guardian of the two long rooms, shuffled to their side. 'Allegorical,' he whispered, bending over the row of pilgrims and laying a finger to his forehead, with the gesture of one who has a harmless madman in his care.

'Allegorical.' The word, though it told so little, served nevertheless a kind of mechanical purpose, passing from mouth to mouth with a series of slight shocks which, gathering scope and momentum, ended at last in an uneasy fidgeting with buckles and catches, a restless scraping of feet.

Soon with a last glance at the strange borderland that had detained them so long, the pilgrims pushed out of their siding. At first they moved forward again in a solid mass. But they had lost their real cohesion. Two of them presently, as though all at once endowed with a propulsion of their own, branched off from the crowd, and drifted separately through the grey hush into an avenue of small side rooms, where they met time after time in front of the same row of grubby Dutch carousals, almost colliding, then parting again, with the sharp twist of a gold-fish into whose pool a pebble has been thrown.

Soon there was a greater disruption. The child, whose first and real fear had been so easily distracted, now began to take fright causelessly at every turn. Soon the discs of the whole family were in its possession. With these in its hand, pausing at every few steps to look back, yet mounting with incredible rapidity, it darted up a steep, dark staircase the very existence of which no one else had perceived. The mother panted after it, followed by the whole family; they did not return. The pilgrims were pushing once more straight through the heavy waxen air. Their course was set; it seemed as though nothing could turn them aside. But like a river in whose banks a breach has accidentally been made, one after another they were drawn through the unnoticed gap, till only a thin trickle of them oozed slowly down the centre of the glassy floor.

The rest, re-animated by the diversion, rose wave on wave. They did not feel the exertion. Their feet perhaps were numbed by so much shuffling and sliding. It was as though by magic that they arrived at the doorway of a low upper room.

They gave a deep sigh of relief. Here at last was no shadow-fair, no hall of mysteries. The air lived, the walls spoke, there were attitudes and textures that they knew.

Military men were frequent; here however not bewigged or helmeted, but bald, or with close-cropped, unlegendary hair. There were stolid queens and princesses whose presence could not bewilder or embarrass the humblest visitor, so rustic and unfashionable were the clothes they wore. There was a schoolboy in an Eton collar cutting a silvery cake into which a sprig of holly was thrust. There was a basket of grey kittens and an orchard full of bloom.

The kittens were high on the wall. Wishing to please the child, to whose inconsequence they owed this breath of solidity, this welcome contact with a sharper, more natural world, one of the pilgrims seized it in his arms and held it close to the picture.

With a cry of delight the child stretched out its hand, but its fingers, that expected warm fur, slid along the glass with a faint creaking sound, not unlike the mewing of an offended cat. Hastily, as though it had touched a thorn, the child drew back its hand, and again burst into tears.

Close by there was a narrow staircase, this time a mere turret stair. It was too insignificant to promise anything of value or importance, but it at least afforded a refuge from the child's cries and, by a simple reckoning, gave hope of a scene intensely actual and alive. They climbed the stairway (the less phlegmatic of the pilgrims) round and round, their hands on the rough stone.

But as they passed towards a door, there struck at them, seen only with the corner of the eye, a sudden, amended vision; solid, purposeful, complete. It was as though a hand had shot out of the future and hooked it into their ken. Incredulous, they wheeled round; the marvel, on the walls was still there. But no sooner had they halted than a huge bell suddenly moved in the tower. The sound, coming from so close, had no time to poise for its flight, but leapt at them as mere uproar and confusion. It rattled along the walls, shook dust from the floor, bombarded the narrow stair.

And through the midst of all the din there sounded too, from room to room, one after another the voices of the guardians rising with a burst of startled energy, as though a box of tin soldiers had suddenly been woken for their roll-call by an invisible power.

There was a halt and crush at one of the doors. Wave after wave of pilgrims broke against a dark, obstructing mass, which proved to be the invalid lady's wheeled chair. It advanced slowly now, and also rather unsteadily. Her two attendants or companions had pulled the newspaper from under her pillow and holding it between them were reading as they went. As though to make up for having abstracted this much of their attention, they were pressing very hard on the back rail with their outer hands – too heavily indeed, and the front wheel was in the air. The lady still looked straight in front of her, just as at the beginning when everything still lay ahead, and with hands tightly folded over the steering-bar guided her wheel through the air on a rigid and unvarying course. The statue guarded the final stairway with an air of confident reality. His face was towards the street. He seemed even to regard with a certain contempt – the loftily averted gaze and fastidious pose of the right elbow suggested it – the polished stretches, the dim lifeless walls.

The galleries were cleared; emptied of their last human drop. Even the invalid lady and her chair had at the last moment vanished – decently spirited away.

The pilgrims were trooping out of the hall. There was light ahead; they were nearing the end of their tunnel. Decked again in the damp properties with which, like soul and body at the Judgment, they were at last re-united, they walked slightly sideways, raising their feet high, down the long series of steps, at every step breathing deeply into their stifled lungs the trivial animation of the outer world.

(*Cornhill*, 1948–49.)

# CENSORSHIP

*(In Chinese Style)*

I have been a censor for fifteen months,
The building where I work has four times been bombed.
Glass, boards and paper, each in turn,
Have been blasted from the window – where windows are
    left at all.
It is not easy to wash, keep warm and eat;
At times we lack gas, water or light.
The rules for censors are difficult to keep;
In six months there were over a thousand 'stops'.
The Air Raid Bible alters from day to day;
Official orders are not clearly expressed.
One may mention Harrods, but not Derry and Toms;
One may write of mist but may not write of rain.
Japanese scribbled on thin paper
In faint scrawl tires the eyes to read.
In a small room with ten telephones
And a tape-machine concentration is hard.
Yet the Blue Pencil is a mere toy to wield,
There are worse knots than the tangles of Red Tape.
It is not difficult to censor foreign news,

What is hard today is to censor one's own thoughts –
To sit by and see the blind man
On the sightless horse, riding into the bottomless abyss.

(*Horizon*, 1941)

# No Discharge

I do not believe that Heaven and Hell are in different places,
I do not believe that the utmost anguish of the damned
Could ever damp the bliss of neighbouring Saints.
I do not believe there have ever been complaints
From any of the Twenty Four Elders or Seven Spirits,
About things like the smell of brimstone. 'At first it seems
     strong'
They confess, 'but one does not notice it for long,
And we keep our incense burning night and day.'
'While for the groaning and gnashing of teeth,' the angels
     say
'What with the noise of golden harps and new song
They scarcely worry us at all.' To a recent guest
Shy at first amid so much goodness, wondering
Whether one can ever really be friends with the Blest,
Gazing down at the unconsumable Phoenix nest,
At the obstinate host whose daily bread is destruction
Yet none can cease to suffer by being destroyed –
To such, a hospitable Elder will often come
Saying, 'Meet me here when it's dark. You have never enjoyed
Beauty on earth such as I will show you tonight –
The fires of Hell reflected in the Glassy Sea.'

349

The hours of evening pass; his golden crown, a little tight,
Tires him at first, his unaccustomed wings
Bewilder him, his fingers on the golden strings
Find disconcerting music, and his own voice
Startles him with its raptures when he sings.
Darkness drops; he stands by the smiling Elder
Wing to wing. Shall he look up or down?
At the rose-leaf Phantom caught in the glacier of Heaven?
At the scarlet Fury prancing over Hell-town?
'It's wonderful to look at it, isn't it,' an Eider once said,
'Surely this alone makes it worth while to be dead!'
So Heaven and Hell live side by side
And such troubles as happen are of the mildest kind.
Now and again the dull, the gentle damned
Stir, and some salvaged Lucifer will try
To organize revolt. Which Heaven does not mind.
What does it mean? A few lost spirits clutching
Charred banners with the motto 'We want wings,'
Or 'Harps for Hell', or 'Golden crown for all.'
The unpresentable, scrap-heap Lucifer flings
A written protest over Heaven's wall.
'They're bound to answer.' 'This time they must do
        something – '
The meek spirits whisper, waiting outside.
Hours go by. Suddenly a terrible light
Flashes over them. Is it some new device
For blistering Hell – for cutting off their retreat?
No! That transcendent whiteness is the Angel of Day
Telling them quietly but firmly to go away.

(*New Statesman*, July 1941)

# BLITZ POEM

There are days when, slipping from the clasp
Of memory, each sound and sight
On some blank shoal of inward feeling
Lies new and separate and bright.
It was so today with the voice
Harsh-edged as Andalusian hills
Of the old Gibraltar woman calling back
Her grandchild that was scraping
Splintered glass from window-sills.

(not published before)

# SONG

I had a bicycle called 'Splendid',
A cricket-bat called 'The Rajah',
Eight box-kites and Scotch soldiers
With kilts and red guns.
I had an album of postmarks,
A Longfellow with pictures,
Corduroy trousers that creaked,
A pencil with three colours.

Where do old things go to?
Could a cricket-bat be thrown away?
Where do the years go to?

*(not published before)*

353

# The Swan

Through a haze of murk and gold
Under the laughing moon and blue sky
In stiff glassy whiteness the self-enchanted
The glorious swan goes by.

And when danger rustles on the shore,
Afraid to break the trance of motionless speed,
Only the small head wakes and swiftly turns
On silver shaft; the body pays no heed.

*(not published before)*

Made in the USA
Columbia, SC
09 April 2021

35898521R00200